Praise for *Dogs Demyst*

"Dog owners are so lucky; Marc Bekoff has done it again. *Dogs Demystified* is beyond fascinating, and Bekoff's sheer wealth of knowledge shines through, creating awe and wonderment. A page-turner!"

— **Dr. Ian Dunbar**, author of *Before and After Getting Your Puppy* and *Barking Up the Right Tree*

"Another terrific resource from dog expert and advocate Marc Bekoff: your canine questions asked and answered!"

— **Jennifer S. Holland**, author of the *New York Times* bestselling Unlikely Friendships series

"Based on Marc Bekoff's lifetime of research, personal experiences, and passion for dogs, *Dogs Demystified* delivers what its title promises — a unique whirlwind tour of the behavior and inner lives of dogs and our relationships with them. Covering topics ranging from animal-assisted therapy to canine zoomies, this book is a delightful potpourri that is both an authoritative reference guide and a great read. I learned something new about dogs on every page."

— **Hal Herzog**, author of *Some We Love, Some We Hate, Some We Eat: Why It's So Hard to Think Straight about Animals*

"In *Dogs Demystified*, Marc Bekoff explains how to understand your dog's personality and behavior and how to care for them. Grounded in science and full of fun, this compassionate and accessible book will appeal to everyone who loves dogs. Everything you ever wanted to know about dogs is here."

— **Zazie Todd**, PhD, author of *Wag: The Science of Making Your Dog Happy* and *Purr: The Science of Making Your Cat Happy*

"*Dogs Demystified* is an easy-to-read reference and is easy to pick up whenever you wish to dig up new dog knowledge. Demystified indeed, as Dr. Bekoff busts myths and explains curious behaviors. You're sure to better understand our best friends if you read this book."

— **Steve Dale**, certified animal behavior consultant, contributing editor of *Decoding Your Dog*, and host of the nationally syndicated radio show *Steve Dale's Pet World*

"With whimsical drawings by Joan Baez and a laudatory foreword by Jane Goodall, Marc Bekoff's *Dogs Demystified* provides a tidy guide to all things dog that will enlighten and amuse everyone who cares about these complex creatures. First-time dog owners and seasoned dog veterans alike should flock to read what Bekoff has to say."

— **Mark Derr**, author of *How the Dog Became the Dog*

"*Dogs Demystified* is the kind of informative, insightful book that one would expect from Marc Bekoff, who combines his award-winning scientific background with his knowledge of what is going on in animals' minds to enlighten and amaze even longtime dog guardians. You will come away fully aware of what complex individuals all dogs are and how each acts in purposeful, unique, and sometimes incredibly surprising ways. This excellent book will help garner respect for dogs for who they are and not who we want them to be."

— **Ingrid Newkirk**, founder of PETA

"Marc Bekoff's insights into dogs' minds are so compelling and important, I never want to miss a word he writes. Everyone should read his work with attentiveness and gratitude."

— **Sy Montgomery**, author of *The Soul of an Octopus*

"*Dogs Demystified* is the ultimate anthology of everything scientific, sentient, and sensational about dogs, brilliantly organized in A-to-Z format. Marc Bekoff has crafted a masterpiece, and staying true to his *dogness*, he gives the reader a choice: You can read in sequence or easily skip around according to subject. I confess to doing both, and they are equally addictive. This book is like crack for dog lovers, filled with so much insight, field knowledge, storytelling, and curiosity. If *Jeopardy* had a canine game-show equivalent, I imagine it would be *Dogs Demystified*. 'I'll take "humping" for two hundred, Alex,' or 'Let's try "zoomies" for six.' With this book by my side, I'll never need Google for anything related to *Canis lupus familiaris* again."

— **Pilley Bianchi**, coauthor of *For the Love of Dog: The Ultimate Relationship Guide* and founder of the Chaser Initiative

"We owe much of our understanding of dog behavior to Marc Bekoff. Dr. Bekoff's books and *Psychology Today* articles are founts of knowledge and wisdom that prompt us to form deeper, more compassionate connections with the dogs in our lives. The fascinating, fact-filled A-to-Z format of *Dogs Demystified* makes it even easier for readers to explore all things dog, and the accompanying illustrations by Joan Baez are wonderful. This is the go-to book for everyone who wishes to learn more about our canine companions."

— **Lisa Tenzin-Dolma**, author and founder of the Dog Welfare Alliance and the International School for Canine Psychology and Behaviour

"Vibrant, fun, and inspiring, *Dogs Demystified* is all about dogness. Dr. Marc Bekoff, an authority in the dog world, shares his remarkable experience and conveys the views of prominent experts in the most accessible way. The rich information can enthuse dog guardians, professionals, vets, and those considering adopting a dog. The dog world is rife with misinformation, untruthful news, debates, and myths, which are frustrating and reflect the struggles of dogs and people. *Dogs Demystified* conjugates clarity with reliable knowledge, making canine science easy for everyone. The A-to-Z entries guide the reader on a captivating journey of discovery, reflection, and transformation. *Dogs Demystified* is an extraordinary tribute to the real nature of dogs and a true gift to the dog-human community and all animal lovers."

— **Marco Adda**, independent scholar, anthrozoologist, and dog behavior consultant

"This is no ordinary book. Beautifully written and delightfully illustrated, *Dogs Demystified* is a journey you can read from cover to cover, a reference you can return to again and again, and an adventure you can open at random to find something surprising and new. Marc Bekoff is a true master of canine ethology — he will answer every question you've ever had about your dog and tell you everything you didn't know you had to know in order to be a true best friend."

— **Dr. Brian Hare and Vanessa Woods**, *New York Times* bestselling authors of *The Genius of Dogs*

"Through *Dogs Demystified*, Marc Bekoff delivers an authoritative yet wholly refreshing take: the latest science, drawing on the minds of hundreds of research professionals around the world, often told through stories, relationships, anecdotes, and personal memories. If dogs could read, I'd tell them to read this book. I have a feeling they would heartily approve of each and every word."

— **Jules Howard**, science writer and author of *Wonderdog: The Science of Dogs and Their Unique Friendship with Humans*

"In *Dogs Demystified*, Marc Bekoff shares his encyclopedic knowledge of dogs and dog behavior. In an easily readable and often personal manner, this book answers most of the questions that you might have about dogs. It should be on the bookshelf of every dog owner."

— **Stanley Coren**, author of *How Dogs Think*

"No one manages to mix scientific knowledge, practical advice, and love for dogs as well as Marc Bekoff."

— **Angelo Vaira**, author of *Dritto al cuore del tuo cane* (Straight to your dog's heart)

"In *Dogs Demystified*, world-renowned dog expert Marc Bekoff gives us a grand tour of all things dog. The short and accessible encyclopedic entries help us understand our dogs better, and, fortified with this understanding, we can appreciate what our dogs need to live full, happy lives. Delightful and informative, *Dogs Demystified* is just what the dog ordered. Read this book. Your furry friend will thank you."

— **Jessica Pierce**, bioethicist and author of *Who's a Good Dog?*

"*Dogs Demystified* joins a growing call to look at dogs as individuals and not just members of their breed or species. It emphasizes their emotional lives and an appreciation for what we can learn from free-living dogs, or 'streeties,' as they are known in my part of the world. This type of open-minded, bold exploration is much needed in the world of dogs."

— **Sindhoor Pangal**, author of *Dog Knows: Learning How to Learn from Dogs*

"There is no mystery to dogs when we open our hearts. They are mirrors of our humanity, and this book offers us some clarity and direction in these times when we are increasingly disconnected from the natural world and fellow creatures wild and domesticated whom we continue to harm."

— **Michael W. Fox**, veterinarian, ethologist, and bioethicist

DOGS
Demystified

ALSO BY MARC BEKOFF

The Animal Manifesto: Six Reasons for Expanding Our Compassion Footprint

Animal Passions and Beastly Virtues: Reflections on Redecorating Nature

Canine Confidential: Why Dogs Do What They Do

The Animals' Agenda: Freedom, Compassion, and Coexistence in the Human Age (with Jessica Pierce)

Animals at Play: Rules of the Game (a children's book)

Animals Matter: A Biologist Explains Why We Should Treat Animals with Compassion and Respect

A Dog's World: Imagining the Lives of Dogs in a World without Humans (with Jessica Pierce)

Minding Animals: Awareness, Emotions, and Heart

Nature's Life Lessons: Everyday Truths from Nature (with Jim Carrier)

Rewilding Our Hearts: Building Pathways of Compassion and Coexistence

Species of Mind: The Philosophy and Biology of Cognitive Ethology (with Colin Allen)

Strolling with Our Kin (a children's book)

The Ten Trusts: What We Must Do to Care for the Animals We Love (with Jane Goodall)

Unleashing Your Dog : A Field Guide to Giving Your Canine Companion the Best Life Possible (with Jessica Pierce)

Why Dogs Hump and Bees Get Depressed: The Fascinating Science of Animal Intelligence, Emotions, Friendship, and Conservation

Wild Justice: The Moral Lives of Animals (with Jessica Pierce)

EDITED BY MARC BEKOFF

Animal Play: Evolutionary, Comparative, and Ecological Perspectives (with John Byers)

The Cognitive Animal: Empirical and Theoretical Perspectives on Animal Cognition (with Colin Allen and Gordon Burghardt)

Coyotes: Biology, Behavior, and Management

Encyclopedia of Animal Behavior

Encyclopedia of Animal Rights and Animal Welfare

Encyclopedia of Human-Animal Relationships: A Global Exploration of Our Connections with Animals

Ignoring Nature No More: The Case for Compassionate Conservation

Listening to Cougar (with Cara Blessley Lowe)

Readings in Animal Cognition (with Dale Jamieson)

The Smile of a Dolphin: Remarkable Accounts of Animal Emotions

DOGS
Demystified

An A-to-Z Guide to All Things Canine

MARC BEKOFF

Foreword by Jane Goodall
Drawings by Joan Baez

New World Library
Novato, California

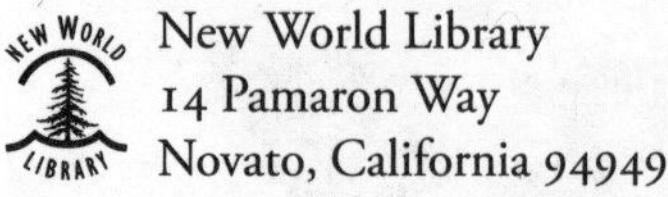
New World Library
14 Pamaron Way
Novato, California 94949

Text design by Tona Pearce-Myers

Library of Congress Cataloging-in-Publication Data

Names: Bekoff, Marc, author. | Goodall, Jane, writer of foreword. | Baez, Joan, illustrator.
Title: Dogs demystified : an A-to-Z guide to all things canine / Marc Bekoff ; foreword by Jane Goodall ; drawings by Joan Baez
Description: Novato, California : New World Library, [2023] | Summary: "An easy-to-read A-to-Z guide of 'all things dog.' The book largely focuses on dog behavior — what dogs do and why they do it — in order to help readers understand, appreciate, and peacefully coexist with dogs." — Provided by publisher.
Identifiers: LCCN 2023009292 (print) | LCCN 2023009293 (ebook) | ISBN 9781608688166 (paperback) | ISBN 9781608688173 (epub)
Subjects: LCSH: Dogs--Behavior. | Dogs--Psychology.
Classification: LCC SF433 .B346 2024 (print) | LCC SF433 (ebook) | DDC 636.7/0887--dc23/eng/20230307
LC record available at https://lccn.loc.gov/2023009292
LC ebook record available at https://lccn.loc.gov/2023009293

First printing, June 2023
ISBN 978-1-60868-816-6
Ebook ISBN 978-1-60868-817-3
Printed in Canada on 100% postconsumer-waste recycled paper

New World Library is proud to be a Gold Certified Environmentally Responsible Publisher. Publisher certification awarded by Green Press Initiative.

10 9 8 7 6 5 4 3 2 1

I dedicate this book to all dogs everywhere.
I hope it will help you all to have the very best lives possible.

Drawing by Joan Baez

CONTENTS

This is Kesey, who was rescued by orthopedic surgeon Dr. Laura E Peycke, DVM. Peycke writes about Kesey: “Hail to the dogs found on the side of the road and who exist as love in a human’s world.”

Drawing by Connie Carpenter Phinney

FOREWORD

Almost everyone thinks that my favorite animal must be a chimpanzee. They are wrong. Actually, chimpanzees share so many characteristics with us that I do not consider them "animals" — any more than we think of ourselves as "animals," although we are. My favorite animal is the dog. When I was growing up, a very special dog came into my life named Rusty. Dogs can be extremely intelligent — Rusty certainly was. It almost seemed he was sent to teach me about animal behavior. He didn't even belong to us, but lived in a hotel around the corner. They did not mind that he left them at around 6 a.m., returning only for his midday meal and to sleep at night, when we told him to go home around 10 p.m. I first met him when I was about ten, and he was my best friend for the next ten years until he died. I would never have gone off to Africa had he still been alive — I could not have betrayed his trust. I still miss him to this day, almost seventy years later, and in spite of all the other wonderful dogs I have known since.

It was because of my relationship with Rusty that I was able to stand up to the professors at Cambridge University who told me, after I had been studying wild chimpanzees for over a year, that I could not talk about their personalities, minds, or emotions — because those were unique to humans. Rusty had taught me long before I began studying our closest relatives that humans were not the only sentient sapient beings on the planet.

Not for nothing have dogs earned the title of "man's best friend" — or perhaps now we should say "humanity's best friend." They have been trained to be eyes for the blind, ears for the deaf, guards for the house. Sheepdogs help shepherds to herd their flocks, and hunting dogs help in the chase. Because of their keen sense of smell, dogs can help track down criminals, find people buried under the rubble of a collapsed building, detect cancer, and predict the onset of epileptic seizures. Dogs can sniff out endangered animals or their body parts being smuggled illegally across borders.

An increasing number of dogs are being taken into hospitals, where they bring comfort to the sick. They provide companionship for the lonely and help autistic children to read because they do not judge. And there are so many wonderful stories of dogs who seek out help when their owners are lying unconscious or wounded after some kind of accident in a remote place. As I watch the horrors of the war in Ukraine, I have seen cases where an abandoned dog (through death or emigration of their person) has been adopted by soldiers. "He's changed our lives," said one soldier, who was based with his unit in a hastily constructed, damp trench. "He warns us if anyone approaches — and he gives us love and raises morale." It was the same story with a dog who was adopted by people sheltering in a basement during air raids in Ukraine.

All those things and more are what dogs do for us. But what about the other way round? What do we do for dogs? How do they want to be treated? Of course, we rescue and adopt dogs and give them homes. A dog with a really good home, understanding human companions, access to the outdoors, and plenty of exercise will be a "happy" or contented dog. Especially if there are two dogs, so they can play and keep each other company. A dog can be a member of the family in a good way — treated with love and respect for their dogness. Others are treated not as a dog but as a human with furry skin, dressed in fancy coats and jeweled collars. This may all be done with the best of intentions, but is this the way dogs like to be treated? Do dogs like being bathed in perfumed shampoo or having their hair shaped in fancy styles?

What of the thousands of dogs who are left alone all day, trapped in a house or apartment five days a week, simply to give their owners a few hours of pleasure in the evenings and on weekends, and who are likely to be dumped in kennels when their owners go on holiday? What of the dogs who have very few opportunities to run off-leash, to interact with other dogs? And what of those who are taken for walks but not allowed to spend time sniffing along the way, gleaning information about the world of dogs, tugged along with irritated jerks of the leash?

If you really and truly love dogs, you need to understand the ways they try to communicate. As Marc Bekoff says in this wonderful book, you need to understand "dog," to learn the meaning of the communication signals your dog is sending you — of pleasure, irritation, displeasure, apprehension, fear. You need to be able to interpret the expression that says, *I want to be a good dog, but I don't understand what you want me to do.* Understand the desperate apology: *I know I shouldn't mess in the house, but you left me so long and I couldn't help it. Please understand and forgive.*

Dogs Demystified will help you to develop a relationship that is two-way with true communication and companionship between human and dog. Above all, dogs are loyal companions who give us unconditional love when they are treated with kindness and respect.

Jane Goodall, PhD, DBE
Founder of the Jane Goodall Institute
and UN Messenger of Peace

Introduction

A DOG BOOK FOR EVERYONE

Dogs Demystified is an easy-to-read, easy-to-use A-to-Z guide — or *canidpedia* — of "all things dog." It largely focuses on dog behavior — what dogs do and how and why they do it — in order to help you see, appreciate, and respect dogs for who they are and not what we want them to be. A large part of demystifying our canine companions is understanding how they sense their world, which is rather different than how we sense our world, and I hope this guide helps you get eye to eye, nose to nose, and ear to ear with dogs. Getting a good handle on what is happening inside a dog's head and heart is how we can minimize the border between them and us. When we can do that, we are better able to help dogs be dogs — to do what comes naturally — in a world where many aspects of their lives are often controlled and compromised by humans.

However, *Dogs Demystified* is really a potpourri. It includes many diverse topics — such as art, culture, ethics, animal welfare and well-being, conservation, and spirituality — and how they relate to canines. Further, as a cognitive ethologist — a scientist who studies the inner lives of all sorts of nonhuman beings, including dogs — I want to introduce readers to animal research itself. In a conversational, nontechnical way, entries explain research terms and how science is conducted, and I cite numerous studies that support what we currently know about dogs. For a list of references, visit marcbekoff.com (see: "Dogs

Demystified / Notes"). Throughout, I blend data with first-person stories, since I think everyday anecdotes are in themselves rich sources of information that often generate subjects for more research.

I also bring an ethological perspective, which means I view dogs as individuals whose behavior has evolved over time. I'm also concerned with how dogs adapt to different habitats, including their human's homes, what causes them to do what they do, and how behavior develops throughout their lives. Everyone knows that domestic dogs originally evolved from a common ancestry of wild wolves, but dogs have continued to change as they have kept adapting to our increasingly human-dominated world. The bottom line is, I hope by reading this book you become more dog literate — fluent in all things dog — and something of a "citizen ethologist" yourself as you increase your understanding of what it is like to be a dog.

Minnie, a canine ethologist, carefully watching a deer. Dogs watch us as we watch them! (Credit: Tom Gordon)

DOGS IN OUR WORLD

Hardly a day goes by that someone doesn't ask me a "dog" question. I find myself saying over and over again something like, "Did you know that dogs do this or that?" Many people are eager to learn more about dogs — about their different personalities and why they do what they do and how the behavior of dogs relates to wolves and other wild relatives such as coyotes. This is one of the main purposes of this book: to answer all those questions about the intelligence, feelings, and personalities — including the quirkiness — of dogs. This book also makes clear how much more there is to learn. When people ask me questions I can't answer, or for which there aren't any simple, definitive answers, I tell them honestly, "I don't know." In fact, the more I learn, the more I realize all that we still don't know about dogs, and that isn't a bad thing. It truly reflects how much we're learning, how we need to look at dogs as individuals, and how much we need to appreciate that every dog-human relationship is unique. I honestly get upset when people make categorical pronouncements about dogs — saying they can't or don't do this or that — and characterize dog-human relationships in a narrow human-centered way.

However, my deeper hope — both with this book and when I speak to people — is that increased understanding will foster more caring. A dog's feelings matter to them, and they should also matter to us. We should take the perspective and emotions of dogs into account in every aspect of our shared lives. This applies to training. I prefer to think of training as teaching and educating dogs about how to live in our human-oriented world — which should be done using only positive, force-free methods. But in reality, dogs are always learning from humans. We often place unrealistic social expectations on dogs, especially homed dogs, who are constantly being asked to do what *we* want them to do. So giving dogs some extra tender loving care is really good for them and for us. You can't "spoil" a dog, nor are there really many "bad dogs." Most of the time, when dogs "misbehave," they're simply doing whatever they have to do to be dogs. Training is a form of education; it's not a way to program dogs so they always please us.

There's no shortage of dogs who will benefit from humans trying to figure out what it is like to be a dog. As I'm writing this book, dogs can be found in around 64 million American households — which accounts for 53 percent of all US homes. In Japan, dog companionship is very widespread, and people like to travel with their dogs, so much so that Japan's Shinkansen bullet trains are creating a pet-friendly carriage in which dogs can roam free and relax as they travel with their people.

Dogs themselves are a very diverse species — *Canis lupus familiaris* is the most diverse mammal. As such, there is no "universal dog." Further, laboratory studies that seek to assess dog behavior and human-dog relationships can provide limited or even skewed results. Many times, the dogs used in studies are captive, highly controlled individuals in restricted settings, and just because those dogs don't do something in a lab doesn't mean other dogs can't, don't, or won't exhibit that behavior when they're free. This makes it impossible to declare that "all dogs" do this or that in any particular situation. Overall, dog breeds don't have distinct personalities, but individual dogs do — so don't judge a dog by their cover. Not every member of a given breed will always perform the way people expect.

Likewise, comparative research on dogs and wolves doesn't allow us to make reliable species-wide conclusions about the cognitive skills of dogs compared with wolves. A lot of research hangs on which tests are used, how they're conducted, and how individuals are raised.

In total, there are about a billion dogs in the world, but many people don't realize that only around 20 percent of those dogs are "homed" individuals — those cared for by people, who (hopefully) provide their dogs with a predictable place to sleep, healthy food, a lot of love and respect, and veterinary care. This means that roughly 750 million dogs are free-ranging or feral and have different amounts of contact, both direct and indirect, with humans. The good news is that globally there are numerous projects concerned with the humane care of these individuals. Of course, some dogs do indeed need us, but many feral dogs can do quite well on their own. What might happen with dogs if humans weren't around is what Jessica Pierce and I explore in our book *A Dog's World: Imagining the Lives of Dogs in a World without Humans*.

Homed dogs also lose countless freedoms, meaning they can't always be who they really are. We're constantly telling dogs what they should or shouldn't do as we helicopter parent their dogness out of them. Too much fussing and pampering of family dogs can actually compromise their well-being. In *The Book Your Dog Wishes You Would Read*, British dog trainer Louise Glazebrook puts it succinctly: "I actually got really emotional, because I saw in lockdown what we as a society were doing to dogs. I remember sitting there one night just crying — we call ourselves a nation of dog lovers, yet essentially, we're [screwing] them over. It felt like this really horrible moment for dogs."

Along these lines, in her book *Love Is All You Need*, Jennifer Arnold notes that dogs live in an environment that "makes it impossible for them to alleviate their own stress and anxiety." According to Arnold, "In modern society, there is no way for our dogs to keep themselves safe, and thus we are unable to afford them the freedom to meet their own needs. Instead, they must depend on our benevolence for survival." Some people even wonder whether we deserve dogs. I frequently ask people to cut their dog some slack when possible because, in our humancentric world, what a dog wants and needs doesn't always mesh with what humans want and need.

I often wonder if the process of domestication — which David Nibert has dubbed "domesecration" — might cause "collective trauma" in nonhuman animals. While we usually only consider collective trauma to be something that impacts humans, there's no reason to think it might not apply to nonhumans.

Often when we tell a dog they're a "good dog" — and most people don't say this enough — we're letting them know that they did something *we* like, not necessarily something that is an expression of being a card-carrying dog who expresses "good dogness." Conversely, when a dog does something that comes naturally — that expresses their dogness — we typically tell them they're being a "bad dog." This causes problems in individuals, and it impacts the species, since it means we are continuing to select for traits that we find appealing, but which might be highly detrimental to what makes a good life for a dog.

For example, I often hear that there's something wrong if a dog doesn't like to play, doesn't eat a meal, doesn't want to go to the dog park, needs alone time, or just seems to be having a bad day. Normalizing certain dog behavior as universal, or being overly simplistic about the reasons why dogs do certain things, is misleading and can cause huge problems. Of course, it is important to note changes in behavior, disposition, or mood, but like us, canines can have good days and bad days, ups and downs. Dogs are not always up and there for us, and that is a normal part of being a dog.

In fact, some of this misguided care is related to the many misleading myths about who dogs supposedly are and what they should do (which I address in several entries). For instance, dogs are not our "best friends," and they don't love all humans unconditionally. When dogs love, it's more than mere attachment — it's real love. If your dog doesn't seem to love you, there's not something "wrong" with the dog; dogs are not unconditional lovers, as they're often touted to be. Dogs have minds and feelings of their own, and they're pretty choosy. Their close association with humans might be because they possess a gene that lowers their stress, so they're more relaxed around people, but that doesn't mean they'll love you regardless of how you treat them.

While dogs can and do love people, and often display remarkable devotion, any given dog is not *always* going to be in the mood to cuddle or play at any given moment. Dogs have different preferences and personalities. In his award-winning book *The 5 Love Languages: The Secret to Love That Lasts*, Gary Chapman identified five different aspects of human-human relationships that are important for keeping a relationship fresh and growing: acts of service, gift-giving, physical touch, quality time, and words of affirmation. How they apply to dog-human relationships is interesting to ponder. My take is that it all depends on context — who the dog is, who the human is, the nature of their ongoing relationship, and what's happening at the moment for each of them, just like in any human-human relationship. All five are an integral part of the language-of-love package, and they're difficult to separate. All are essential and important for staying in love and keeping a relationship fresh and growing amid the demands, conflicts, and boredom of everyday life. In other words, to understand your dog's behavior, you always have to consider the context for your dog. That means paying close attention to who the dog is, who you are, and the nature of your unique relationship. That's why there are so many mysteries and too many myths floating around. Each dog and every dog-human relationship is unique. We can't assume there are quick, simple, cut-and-dried answers to all our questions about what makes dogs tick.

In this book, rather than provide one-size-fits-all explanations, I try to offer wide-ranging explorations that convey what dogs are capable of and that hopefully leave you excited about how much more there is to learn and discover, both about dogs in general and about your dog in particular.

Drawing by Joan Baez

SEEING, STUDYING, AND RETHINKING DOGS

In order to understand dogs, we have to actually *see* and appreciate dogs for who they are. We also need to pay attention to *how* we are looking — are we bringing any preconceived notions about the cognitive and emotional capacities or limits of dogs? Those assumptions can affect what we see, who we see, and our conclusions. I often encourage people to conduct their own citizen science with their own dog or with the dogs they meet. I ask them to try as hard as they can to see the world from a dog's perspective or to "become a dog" in the way an ethologist would. *Seeing* dogs rather than merely looking at them allows us to get into their heads and hearts.

For me, it's really a lot of fun to watch and study dogs, and you don't need to be a trained, credentialed, card-carrying scientist. Anyone who retains their childlike curiosity and who wants to know more about dogs can build a database of canine behavior and draw useful, practical conclusions. In this way, dogs can rekindle our youthful curiosity. To help foster this, I've included entries in this book on research terms and methods, which you can try out and adapt in your own ways. Historically, citizen science has contributed a lot of detailed and useful information about dogs, and you can use what you learn to help you decide which behaviors you should encourage and which you should discourage — with the main goal being to allow your dog to be as much of a dog as possible, rather than imagining them like a furry human running around on all fours.

Minnie proofreading my book
(Credit: Tom Gordon)

Citizen scientists are amateur naturalists — and curious naturalists — who have contributed to the knowledge base for a wide variety of nonhumans. I talk with people a lot when I'm at a dog park or in nature as their dogs are playing, peeing, and just doing what dogs do, and I always learn something. During the Covid pandemic, when many people had to work at home, I received many emails telling me that as people were spending more time with their companion dog, they were learning more about who they were and appreciating them more. One hard-core scientist — in his own words — told me that he came to respect the field of animal behavior more because figuring out what his dog was doing was a challenge, one that was no less difficult than his field of particle physics.

Understanding what dogs are feeling is critical to any attempt to figure out why they do what they do. Dogs have rich and deep emotional lives, and we must honor and respect this bona fide scientific fact whenever we interact with them. Treating dogs as if they don't have emotions is antiscientific, and it damages the relationships dogs form with us and other dogs. Dogs not only care about what happens to themselves, but they also care about what happens to other dogs and their humans. They read us well; what we're feeling goes down leash. Healthy dog-human relationships are a two-way street and require mutual tolerance and respect, and it can be a lot of fun building and maintaining strong and enduring bonds — which is a win-win for all. We need to meet dogs halfway to build and maintain reciprocal, give-and-take relationships. It isn't all about us. We must learn to know "dog," and dogs must learn to know "human." In other words, dogs depend on the people who live with them to become fluent in dog — to be dog literate — so we humans can understand what our dogs are trying to tell us.

A good analogy is that a dog-human relationship is a puzzle, and our mutual goal is to assemble an entire puzzle that works for all concerned. Of course, the shape of the pieces is constantly changing, and this is part of the game I find especially fun and exciting. The main challenge is fitting the pieces into a coherent whole while recognizing that the "best fit" will vary from dog to dog and relationship to relationship and even over time.

The number and shape of the pieces can vary depending on the personalities of the dog and their humans. Humans must adjust their lives to accommodate their dog's needs, and dogs must learn and unlearn certain behaviors — like peeing wherever they like, chasing, humping, jumping on people, sniffing crotches, and so on — to adapt to their human-oriented world. To work on your puzzle and gain a better understanding about what's happening for your dog, make a list of the different variables and make a drawing of a dog's head, ears, tail, mouth, facial expressions, gaits, and postures, and then consider odors, sounds, and visual signals in the different situations in which you and they interact. One guiding principle for me is that I imagine it's every dog's wish to be able to pee on everything in the world, and it's my job to restrict these peeing proclivities without damaging their dogness or self-image.

It can be quite challenging to make sense of the inflowing and outgoing information, but it also can be loads of fun. By doing this, you get to know your own dog better, and they get to know you better, and these shared emotions and knowledge can function like "social glue," which is mutually beneficial.

Some people might think: *What a pain this is! I just want a dog and I want them to be happy.* But in the long run, if you take the time to get to know your dog better, it's a win-win for everyone. Looked at this way, it's a gift rather than a chore.

We strip far too many dogs of their dogness, and surely we can do better — much better! Some people also try to strip dogs of their rich and deep emotional lives, which flies in the face of loads of scientific data — dogs are not simply a bundle of unthinking reflexes. In fact, we can learn about our encounters with other humans by paying attention to how dogs interact with dogs and us. Dog aficionada Sarah Murphy told me, "I have raised three kids, and worked in multiple high-profile management jobs, and yet I have learned more about raising, partnering with, and working with humans from my dogs than anything else in my life."

Of course, I hope this book helps you understand the world of dogs, but I really hope it helps you understand your own dog — by inspiring you to get to know them for the individual they are and to build a life together based on mutual understanding, respect, and love.

In many ways, we're a planet of and for the dogs. So let's do the best we can because it would be a lonely planet without these amazing beings.

WHY DO YOU DO THAT?: QUESTIONS FOR OUR DOGS

In November 2021, Jessica Pierce and I did a presentation for our book *A Dog's World: Imagining the Lives of Dogs in a World without Humans.* In the audience feedback, we learned that so many people, even those who "know" dogs, wanted to know more, and that's partly what inspired me to write this book. Then, when I started writing it, I asked people I knew — both dog experts and personal friends — to share with me some of the questions they wished they could ask their dogs. If dogs and humans spoke the same language, what would people want to know about how their dog feels and what dogs think about us, their lives, and the world we share?

What follows is a selection of the responses I received. To one degree or another, as best I could, I tried to address all the topics people raised in this book, even if my answer is often, "I don't know."

Minnie launching into a zoomie (Credit: Lisa Kalfas)

Personally, one question I would have asked each of my dogs is, "Why do you play so much?" My dogs were all players, and my guess is they would have said they play because they enjoy it — because it's fun — and because they love mixing it up with their friends and others.

There are some general trends in people's questions. People want to know if their dogs are happy and content and what their humans could do to improve their lives. They want to know their dog's history — what happened to the dog before they were adopted, and how dogs experience their own canine families. Some people, recognizing individual differences, asked different questions for each of their dogs. I hope these questions inspire you to make your own list as you explore this book.

I also wonder what dogs would ask of us. This is an equally important question to consider. Jethro, the last dog with whom I shared my home and heart, was a large couch dog. Nothing pleased him more than plopping down next to me — all his ninety pounds of muscle and often unpleasant odors — and simply staring at me, as if to say, *What do you want from me?* If he could have, I'm sure he would have sat like the dog in Joan Baez's drawing below, pondering the world and considering whether to write a book about humans!

Drawing by Joan Baez

Marco Adda, dog researcher and behavior consultant

Hey dog, if you were given a chance to speak at the Global Dog Conference, what would you say? What are the urgent topics you would want to discuss with all the dog delegations from all around the world?

Mary Angilly, dog trainer

Are you happy? How can I increase your happiness?
What are three things you wish we did more or less of?
What was your life like before I adopted you? Do you miss it?

Sayli Benadikar, head of animal interaction and behavior at Companion Software Development

Questions for my dog Lyra:

Can you smell the time of day?
Who was the most challenging puppy in the litter you had, and why?

Questions for my dog Draco:

How are you feeling differently between when you howl to a siren, or when you howl in unison with Lyra when she is in heat, or when you howl in the car crate on your way to a run?
Did you enjoy spending time with your littermates in the first nine weeks of your life or would you rather have been a singleton?

Deborah Pilley Bianchi, writer, producer, and founder of the Chaser Initiative

What did you hear, feel, or see to evoke that haunting eulogy of a bark?

Backstory: My father, researcher John Pilley, was the parent of Chaser, who was dubbed "the world's smartest dog," and the two of us taught Chaser together. In 2018 my father was diagnosed with a rare form of leukemia and went downhill very rapidly. After three weeks in the hospital, he spent his last six days in the serenity of hospice as he slipped in and out of consciousness. Chaser spent those last days with us, mostly wandering in and out of the room and quietly accepting my dad's outstretched arms for a weak hug. But on his last day, she silently stood up, positioning herself directly in front of his bed. Her tail was down, tucked against her hind quarters, with her shoulders squeezed tight against her chest, and her head was low with her ears pinned back against her head. She stared at him for several seconds and then let out one very loud, sharp bark, standing stock-still as she continued to give him her "border collie eye." It stunned us into silence as we looked from one to the other, goose bumps creeping up our arms and down our necks.

Jack Brooks, Turkish Delight manufacturer and Floppy's human

Floppy, why do you like to eat leaves so much?

Mark Derr, author and dog expert

Do you think about your situation in the world? If so, what is it?
What is one thing you would change about your life that would make it better?

Yannick Eckmann, product developer at Cuore of Switzerland and former professional cyclist

Why are you always lying down when you see other dogs?

Hope Ferdowsian, author and president of the Phoenix Zones Initiative

Sugar, what makes you feel the safest?
Stella, how can we make it easier for you to interact with your dog friends?

Camilla Fox, founder and executive director of Project Coyote

Mokie, why are you itching so much, and what can I do to alleviate the itching?
Are you happy alone with me or would you prefer more dogs in our life? How would you feel if we added a cat to our household?!

Jenny Gerson, senior director of sustainability for DataBank

Kaia, what would your perfect day consist of?
How much of what I say to you do you understand?

Tom Gordon, retired outdoor gear specialist

Why do you love to roll and rub your neck on dead things?
How do you perceive dogs and their people walking more than a block away when you bark and warn us of their presence?

Brian Hare, professor at Duke University and coauthor of *The Genius of Dogs*

What is it like to be so positive?
Why does fetch make you so happy?
How can I be more like you?

Lauren Harris, actress, director, and producer

Can you walk me through what you've been through — having been abandoned by your owner and placed in a high-kill shelter in South Korea? What were your first impressions of Los Angeles and me?
Why does it bother you so much when I try to brush your teeth?

Jules Howard, zoologist and author of *Wonderdog*

The first question I'd ask Ozzy (our lurcher) would be, predictably, "Is this love?" I've thought for a long time about dogs and what we can infer about their emotions (and the strength of their attachment) by considering their day-to-day interactions with us. Of course, it's clear that they can feel something we would describe as love.

The second question would be a little more left field. I often wonder about the emotional responses Ozzy gets from sniffing certain smells. It would be fascinating to know whether these smells elicit in Oz memories of events long gone, as seems to happen in humans.

Jon Knoll, former global category manager for Pearl Izumi USA

What do you think we are — big, smart dogs; servants; Gods?
Do you understand our affection?
What do you wish for?
What concerns you most?
Why all the barking?

Paul McCartney, musician, songwriter, and animal advocate

My wife Nancy, stepson Arlen, and I have a lovely little dog called Rose. She was a rescue, and when she arrived with the name Rose, we thought it suited her and decided to keep it. She and her family had been abandoned on the streets in South Carolina, and the rescue facility had the requirement that the dogs had to be picked up before Friday or they would need to be put down because the facility didn't have enough money to keep them longer than that. Fortunately for us and Rose, she was picked up on the Thursday by the Animal Rescue Fund, where we finally met her. It was love at first sight, and she went from being a cruelly abandoned dog to being the queen of our hearts.

The question I would ask is: Who abandoned you and left you out in the streets?

Heather McWilliams Mierzejewski, avid doggie foster mom, cycling buddy, and marketing director at Tribute Technology

I don't think I have just one question because I would ask every dog something different. They are all so different. For instance, my current dog Jett pretty much tells me things already. So, if I want to know something, I just ask him.

Our dog Zoey does this thing where you call her and she runs to the couch, where she waits to be patted or picked up, instead of running to us. I kinda want to know why.

If I truly only had one question, I would ask, "How self-aware are you?" That question feels really loaded with "human" and not so much "dog." I'm curious, though, because if animals are truly self-aware the way humans are, it should inform a lot of change in our society with regards to how we treat nonhuman animals.

I'd also ask, "Are you ready to die?"

Ádám Miklósi, dog researcher and director of the Family Dog Research Project

Do you like what you get as food?

Ingrid Newkirk, founder of People for the Ethical Treatment of Animals (PETA)

We were given a dog named Muffy who was rescued after eight years of life on a chain in someone's backyard, appallingly neglected. She came to live with us. Once I picked up a broom, and she flattened herself onto the floor, giving an indication of how her interactions with humans carrying a stick, a rake, a broom, something like that, had been. When there was a thunderstorm, she dug frantically into the bed as if to burrow to China, and even tried to burrow into me, desperate to escape.

I would have liked to ask her: Out there, alone in your back garden, tied up so that you could not run from it, what happened? Did lightning ever strike close by or did a tree fall down perhaps that you are so incredibly afraid, or is that always how you've felt?

Jessica Pierce, bioethicist and author of *Run, Spot, Run*

I would like to ask Bella how much of her daily life she would describe as boring: 0 percent, 25 percent, 50 percent, 75 percent, 100 percent.

I would also ask whether she likes it when we talk to her or whether she finds it annoying.

Anne Carver Rose, professor at Pennsylvania State University

How do you feel when I scold you?

My question is *not* about whether she understands why she misbehaved (there is so much advice about this on the internet). It's about how she processes that someone who is generally nice to her can turn around and raise her voice and look upset. Being an empathetic animal, she knows I am genuinely angry.

Why don't you believe that, when I go out, I will come back?

Marian Salley, psychotherapist and social worker

What was it like to leave your mother and/or siblings and to have them leave you?

How does it feel to be told what to do all the time? How do you experience yourself relative to a sense of agency in your life?

Margaret Wallace, retired schoolteacher and Arley's human

Arley, when we push up the blinds by the bed so that you can see out, are we putting you on duty to keep track of everything, or is that your choice?

When you play with a toy or small, squeaky ball as if it's a small animal, are you actually pretending that it is alive and might run away?

Vanessa Woods, director of Duke Puppy Kindergarten and journalist

What did you dream about last night?
What is your earliest memory?

Sonny and Lennard Zinn, owners of Zinn Cycles

Three questions we would like to ask our dog, Eleven:

1. When you roll in something, what is it that attracts you – why do you do it?
2. Why are you licking your belly so much? Is it food-related or anxiety? Your belly skin wants to know as much as we do!
3. Why are you so afraid of thunder and fireworks? Is there more (than the CBD and ThunderShirt) we could do to support you through these events?

WHERE TO FIND REFERENCES AND NOTES

This book is based on a good deal of science, and readers can find the references at marcbekoff.com (see: "Dogs Demystified / Notes").

AN A-TO-Z GUIDE TO ALL THINGS CANINE

Drawing by Joan Baez

A

abnormal behavior. This could be any problematic behavior that falls outside of what we normally might expect. When identifying "abnormal dog behavior," a good deal hangs on the words *normal* and *expect.* What we might label as *normal* can vary by breed, context, and individual.

We need to be very careful in labeling something as *abnormal* — by normalizing behavior — because we know that dogs and many other animals show great variability in behavior depending on *context*, including what's happening around them, who's there, and where they are. *Abnormal* could refer to unusual or excessive behavior, such as aggression or barking, but often when a dog is doing something we call abnormal or excessive, it might be just what one would expect when different aspects of context are considered. Their behavior might be entirely dog appropriate — butts and noses are very important to dogs — and we need to consider the dog's point of view.

One very large study of 4,114 dogs and 2,480 guardians, titled "Demographics and Comorbidity of Behavior Problems in Dogs," reported that 85 percent of people living with dogs experienced behavior problems, including "fear/anxiety, aggression, jumping, excessive barking, coprophagia, obsessive-compulsive/compulsive behaviors, house soiling, rolling in repulsive materials, overactivity/hyperactivity, destructive behavior, running away / escaping, and mounting/humping."

Of course, these can be problematic behaviors, such as what people sometimes call "excessive barking." However, if we consider what a dog is thinking or feeling, what we call excessive might be entirely dog appropriate to the particular situation at hand. The bottom line is simple: We must consider what's happening in a dog's head and heart and take their perspective — the point of view of each unique individual.

Dogs will bark in situations in which it seems to us that barking is unnecessary or over the top. They may be smelling, hearing, or seeing something of which we are totally unaware, or simply be feeling down and out or afraid. Perhaps they are having trouble figuring out what's happening and are scared out of their mind. Or maybe they had a bad dream, which is quite possible. *See also* **barking**; **dreaming**; **humping**; **rolling in stinky stuff**.

abuse. Dogs suffer a good deal of abuse in our world, which includes neglect, dog fighting, obesity, use in research, and many other examples. For instance, beagles have been force-fed fungicides because animal testing is required in Brazil. Breeding facilities are also guilty of rampant abuse. Dogs who are rescued from laboratories and breeding facilities need a lot of care and love when they are rehomed. In early July 2022, more than forty-five hundred beagles were freed from a laboratory in Virginia by the order of a district court judge. Unfortunately, humans are not always a dog's "best friend." *See also* **best friends, dogs as our**; **scientific research, dogs used in**.

accomplishment, sense of. When dogs do something good or have something that makes them or us happy, I often wonder if they feel a sense of accomplishment. Perhaps they're proud of themselves. After he found some treats I had hidden on my mountain property, one of my dogs, Jethro, would parade around with his head and tail held high either chewing or playing with a piece of food in his mouth. He did this especially when other dogs were around to see him. Was he proud and showing off and saying something like, *Look what I have, aren't I cool?*

I also remember one of my friend's dogs who was a master Frisbee catcher. He would run at blazing speed tracking a Frisbee and jumping and catching it in midair, and right after he landed, he would run back to us and proudly parade around with his catch, head held high as if saying, *Look what I just did!* Crows also may engage in similar behavior. Someone once said to me, "If crows do this, then surely dogs can, too." Well, yes and no. The person assumed birds must be dumber than dogs — they're "bird brains," after all — and he didn't realize that crows are very bright and emotional birds who play and grieve. However, I feel comfortable saying that, when the proper studies are done, we'll learn that dogs and other nonhuman animals feel a sense of accomplishment.

"acting like an animal." A demeaning expression usually implying that a person is doing something that's below them. The phrase is often used when a person acts with excessive violence or is eating in a wild or gluttonous manner. The expression does a disservice to nonhuman animals, including dogs, who commonly exhibit a wide range of positive prosocial behaviors, such as compassion, cooperation, empathy, fairness, and justice. In fact, humans tend to be more violent and xenophobic (afraid of strangers) than other animals in many situations.

acting out. We rarely think of dogs or other nonhumans throwing fits and having temper tantrums out of anger or frustration, but there's no reason to think that other animals don't occasionally act out, just as humans do, to relieve tension or to send a message that they are highly stressed.

activity patterns. The different patterns of behavior dogs perform throughout the day and night. Activity patterns are strongly affected by people, particularly "helicopter" humans. For example, we tell dogs when they're allowed to eat, pee, poop, play, and walk and who they're allowed to interact with and where. *See also* **helicopter parenting**.

adaptability. When a dog alters their behavior to accomplish a goal. Donald Griffin, often called "the father of cognitive ethology" (the study of animal minds), suggested that flexibility in behavior is a marker of consciousness, since an individual has to think through what is happening, think about what they want to happen in the future, and adjust their behavior accordingly. That is, adaptability is the opposite of hardwired thinking, or performing an action or string of actions without considering the impact of what is being done and what might result in the future. *See also* **learning**.

ad libitum sampling. A research sampling technique in which a person tries to record everything an individual does, often including what others are doing to that individual. In the best of all possible worlds, this would be the research method of choice, and using video to record who's doing what to whom can produce these data. *See also* **research techniques**.

adolescence. The period of life between puberty and adulthood. For dogs, adolescence can extend from around six to eight months to two to three years. Dogs might show an extended period of adolescence when compared to their wild relatives, especially when there are humans around to make life easier by providing shelter, food, and medical care.

Dogs, like humans, can get difficult when they reach adolescence. In one 2020 study, Lucy Asher and her colleagues learned there was "an association between earlier puberty and an insecure attachment to a human carer.... When dogs reached puberty, they were less likely to follow commands given by their carer, but not by others." They also wrote, "Conflict behavior is associated with less secure carer attachments during an adolescent phase, because behavior indicative of insecure or anxious attachments was only associated with obedience at an age that corresponds with adolescence."

Barbara Natterson-Horowitz and Kathryn Bowers, authors of *Wildhood: The Epic Journey from Adolescence to Adulthood in Humans and Other Animals*, call adolescence "wildhood," which is a tumultuous time ruled by the "teenage brain" across many different species. Human teenagers can experience or suffer from anxiety, suicidal tendencies, sexual vulnerability, and dangerous risk taking, but research is showing that rodents, dogs, and numerous wild species experience behavioral disturbances during adolescence that can reduce their survival later in life. *See also* **developmental stages**.

adopting a dog. Choosing to share your life, home, and heart with a dog is a huge decision and a life-changer that shouldn't be taken lightly. One UK study showed that nearly 20 percent of dog owners thought that raising a baby is easier than training a puppy, with the first two years being the most difficult. Knowing what to expect and learning the basics of dog behavior can go a long way toward helping make the journey much less difficult. Numerous people also don't anticipate the financial commitment of living with a dog. When times are tough, as many as 50 percent of dog guardians worry about providing adequate veterinary care to their canine companions and a large number worry about affording dog food.

When people can't make ends meet when living with a canine companion, relinquishment occurs at higher rates than usual. Upward of twenty-three million American households adopted a companion animal during the Covid-19 pandemic — around 20 percent. In Canada, around nine hundred thousand people became new pet owners during the pandemic, in many cases as "accessories." In 2019, nearly four hundred thousand shelter dogs were euthanized across North America and the number of surrenders skyrocketed. Many sheltered dogs experience high levels of stress, as evidenced by higher levels of the stress hormone cortisol in their urine.

During the pandemic, when many people worked from home, around 70 percent of people found working at home and training a dog was much trickier than they thought it would be. However, data from the APPA National Pet Owners Survey in 2021–22 showed that 71 percent of dog owners in the United States would be likely to take a remote job over an in-person one to be able to effectively look after their dog; around one-third of dog owners would consider changing their job if they were not allowed to bring their dog to the office; and 44 percent of pet parents would not accept a new role if they did not allow dogs in the office. In addition, 75 percent of people who live with dogs choose dogs in the office over unlimited vacation.

An excellent guide for raising a puppy using force-free, positive methods is *How to Raise a Puppy* by Stephanie Rousseau and Turid Rugaas. *See also* **pandemic puppies**.

aerobic and anaerobic exercise. Cardiovascular conditioning that uses oxygen (aerobic) or produces energy without using oxygen (anaerobic). Dogs, like other animals, including humans, engage in both types of exercise. For wild animals, both are important to survive when they must find food or a place to live and possibly defend those things from others. *See also* **exercise**.

affective dog behavior (ADB). A training approach based on the rich and deep emotional lives of dogs. Emotions affect behavior. Understanding basic human and canine neurobiology can greatly help us in working with another species. Since the canine brain and human brain are very similar, affective dog behavior training is all about mental health, emotional and physical safety, and social and emotional connections.

ADB does not use rigid protocols or particular methods, as these are mostly created with the human, not the dog, in mind. Additionally, dogs have their own individual "protocols" for dealing with the ups and downs of life, and most human protocols don't consider the dog's internal processes. Ideally, your dog will look to you to feel safe — if a dog is triggered, it means they do not feel safe *in that moment*. We can't undo the past by protocol, but we can help dogs feel safe in their own way with our emotional support and recover together afterward.

ADB is not a training program but an educational program. More emphasis is placed on connection than on changing behaviors, simply because many so-called problem behaviors either become less of an issue or are greatly eliminated once a dog feels heard, wanted, or acknowledged. The need for connection is innate, and even millions of years of evolution have not undone something that has served social animals so well.

ADB looks at internal processes to learn why and how behaviors happen, and it emphasizes the importance of all seven of the primary emotional systems identified by neuroscientist Jaak Panksepp. The understanding is that, when a dog goes into a nonsocial state of fear or rage, it is due to an unmet need, and this state is only temporary before the brain will go back to being more social. Thus, this training helps the dog want to be more social again on *their* terms and *their* time. None of these internal processes can be switched off, and coping is up to the individual, yet it's easier with a friend. If dogs are being coerced to suppress their emotions, they don't have much room to express themselves. *See also* **hierarchy of dog needs**; **training**.

African wild dogs (*Lycaon pictus*). Also called African hunting dogs or painted dogs.

age, calculating a dog's. Many people try to translate a dog's age into human terms, but it's not as straightforward as it's often made out to be. You can't simply multiply a dog's age by seven, as is often suggested. A dog's size is important to consider. For example, it's estimated that a small ten-year-old dog would be similar to a fifty-six-year-old human, whereas a large ten-year-old dog would be similar to a sixty-six-year-old human. *See also* **life expectancy**.

agency. Allowing an individual dog the freedom to make their own choices. Jessica Pierce notes, "If I could identify the single most significant problem facing homed dogs right now, it would be lack of adequate agency. Dogs have very little control over their sensory environment, their social interactions, and the basic elements of daily survival, all of which are orchestrated by human guardians. This lack of control — a near-total loss of agency — has significant fallout for their physical and especially their psychological well-being." Fortunately, there are many ways to allow dogs (and other animals) to have more control over their lives and to empower them. *See also* **consent**; **personhood**.

aggregation. An unorganized group of individual dogs. Individuals may be attracted to a particular location because there's food or shelter, or they feel safer and more protected in a group, but they don't necessarily work together as a coordinated unit like a wolf pack.

aggression. Some people differentiate between offensive aggression — in which a dog attacks another dog for no apparent reason, at least to us — and defensive aggression, which occurs when an individual defends themselves when they are threatened or attacked. Breed is not the only predictor of aggression or of competitive, hostile behavior.

An email I received from Sarah shows that often it's very difficult to figure out what is actually happening in a dog's mind when they behave aggressively.

> I was wondering if I could have some more insight into dog behavior from your perspective. I'm a dog trainer now, but I have two male

dogs of my own who absolutely despise each other. They are both unneutered, so I know that plays a role, but it's strange because they have no problems with any other unneutered dogs. They will go into each other's rooms (where the crates are) and antagonize each other. If my corgi even thinks my German shepherd is being let out, he goes crazy. There hasn't been any trauma since I've had them as puppies, and they used to get along. What could cause this?

Unfortunately, I wasn't able to offer any specific advice. It's impossible for me to say anything without seeing it "in person" — or "in dog," as it were — and even then it can be difficult to know. I don't know whether being unneutered was significant, and my advice was to seek out a force-free positive trainer, someone who could see what was happening and make suggestions.

agility training. This refers to teaching dogs to run a predetermined obstacle course in a set amount of time. I've been told that many, if not most, dogs enjoy agility training because it provides exercise, it enriches their lives, and it's fun. Nevertheless, there are risks of which people should be aware, such as the dog twisting an ankle or shoulder. One study showed that 41.4 percent of almost forty-two hundred dogs who engaged in agility training suffered injuries, of which 15 percent were severe and lasted more than three months.

agonistic behavior. Behaviors seen in aggressive and defensive encounters. These include fighting, threatening, submitting, appeasing, and fleeing.

agoraphobia. I've known a few dogs who seemed afraid of being outside and hesitant to leave a small room. All of them had been rescued from abusive laboratory situations, and all but one eventually stepped outside, explored here and there, and felt comfortable doing so from that point on. A few people thought that a dog's refusal to go outdoors was abnormal, but it wasn't. These dogs had no idea what being free really meant because they had been horrifically abused for their entire lives.

allelomimetic behavior. When dogs do what other dogs are doing — aka follow the leader. This is a form of social contagion. *See also* **emotional contagion**.

allomones. Chemicals, similar to pheromones, that a dog releases to communicate with other dogs. *See also* **pheromones**; **scent marking**.

alloparental behavior. Aka babysitting. This is also often called "helping behavior." Helping behavior has been observed in free-ranging dogs, and those providing care can include proxy parents, such as grandparents, aunts, uncles, older siblings, and other adults. Who provides care depends on the social organization of a group and who is available and willing to help. In some animals, helping occurs when there is enough food to support all the individuals who are present.

allopatric. Animals living in different, nonoverlapping areas.

alone time. Most dogs need both social interactions and time on their own, and it's important to give dogs plenty of both. If a dog seems uninterested in socializing or playing with their humans, there's no reason to take it personally or to feel snubbed.

It is important for every dog to have a "safe zone" — a place they can retreat to and feel safe, where they are allowed not to interact or be touched. Mishka, a somewhat zaftig husky with whom I shared my home, loved to nestle in a corner behind a bed when she'd had enough of her humans. She made it clear what she was doing, and there was only room for her. When she was ready to interact, she'd have to back out of her husky cave, which she did with impressive agility. Some people provide their dog with a crate or kennel — with the door always open — that is designated "dog property" and is off-limits to children and other humans in the house.

Every dog is different, and how much time they need or prefer to spend with humans varies, but learn to recognize the signs of separation anxiety if dogs are left alone for long periods (such as over five or six hours). It's also possible that when a dog is spending what seems to be too much time alone, there's something wrong, and you should consult a veterinarian. For example, heightened sensitivity to noise can indicate a dog is in pain. This is why it's essential to know your dog well. *See also* **safety, sense of**; **separation anxiety**.

alpha dog. The "top dog" or highest-ranking individual in a group. This status can be attained with or without fighting. Dogs, wolves, and other canids form dominance relationships in which there is an alpha individual, but it's a myth that dominance-based training works for dogs. It doesn't. *See also* **dominance**; **pack formation**.

altricial. Dogs and other animals who are born in an undeveloped state and require parental and/or alloparental care. *See also* **precocial**.

altruism. Typically, animal researchers define this as selfless behavior that benefits another individual at the altruist's expense. Individuals who perform altruistic behavior are called *donors*, and those who benefit are called *recipients*. There are very few examples of true altruism in nonhumans in which the donor actually suffers a permanent loss of reproductive output or fitness. However, the word is often used to refer to situations in which an individual dog or other nonhuman animal does something beneficial, nice, or risky to help someone else with no obvious benefit. *See also* **reciprocity**.

anal gland. A small gland near the anus in many mammals, including dogs and cats. This gland can exude stress pheromones that tell other animals that an individual is stressed.

animal-assisted play therapy (AAPT). Authors Risë VanFleet and Tracie Faa-Thompson define AAPT as "the integrated involvement of animals in the context of play therapy." In their book *Animal Assisted Play Therapy*, they write, "Trained therapists and animals engage with clients primarily through systematic playful interventions, with the goal of improving clients' developmental and psychosocial health, while simultaneously ensuring the animal's well-being and voluntary engagement. Play and playfulness are essential ingredients of the interactions and the relationship."

They also stress that not all animals are cut out for this type of work, and it is better for everyone — client, animal, and therapist — when the needs of the animals are always considered and acted upon. All in all, the animals must have a "voice and choice." I am thrilled that the well-being of the animals is given so much attention, as it should, with AAPT. Both the animals and humans have to get something positive out of animal-assisted play therapy and the relationships that are formed.

animal-assisted therapy (AAT). Using dogs or other nonhumans to give emotional support to humans. Animal-assisted therapy can take many forms, from simply having a dog or other animal present to having a person become responsible for the well-being of the animal. Therapy dogs are not service dogs.

Whether or not therapy dogs actually work to help humans along is a mixed bag. They certainly are not cure-alls or panaceas. My take is that it works for some people, and it doesn't for others, so if it works for you, use a therapy dog. If not, find another method to address your issues. Hal Herzog reached the same conclusion, noting, "For most outcomes, having an assistance dog has no effect on psychological health and well-being."

Many people are concerned about the welfare of therapy dogs or other therapy animals. However, one study found that, despite concentrations of cortisol in therapy dogs as they participated in animal-assisted therapy, this didn't indicate heightened stress. Dog researcher Stanley Coren wrote, "Although the sample size is small, the investigators still felt that they could assert that this study indicated that dogs were coping well with animal-assisted therapy sessions and were not responding in a stressful manner to the interactions associated with being a therapy dog."

My best guess is that further research will show that while some therapy dogs are more stressed and distressed than other homed dogs, some aren't. General comparisons across groups are very limited in meaning. The critical assessment of how a dog is feeling must focus on each individual. What works for one or some dogs might not work for others, and the unique personality of each dog, each human, and their relationship must always come first. Further, dogs, humans, and the nature of their relationships can change with time. Each dog-human relationship needs to be considered on a case-by-case basis. *See also* **emotional support animal (ESA); service dogs.**

animal communicators. This refers to people who have a close, often-telepathic connection with a nonhuman animal. I wanted to know more about animal communicators — what they do and why — so I asked one of the deans of animal communicators, Penelope Smith, to answer a few questions. Here's what she said:

Marc Bekoff: You are one of the pioneer animal communicators. Why did you decide to pursue this field and how would you characterize or define it?

Penelope Smith: Since I was a child, I was aware of my purpose in life to help people remember who they are as spiritual beings and to help them follow their purpose in the best way possible for them.

I have always loved animals and been aware of telepathically communicating with them my whole life. I understood them and they understood me.

When I became a spiritual counselor for people, I ended up applying with animals the same counseling techniques that helped people get through emotional traumas and handle problems with great results. Animals responded easily and quickly to lift out of their negative feelings and patterns and shift their behavior positively.

In the 1970s, my communication work with animals and their people grew. I saw incredible results when people realized more about their animals' emotional and spiritual nature. Besides improving their relationship with their animal friends, people opened their own awareness of themselves as spiritual beings and improved their attitudes and lives. I loved the work, which helped both animals and their people.

The field is called animal communication or more accurately interspecies telepathic communication. It involves understanding animals through receiving their thoughts and feelings through telepathy, which is direct mental and spiritual communication through all the spiritual, internal, or extended senses, which mirror our physical senses, but could be considered a finer-tuned energy transmission.

MB: When you work with clients, are there any questions that come up much more than others, or is there a broad range of questions that come your way?

PS: There are a broad range of questions, such as "Why does my dog/cat/horse do that behavior?" "How can I get my dog or other animal to change a behavior, such as excessive barking, aggression toward other animals or humans, separation anxiety?" "How will I know when it is my animal's time to die?" Or, "Does my (very ill) animal want to live or die now?" "How is my dog/cat/bird feeling physically, does she hurt anywhere, how does the treatment from the vet feel to my animal?" "What does she feel could improve her well-being?" "How does my animal friend feel about me?"

MB: Why do you think people, especially scientists, are skeptical about what you do? I'm a scientist and remain open to animal communication.

PS: People are skeptical when they don't understand what animal communication is and how it works. Once people see how animals communicate about specific things in their lives that the animal communicator knows nothing about and see the results of communicating telepathically in resolving situations, with the animals demonstrating positive changes, they are generally more open to what is happening and to understanding animal communication.

MB: Is there anything else you would like to say?

PS: Interspecies telepathic communication opens the door to a wide range of benefits for people and other animals. These include changes in people's relationship to other animals and all of nature and the cultivation of qualities of being that other animals share, such as compassion for others and awareness of themselves as spiritual beings with a purpose in life and how we assist each other on our Earth journeys.

See also **extrasensory perception (ESP)**.

animal studies. I can't describe this emerging field of study any better than Wesleyan University, which says animal studies "builds on scholarship in the humanities, social sciences, and sciences to investigate past and present relations between human and nonhuman animals, the representation of those relations, their ethical implications, and their social, political, and ecological effects in and on the world. It is a field of critical importance today as the complex but fragile interdependence of all life becomes increasingly apparent, and as scholars, artists, and activists seek ways to understand and enhance the lives of all animals." Clearly, dogs fit well into the arena of animal studies.

Anthropocene. An epoch characterized by human domination of the entire planet — on land, in the water, and in the sky. While the term stands for "the Age of Humanity," I prefer to call the Anthropocene "the Rage of Inhumanity." We humans are all over the place, and there aren't many, if any, places in which our destructive footprints aren't significantly impacting the lives of countless other animals. This includes dogs and just about every species.

anthropocentrism. A human-centered view of the world. Sometimes called human exceptionalism, this often results in our doing things in our own interests — in the name of humans — rather than incorporating the interests of nonhumans and nature, which all beings need to survive and thrive.

anthropodenial. This term was coined by primatologist Frans de Waal, and it refers, he writes, to "ignoring or dismissing the human-like characteristics of animals, or the animal-like characteristics of ourselves."

anthropomorphism. The attribution of human traits, emotions, or intentions to other animals. Most people use anthropocentric language when speaking about other animals, and I feel it's important to try to take the animal's point of view when talking or writing about them.

Inappropriate anthropomorphism is always a danger, since it is easy to get lazy and presume that the way we see and experience the world must be the way other beings do. It is also easy to become self-serving and hope that because we want or need animals to be happy, they are. In fact, the only guard against the inappropriate use of anthropomorphism is knowledge, or the detailed study of the minds and emotions of animals.

Many researchers now recognize that we must be anthropomorphic when we discuss animal emotions. When done appropriately, it represents what I call *biocentric anthropomorphism*, which gives consideration to the animal's point of view. Being anthropomorphic is speaking in a way that comes naturally to us. Most agree that animals and humans share many traits, including emotions. Thus, we're not inserting something human into animals, but we're identifying commonalities and then using human language to communicate what we observe. Similarly, Gordon Burghardt argues for scientifically based *critical anthropomorphism*. *See also* **zoomorphism**.

anthrozoology. The interdisciplinary scientific study of human-animal interactions. Meanwhile, *cynology* refers to the study of the relationship between dogs and people. *See also* **animal studies**; **human-animal interaction (HAI)**.

anticipating. Dogs obviously think about the future, such as when they expect to be taken on a walk or anticipate the arrival of their humans at a certain time. Dogs also anticipate the path of a Frisbee or tennis ball while in flight. Someone once asked me how dogs "do the geometry," and I don't think anyone knows.

antipredatory behavior. Evolved responses by a dog or other nonhuman animal to avoid being caught, killed, and eaten. Antipredatory behavior includes simply fighting back, random protean flight, freezing, and remaining still and playing dead, which is also called tonic immobility or "playing possum."

antithesis, Darwin's principle of. In the context of animal emotions and behavior, Charles Darwin defined *antithesis* as the way opposite emotions result in opposite behaviors. He then famously used an example of a dog to illustrate this:

> When a dog approaches a strange dog or man in a savage or hostile frame of mind he walks upright and very stiffly; his head is slightly raised, or not much lowered; the tail is held erect and quite rigid; the hairs bristle, especially along the neck and back; the pricked ears are directed forwards and the eyes have a fixed stare. These actions, as will hereafter be explained, follow from the dog's intention to attack his enemy, and are thus to a large extent intelligible. As he prepares to spring with a savage growl on his enemy, the canine teeth are uncovered, and the ears are pressed close backwards on the head; but with these latter actions, we are not here concerned. Let us now suppose that the dog suddenly discovers that the man he is approaching is not a stranger, but his master; and let it be observed how completely and instantaneously his whole bearing is reversed. Instead of walking upright, the body sinks downwards or even crouches, and is thrown into flexuous movements; his tail, instead of being held stiff and upright, is lowered and wagged from side to side; his hair instantly becomes smooth; his ears are depressed and drawn backwards, but not closely to the head; and his lips hang loosely. From the drawing back of the ears, the eyelids become elongated, and the eyes no longer appear round and staring. It should be added that the animal is at such times in an excited condition from joy; and nerve-force will be generated in excess, which naturally leads to action of some kind. Not one of the above movements, so clearly expressive of affection, are of the least direct service to the animal. They are explicable, as far as I can see, solely from being in complete opposition or antithesis to the attitude and movements which, from intelligible causes, are assumed when a dog intends to fight, and which consequently are expressive of anger.

anxiety. Dogs certainly feel anxiety, stress, and uneasiness, and there is evidence that dogs pick up and mirror the anxious feelings of their humans.

appeasing. To make nice and appease another individual, a dog might approach another dog and lick their muzzle or lower their body as they approach them and flip over on their back. These gestures let the other dog know all's well.

appetitive behavior. When a dog is looking for something they want. This doesn't necessarily mean dogs are hungry, but they have an appetite for something. They seek to satisfy some need.

approach-withdrawal. When a dog approaches and then withdraws or circles around an object or individual. This behavior indicates mixed feelings or uncertainty about how to deal with a situation, and dogs engage in this as they decide what to do.

artificial insemination. A medical procedure to inject semen into a female dog. This is most often done to breed certain types of dogs people desire, and there are growing global demands for this sort of reproduction. However, this type of human selection gives dogs no choice in the matter, which raises ethical issues, and it entails the risk of psychological and physical trauma. There also are biosecurity concerns and possibilities of spreading diseases via unhealthy semen.

artificial selection. Aka human selection, the human control of breeding. As opposed to natural selection, this is when people decide who mates with whom in order to select for traits that we prefer or find useful, such as making animals bigger or smaller, changing their coat color and texture, and reshaping other morphological features like ears, snouts, and tails. In many cases, selective breeding doesn't necessarily harm the animal (or can even be potentially beneficial), but humans often take artificial selection to unhealthy extremes with dogs. For human-centered reasons and selfish desires, people produce individuals and breeds who are destined to have highly compromised lives, such as hairless French bulldogs who have trouble breathing. *See also* **commodifying dogs**; **designer dogs**; **natural selection**.

assistance dogs. Dogs trained to help people with a disability. Be aware that sometimes people "fake it" and claim a dog has been trained to be a service dog to get special treatment in a restaurant or store. *See also* **animal-assisted therapy (AAT)**; **emotional support animal (ESA)**; **service dogs**.

assortative mating. Mating between individuals who share similar characteristics, such as size, shape, color, or behavior. There's no evidence dogs prefer to mate with members of their breed or mix. *See also* **mating preferences**.

attention, dogs recognizing human. In a 2004 study, researchers found that the ability of dogs to discriminate between "attentive" and "inattentive" humans varied depending on the orientation of the person's body and head and whether dogs could see the person's eyes. That said, the flexibility of dogs to recognize human attention in different situations was greater than chimpanzees. *See also* **human gaze, dogs following**.

attention-deficit/hyperactivity disorder (ADHD). A condition characterized by limited attention, hyperactivity, and impulsiveness. Though mostly associated with humans, ADHD also occurs in dogs (and other animals). A 2021 study involving some eleven thousand dogs found that ADHD symptoms in dogs can be related to gender, age, and breed, in addition to any behavioral problems and certain environmental factors.

avoidance. Dogs practice avoidance in a variety of ways that are similar to humans: by leaving, running away, or escaping; by choosing not to do something; and by not interacting with another individual even while remaining in the same area.

awe. One big question is whether dogs and other nonhumans feel awe. Can they be "beside themselves" in amazement, overcome with positive feelings of beauty and wonder, or overwhelmed by existential terror? Some speculate that they can, but we don't really know. *See also* **spiritual experiences**.

B

baby talk with dogs. Recent research shows adult dogs, not just puppies, prefer high-pitched rhythmic dog-relevant words, which help to get their attention and improve bonding. I was happy to learn about this because it has practical applications. People ask me all the time why they and others naturally use baby talk with their dogs, such as when saying, "You're a good dog," or "I love you so much." Now I can tell them there are good reasons, even if they don't know why. If using baby talk can help with bonding and socializing, then all people who live and work with dogs, including veterinarians and shelter employees, can use it freely. It's a win-win for all.

back arching. Aka kyphosis. Dogs arch their backs for different reasons in different contexts. It can be an indicator of gastrointestinal problems or pain in the spine; a dog might simply be stretching; or a dog might be trying to increase their apparent size when threatened.

"bad dog day." When his dog seemed "off," a friend of mine would say he was "having a bad dog day." However, I wonder if the dog might have been reading my friend and knew that something was wrong, and so he mirrored his human's feelings. Dogs read and smell us well, using a composite signal made up of visual, auditory, and olfactory cues. When dogs see angry human faces, they lick their mouths, which might clue us in that we are angry, perhaps without our knowing this.

I also often wonder if, when a dog is having a "bad dog day," they can get over it by anticipating what's going to happen later on, like going on a walk or meeting their friends. *See also* **composite signals**; **lip licking**.

bared teeth. Bared teeth can mean several different things. Bared teeth are used when a dog threatens another individual, but the teeth also are exposed when a dog displays a submissive grin or is simply grinning. As with so many dog behaviors, it's important to consider context — who's interacting with whom, where they are, and what's at stake. Bared teeth also can be part of a composite signal, and it's important to consider a dog's gait and their tail, ear, and body postures or positions.

barking. We know surprisingly little about all the different sorts of barks dogs produce — how many there are and the messages they convey. Of course, when evaluating what a dog's bark might mean, we have to consider the context most of all.

Do dogs bark "too much"? This is a very human-centered question that presumes dogs will bark unnecessarily. When dogs bark a lot, there's usually a good reason, and we need to consider their point of view. Typically, we don't. A good example is the town of Aurora, Illinois, which passed a law allowing fines for dogs who bark more than fifteen minutes and also put a limit on the number of domestic animals allowed in a home (no more than four).

I'm often surprised by how little we know about common canine behaviors like barking, which just shows how much there still is to learn. This is what makes studying dogs so interesting and exciting. *See also* **abnormal behavior**; **baying**.

"barking at the moon." A saying that means doing something in vain.

baying. Also called "trail barking," baying is a highly variable sound that hounds make when tracking. Baying alerts other dogs and humans that a dog has a scent and can help to coordinate a hunt.

beauty, human standards of. There are some interesting studies emerging on how seeing other animals as "beautiful" influences the way in which humans view, value, and relate to nonhumans. Hal Herzog wrote about a study of animal images by Catarina Possidónio and her colleagues, and Herzog noted that whether people care about animals is more related to how cute they are than their capacity to think and feel or how harmful they are. Similarly, a study of South African farmers found they tolerated animals perceived as beautiful or charismatic more than those who weren't. Herzog calls this "beauty speciesism."

People have enormously varying definitions of what makes a "beautiful" dog. But one thing is clear: Canine attractiveness is a major driver of selective breeding, which mixes and adjusts traits like size, shape, and facial features to satisfy human aesthetics.

bedroom behavior. It's OK for dogs to sleep in their human's bedroom if everyone likes it and shares in the love. Suggestions that sick, old, or young dogs should sleep elsewhere are absurd and totally human-centered. Dog snoring, however, can have negative impacts on everyone, impacting the relationships between dogs and their humans and between humans. One study found that 76 percent of homeowners allowed their dog to sleep with them, and 33 percent of married couples said their best quality of sleep came from sharing their bed with only their dog. *See also* **conflicts over dogs**.

begging. Dogs can be very creative when it comes to begging, which can take many forms and vary from humble to urgent, depending on the dog, the human, and what the dog wants. Behaviors include sitting and staring, sidling into your body, and pawing at you. My dogs would sometimes beg for some of my meal, and when I gave them something else, they looked at me in surprise, as if saying, *I want what you're eating*. I would tell them nicely that beggars can't be choosy, and invariably they happily accepted their second or third choice. Then they often returned to begging, hoping that what they really wanted would come their way, and often it did.

behavior. There are many definitions of behavior. It can be simply defined as something a being does — how they act or conduct themselves — in a way that can be seen, heard, or smelled. Of course, the sensory systems of dogs are rather different from ours, and so dogs might be doing something or reacting to stimuli of which we are unaware. That is why it's essential not to jump to conclusions or assume that dogs are happy or upset, or that there is no reason for some behavior like "barking too much."

Nobel laureate Konrad Lorenz, who famously wrote about imprinting and had geese follow him around his research center in Germany as if he were their father, noted that behavior is something an animal *does* as well as something they *have*. He also proposed that behavior is subject to the forces of natural selection, just like traits such as body size and shape. I totally agree, and that understanding is what drives a good deal of ethological research. *See also* **ethology**.

behavioral ecology. The study of how behavior is influenced by local environmental conditions, such as how much and what kinds of food are available. This is also called "social ecology." For homed dogs, there isn't much to learn about behavioral ecology other than what's happening in the homes where they live — which are their habitats — but for free-ranging and feral dogs, a good deal of research is being done that shows that they alter their behavior depending on local conditions. This includes food availability, areas where they can rest safely, safe places to den and have children, and who else is around and how they might impact coexistence, cooperation, or competition.

behaviorism. Behaviorism is the proposal that behavior can be explained by different types of conditioning and that thinking and feeling play little to no role in how and why individuals express different behaviors. A decreasing number of researchers still believe in this mechanistic and reductionist view, which doesn't account for large amounts of individual variation and flexibility that many animals, including dogs, display. When people call me a behaviorist, I politely correct them and let them know that I'm an ethologist, which means I recognize that dogs are fully sentient and intelligent canids. *See also* **ethology**.

behavior modification. This refers to changing patterns of behavior using rewards and/or punishments, which is the essence of dog training. Behavior modification can involve processes such as desensitization, counterconditioning, flooding, and environmental enrichment. *See also* **training**.

best friends, dogs as our. It's a tiresome myth that dogs are our best friends, and it can have harmful effects on dog-human relationships. It's easy to say dogs are our best friends and use it to sell books and entertain audiences, but it's a characterization that should be stopped. *See also* **myths about dogs**.

Beston, Henry. Henry Beston was an American naturalist and writer famous for the following quotation from his book *The Outermost House*. His critique of how people view nonhuman animals applies very well to dogs.

> We need another and a wiser and perhaps a more mystical concept of animals. Remote from universal nature and living by complicated artifice, man in civilization surveys the creature through the glass of his knowledge and sees thereby a feather magnified and the whole image in distortion. We patronize them for their incompleteness, for their tragic fate for having taken form so far below ourselves. And therein do we err. For the animal shall not be measured by man. In a world older and more complete than ours, they move finished and complete, gifted with the extension of the senses we have lost or never attained, living by voices we shall never hear. They are not brethren, they are not underlings: they are other nations, caught with ourselves in the net of life and time, fellow prisoners of the splendour and travail of the earth.

"Big Black Dog." A song written by Emmylou Harris. Emmylou runs a dog rescue shelter from the back garden of her property, called Bonaparte's Retreat. To date, Bonaparte's Retreat has saved more than four hundred dogs, and their focus is on rescuing the neglected and forgotten — senior dogs, large dogs, special needs dogs, or dogs in need of imminent medical care or surgery. This song tells the true story about a black Lab mix named Bella who Emmylou rescued from the Nashville Metro pound. Bella provided Emmylou with company when she was on the road, and the song "Big Black Dog" captures the sad lives of far too many dogs who are abandoned by humans. Emmylou explained in 2011: "She goes on the tour bus with me now, along with another one of my rescues. I think of all the years on the road I wasted without a dog. They make it so much more pleasant. I'm making up for lost time now, that's for sure." Emmylou told me dogs are a sacred responsibility, dogs make us better humans, and dogs are one of the universe's best gifts. I couldn't agree more.

biodiversity. A measure of the different types of animal and plant life in a given area. The term was coined by ecologist Thomas Lovejoy in 1980. Dogs are not usually counted in these sorts of measurements, but when they go wild, they become active members of wild communities and should be included.

biting. In general, in any context, dogs exhibit many different types of bites, from soft and inhibited mouthing to hard bites. Bites are directed to various areas of the body; on dogs, this includes the face, muzzle, torso, tail, and scruff. How and when dogs bite other dogs depends on context — who's doing the biting, who's getting bitten, and the nature of the social encounter. Some bites are playful, some curious explorations, and some aggressive. There's evidence that ancient dogs, who had more of a meat diet, had stronger bites and cutting teeth than modern dogs.

When I talk with people, they are most concerned about dogs biting humans. It's estimated that in the United States around 4.5 million people are bitten by a dog each year. A few years ago I conducted an interview with the editors of a book called *Dog Bites: A Multidisciplinary Perspective.* I asked these experts if they could briefly summarize their findings, and one of them answered: "Oh, that's a hard one. To me, the main thing to appreciate is that we know very little with much confidence. Generally, the data is very poor, but that does not mean that all solutions are equally valid. I think if we can be more critical, we can perhaps at least have better pragmatic solutions until the research catches up."

In 2017, a comprehensive study of dog bites showed that dog-bite prevention goes beyond just knowing about dog behavior, and people can play a large role in prevention. Here is a summary list of their conclusions:

- No significant differences in bite severity were observed between contexts.
- Male victims were more numerous across all bite contexts.

- Only the age of the victim was predictive of bite severity: adults were bitten more severely than infants, and infants more severely than children.
- Children and infants were considerably more common victims than adults. Among adults, most bites were to the limbs. Among children and infants, bites to the face and neck area were more common.
- Nonneutral dog body posture and some displacement and appeasement behaviors increased approximately twenty seconds before the bite, and humans made more tactile contact with dogs twenty-one seconds before the bite.
- From nine seconds before the bite, more codes for movement away from the dog were noted.
- Bites during play and benign interactions were particularly common.
- Standing over a dog, petting, and restraining a dog were seen proportionally more frequently closer to the bite, increasing approximately twenty to thirty seconds before.

bloodsport. This term usually refers to dog fighting, but some also use this word to refer to greyhound racing.

bluffing. Dogs definitely try to fool or deceive other dogs and people by bluffing. A threat might be a bluff, or a dog might look at something in the distance in order to distract another dog to also look. *See also* **deceiving**; **lying, dogs recognizing**.

body language. Dogs have very complex body language. They use various parts of their bodies to send different messages, often using composite signals that combine visual, auditory, and olfactory cues. *See also* **hackles**; **play bows**; **tail flagging**; **teeth baring**.

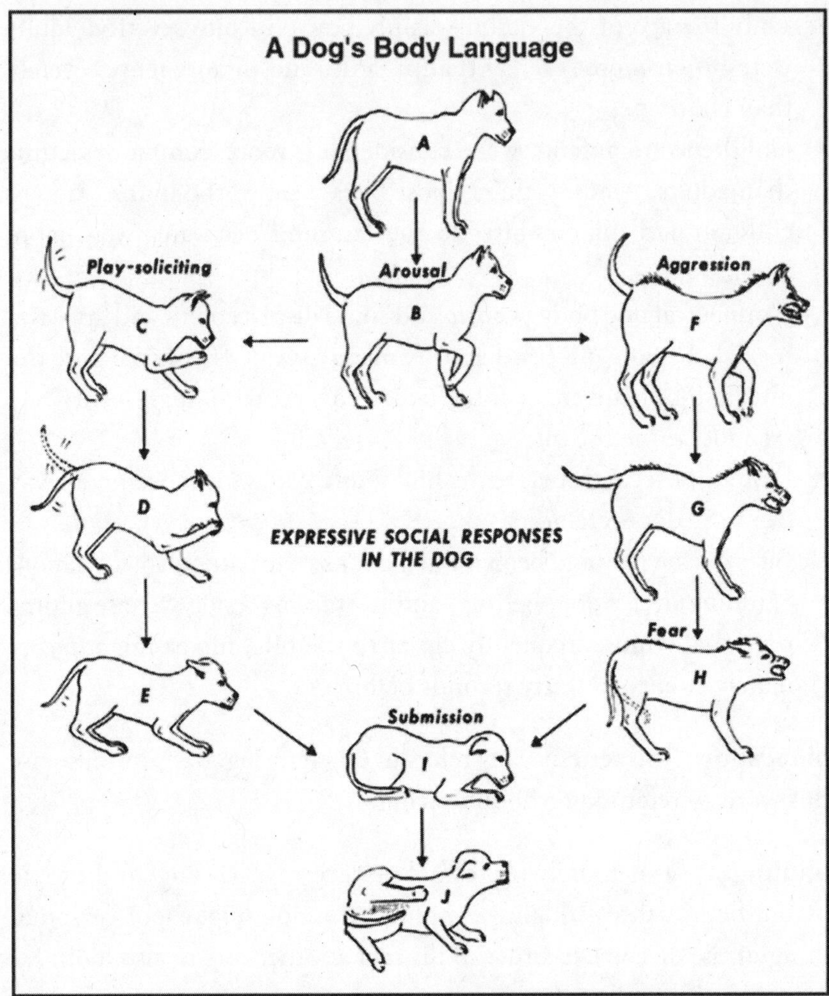

A dog's body language. A-8, neutral to alert attentive positions. C, play-soliciting bow. D-E, active and passive submissive greeting, note tail wag, shift in ear position, and the distribution of weight on fore and hind limbs. I, passive submission with J, rolling over and presentation of inguinal-genital region. F-H, gradual shift from aggressive display to ambivalent fear-defensive-aggressive posture.

Courtesy of Michael w. Fox.

Summary of the dog's body language in social interactions, from Michael W. Fox, Dog Body, Dog Mind, *The Lyons Press. Used by permission.*

body size. Modern dogs obviously come in a wide variety of body sizes, based on what people desire. But now a study has found that the single gene called insulin-like growth factor-1 (IGF-1), which gave rise to tiny dogs, existed in ancient wolves at least fifty thousand years ago, before domestication began. One of the researchers, geneticist Elaine Ostrander, says, "This gene was around at the time humans started to domesticate dogs, so people were able to start selecting for it.... This allowed humans to manipulate body size very quickly to breed for big dogs to guard, smaller dogs to herd and even smaller dogs to rat." Dog expert Mark Derr notes that the split between small and large dogs may be the most ancient divide.

bomb-sniffing dogs. Dogs can be trained to locate bombs and land mines because of their incredibly sensitive noses. When they detect the smell of explosives, they become upset and sit where the explosives are located. Dogs can also be trained to sniff out drugs and mineral deposits. *See also* **military dogs**; **smell**.

bookkeeping. A term for how animals keep track of the presence of other animals and of food and food caches. Fox researcher and biologist David Henry discovered that wild red foxes urinate where they've cached and then removed the food so they don't return to an empty cupboard.

No one has done a careful study of food bookkeeping in dogs. Several times, I have buried food on my mountain property, and my dogs and their friends have gone on a scavenger hunt. I have seen them keeping track of where they have buried and then taken food, but I don't know how they do it. One of my neighbors told me that she was sure that her dog Rachel carefully watched other dogs find food and didn't go back to an empty cache. Because the wild relatives of dogs cache food for later use, it's not surprising that dogs also would do the same thing. Like red foxes, they seem to remember where there aren't any goodies left. *See also* **episodic memory**.

boredom. In his book *Ethics and Ethology for a Happy Dog*, Swedish psychologist Anders Hallgren, who works closely with dogs, calls boredom "the agony of all dogs."

bracelet. The unshaven hair on the hindlegs of poodles.

brachycephalic. Dogs with wide or broad heads, such as pugs and French bulldogs. Brachycephalic dogs can have difficulty breathing, and they are the product of humans selecting for this trait — it's an example of artificial selection. It's difficult to imagine that brachycephalic dogs would be able to survive without human care. There have been calls to ban breeding these and other flat-faced dogs. For instance, the UK's Brachycephalic Working Group asks people to "stop and think before buying a flat-faced dog." Research shows that short-headed dogs are more reactive to negative stimuli than are long-headed dogs. *See also* **artificial selection**; **commodifying dogs**; **designer dogs**.

breed. A group of animals (or plants) of the same species. Among dogs, a mongrel or mutt is a mix of two different breeds (while the term *hybrid* refers to a mix of two different species). Dog breeds usually have been produced by humans purposely selecting for various traits, even when certain traits don't necessarily help the animals. In his wonderful book *A Matter of Breeding*, dog expert Michael Brandow hopes that when people learn how our trying to "improve" different breeds has actually harmed many dogs, we will take the dogs' perspective into account and put an end to many breeding practices. We shouldn't make individuals pay a high price for being cute or otherwise appealing to us. He concludes, "Dog shows, registries, breed clubs, breeders, and social-climbing consumers are largely responsible for what seems to be turning into an all-out pedigree health crisis."

The University of Manchester's Michael Worboys, who has extensively studied the origin and maintenance of dog breeds, feels that they are "mere Victorian confections, neither pure nor ancient." Many people pay a lot of money to get the breed of their liking, and many breeds have vanished. On occasion, a new breed is discovered, such as a South American sheepdog who lives between the Chilean coast and the Patagonian mountains. *See also* **hybrid**.

breedism. Aka breed stereotypes. Research shows that breed stereotypes, or prejudices based on what dogs look like, are unfounded. Individual differences among dogs need to be given serious attention because, while there may be some general trends in terms of how a member of a given breed or mix will behave, even littermates differ and expectations can be misleading. All in all, the best way to view a dog is to consider them as an *individual* and not as a member of this or that breed.

An extensive 2022 study published in *Behavioural Processes* showed that morphological characteristics and a dog's age were more important than their breed in influencing the expression of temperament and emotional reactivity. Another comprehensive study published in *Science* magazine showed that a dog's breed accounted for only around 9 percent of the variation in their behavior and that aesthetic traits were more important in distinguishing among them.

Dog breeds don't have distinct personalities, but individual dogs do, so it's best not to judge a dog by their cover — or what they look like. If you're picking a canine companion, instead consider where you live, your household, and what traits will fit best given your lifestyle and location. If you live in a small home with few opportunities for a dog to be outside and run to their heart's content, make sure not to get a dog who likes to run and run and run, no matter what their breed.

breed popularity. Labrador retrievers have been the most popular breed for the past thirty years. Of course, the popularity of various dog breeds has shifted dramatically over the years, but studies show this has more to do with fashion than function. A study of breed popularity between 1926 and 2005 considered the impacts of breed health, longevity, and behavioral qualities (such as aggressiveness, trainability, and fearfulness) on breed popularity, and it found that fluctuations in popularity, or the rates of increase and decrease, showed no correlation with these traits. In other words, winning best in show at the Westminster Dog Show usually causes little or no increase in a breed's popularity, but if a dog becomes a movie or TV star, their stock rises dramatically. This is what Hal Herzog has dubbed the "dog movie star effect."

Data also suggest that some people actually do tend to choose dogs who look like or act like them. Stanley Coren notes that, in one study, "judges were able to correctly match purebred dogs with their owners in about two-thirds of the cases. This seems to confirm that dogs and owners may tend to look alike." *See also* **movies, dogs in**.

breed recognition among dogs. People often want to know if dogs know others of their breed or of their particular mix. Of course, they don't have names for them as we do, but do some dogs recognize other dogs as similar or different? I've often thought about this. I can't find any research on this topic, but I don't think they do. While dogs have close friends whom they prefer over other dogs, there is no evidence that it is related to breed or any specific mix of different breeds. *See also* **imprinting**.

breed specific legislation (BSL). Laws that dictate what breeds are dangerous and where they can and cannot live. Many people would like to end breed specific legislation, which exists in many places, saying the guiding standard should be "deeds, not breeds." *See also* **Dangerous Dog Act**.

bullying. It's often difficult to know if a dog is actually intimidating other dogs, pushing them around, or being a bully or bossy. Bullying is not synonymous with being aggressive, and it's essential to consider context — who the dogs are, what they're doing, and where the behavior is happening. In countless hours of watching dogs in different venues, I've only seen what I would call genuine bullying a few times, and even then, I wasn't 100 percent certain.

Buttbook. A dog's social media equivalent of Facebook.

butts. A critical canine communication center. People often ask me why butt sniffing is important for dogs, which is an activity we find uncomfortable, awkward, and disgusting. We really don't know much from formal studies, but it's clear that most dogs like butts and likely gain information from sniffing them. For instance, they might get information about individual identity — Russ smells like this, Rachel smells like that, and so on. It's also possible they gather information about gender, about reproductive status, and about emotions. While a dog's nose is traveling around a butt, they might also be picking up information from the anal gland.

Sometimes dogs lick their own butts, and when done excessively, it can indicate an infection. *See also* **smell**.

C

caching. Burying or hiding food. This can include bookkeeping, in which dogs keep track of where food is and whether or not it's been consumed. *See also* **bookkeeping**.

calming signals. Actions dogs use to help calm down other dogs. These stress-reducing behaviors may include lip licking, sniffing the ground, yawning, looking away, play bowing, sitting, lying down, or even blinking.

The idea was formalized by Norwegian dog trainer Turid Rugaas in her book *On Talking Terms with Dogs: Calming Signals*. Many dog trainers and I have learned a lot from her work, but not everyone is convinced of the ubiquity of calming signals. Of course, dogs don't always intentionally perform these behaviors all the time. Dr. Karen London, an applied animal behaviorist and professional dog trainer, cautions that we really don't know whether calming signals always work and whether they are used intentionally. Her conclusions are based in part on a research study of calming signals by Chiara Mariti and her colleagues.

One thing London notes is that "the term 'calming signals' entered the lexicon without much analysis, which is problematic. Using a term that ascribes functionality to behavior patterns prior to scientifically testing whether that's true creates challenges and is a big no-no in ethology."

That is, claiming that certain behaviors are "calming signals" creates a bias so that people tend to accept that this is, in fact, what these behaviors do. While the idea of calming signals is an intriguing hypothesis, there needs to be more rigorous scientific study to determine whether the various behaviors serve this and/or other functions. As with so many aspects of dog behavior, we still have much to learn. *See also* **lip licking**.

canid. A member of the taxonomic family Canidae, often called the "dog family." There are thirty-six living canid species, including dogs, coyotes, wolves, dingoes, jackals, and foxes. *See also* **taxonomy**.

canine exceptionalism. A phrase used to convey that dogs should be recognized and treated as exceptional beings. I would expand this and say that all nonhumans are exceptional in their own right. Jessica Hekman used this phrase as a title for an essay about dog training. She writes: "The perspective of dog trainers, with their deep experience in real-world canine abilities, provides a rich source of theories for academics to test. Collaboration between dog trainers and research scientists could lead to a partnership that deepens our understanding of canine cognition. Dog trainers will keep exploring dogs' learning limits. Now it's up to the scientists to reach out and use this resource. If only the trainers could say to the scientists: 'Do it!'"

canine transmissible venereal tumor (CTVT). An extremely rare and relatively easy-to-treat cancer found mainly in male dogs that is transmitted by sniffing the genital area.

cannibalism. A former graduate student of mine, Dr. Tom Daniels, has observed cannibalism in free-ranging dogs, but it's not known whether this is common or rare among dogs.

captivity effects. Dogs exhibit behavioral changes due to being restrained, caged, or held in captivity for long periods. These include stereotypic pacing, self-mutilating, rocking back and forth, high levels of aggressiveness, and depression.

Though they are not kept in captivity, most homed dogs live highly controlled, even restrained lives, especially compared to free-ranging and feral dogs. Family dogs might not display the most serious and extreme behavior patterns, but the fussing and pampering they receive can compromise their well-being. This means that it's important to pay attention to your dog and give them as much freedom of choice and mobility as possible.

The effects of captivity also impact research studies of dog behavior. We need to be careful to distinguish information collected from studies of homed dogs and captive animals from studies of free-ranging dogs. There's a lot of good science, but the results may not always be comparable. We need to be very careful not to make sweeping generalizations about some sort of "universal dog," since there is so much variation among individual dogs and among breeds, upbringings, and the places dogs call home. For instance, we can't always draw conclusions from studies of captive individuals and claim that wild relatives do or don't, or can or can't, exhibit certain behaviors.

In her book *Wisdom of Wolves*, Elli Radinger also cautions about making comparisons between captive and wild wolves, noting that leadership and other behavior patterns can be very different.

Homed dogs are typically studied in labs, but they constitute only a small percentage of the billion or so dogs in the world. Some studies also suffer from small sample sizes. These aren't "fatal criticisms" of research, as one of my colleagues puts it, but rather these limitations simply need to be acknowledged.

Personally, I think it's better to admit "stupidity" — to say we don't know if we really don't know. I often say, "The more I know, the more I say I don't know." Dogs far too often are victims of partial knowledge, misinformation, meme-like myths, and "quick" answers. It's important to respect their individuality, appreciate the large amount of diversity among these wonderful beings, and pay close attention to how research is conducted and what the results really mean. *See also* **research techniques**.

carnivore. Animals for whom different forms of meat make up the major portion of their meal plans. The order Carnivora is comprised of 279 species of placental mammals, including dogs. That said, some carnivorans are omnivorous and eat both animals and plants, such as raccoons and bears. Then, a few, like pandas, eat a more limited and specialized diet and are primarily herbivores.

castrating. Removing male sex organs. *See also* **neutering**; **spaying**.

cause and effect, understanding of. In behavioral research, it's important to distinguish cause-and-effect or causal relationships from correlative relationships, which simply means when two unrelated events just happen to occur together. It's sort of a mantra that correlation does not mean causation. Simply put, if I get up out of my chair and a wind comes up and knocks over the chair, these events are correlated but not causally related.

As for dogs, they clearly understand cause and effect, but some people wonder whether they do it as well as wolves, which remains unclear. In 2017, Michelle Lampe and her colleagues studied awareness of cause and effect in dogs and wolves by comparing the reasoning abilities of fourteen dogs and twelve captive human-socialized wolves. They reported that some of the dogs and wolves were able to find hidden food using human cues, such as direct eye contact and pointing gestures. Their ability to find hidden food also was tested using behavioral cues that didn't include eye contact or pointing, such as reaching out to the food, and using noise produced by an object containing the food when it was shaken.

The data are very interesting but also rather preliminary. Since the wolves were captive, it would have been very interesting to also study nonsocialized wolves or individuals who had minimal or different degrees of socialization, as well as to control for the wolves' persistence. Further studies clearly are needed.

In this study, the authors' wrote: "Our results seem to imply that domestication impaired dogs' ability to understand causal relationships, as in this condition, wolves outperformed pack dogs and were the only group to perform above chance level." All well and good, but the phrase "seem to imply" caught my attention and that of someone who wrote to me. Further, how all these data relate to the process of domestication remains open to discussion. *See also* **domestication**; **human pointing, comprehension of**.

C-BARQ. Aka the Canine Behavioral and Research Questionnaire. C-BARQ allows for standardized evaluations of the temperament and behavior of dogs.

cephalic index. Dividing the widest part of the skull (in millimeters) by the length of the longest part of the skull and multiplying by one hundred.

chaining. Tethering a dog so they can't move. Chaining a dog is often a very inhumane way of making sure a dog doesn't run away, since it compromises the dog's ability to get away from dangerous situations or out of cold, hot, or wet weather. Some states have banned chaining, whereas others have imposed a time limit or certain other restrictions.

character traits. While all dogs possess distinct personalities and a wide range of character traits, how many and to what extent are open questions. In an essay titled "My Dog Is Quite a Character," behavioral researcher Michael Matthews notes that some of the twenty-four character traits that positive psychologists apply to humans may also apply to dogs. Matthews writes, "Anecdotal observations suggest that love of learning, bravery, persistence, leadership, love, social intelligence, self-regulation, gratitude, and sense of humor seem to vary among dogs." He also says, "Dogs who observed their owner interacting with another dog demonstrate behavioral signs of jealousy." *See also* **personality**.

cheating. Dogs rarely cheat during social play with each other. They almost always play by the established dog rules, although when an individual does act unfairly, it attracts a lot of attention from the cheated dog and possibly others who see what has happened; this occurs in groups of coyotes. That said, dogs will engage in deception in other situations, both with other dogs and humans. *See also* **deceiving**; **fairness**; **golden rules of play**.

Chernobyl dogs. After the Chernobyl nuclear disaster on April 26, 1986, the dogs who had lived there with people were abandoned to survive on their own. However, the dogs weren't entirely left alone, as many people think. Guards fed them and cared for them. This is important to note because the dogs of Chernobyl shouldn't be used as examples of how dogs would do on their own if humans disappeared.

chewing. Most dogs love to chew on a wide variety of objects, which can be a form of self-play. Young dogs often chew to relieve the pain of incoming teeth, and chewing also exercises jaw muscles, can help to keep dogs' teeth clean, which is extremely important, and might relieve stress and anxiety. Of course, humans find chewing annoying when it destroys shoes, chairs, children's toys, couch cushions, and so on. If a dog seems to be chewing excessively, it can indicate some sort of problem that requires a visit to a veterinarian.

Dog expert and veterinarian Paul McGreevy thinks that not allowing dogs to chew, which their wild relatives do very frequently, deprives them of a basic need. He told me, "To chew is to be a dog." I agree. Free-ranging and feral dogs chew a lot, as do unrestrained homed dogs.

chin resting. When a dog rests their chin on the back or shoulders of another dog. Chin resting can mean many different things, but it is often a friendly move used to make contact.

chocolate. Many dogs are highly allergic to chocolate, which can make them very ill. Some of the dogs I've lived with stole chocolate bars and chocolate cake but were fine, but I never offered them chocolate as a treat and I encourage others not to do so.

circling. It's a myth that dogs always circle before they lie down. When they do circle, they may be looking for firm ground or scanning to see who's around — whether friends, foes, or no one.

citizen science. Research conducted by people who are not formally trained in research methodologies. Citizen scientists often collect useful, interesting information that helps us understand dog behavior, and I learn a good deal from them. Their observations can inspire formal studies.

For example, Alexandra, an eighth grader at a Boulder middle school, once emailed me to ask if I would help her with a science fair project on play in dogs. Alexandra and I decided to focus on the question of whether familiar dogs play differently than unfamiliar dogs. Alexandra thought that simple question had been studied extensively, but it hasn't been explored in depth.

Alexandra studied her two dogs — Tinkerbell, a highly social dog who loves to play with any dog, and Huggins, who is pickier about his playmates — as they played at a local dog park in Boulder. Alexandra discovered that play was more rough-and-tumble when familiar dogs interacted. When they know the dog with whom they're playing, dogs aren't as worried about formalities, and they jump right into play without taking the time to sniff and greet each other. Dogs who don't know each other are more formal and respectful, and they take the time to get to know the dog with whom they are about to play by sniffing and nose bumping.

Obviously, this question centering on familiarity and play patterns needs further research, but I'm proud that Alexandra became a citizen scientist to help answer it. As she and her family told me countless times, it was a lot of fun to do, and they learned a lot about dogs. Alexandra also won a science fair award for her research.

I always encourage citizen scientists to make observations in their everyday lives and try to find out more about the dogs they encounter and live with. As it did with Alexandra, this research always increases our appreciation for dogs and can occasionally uncover important data. *See also* **research techniques**.

classical conditioning. Learning through association. This is also called Pavlovian or respondent conditioning, and it occurs when two stimuli are linked together to generate a new response. Ivan Pavlov made this famous by getting dogs to salivate when they heard a bell ring. *See also* **conditioned response**; **Pavlov, Ivan**.

Clever Hans. A performing horse in Berlin, Germany, in the late 1890s and early 1900s who could supposedly count and solve complex math problems. It turned out that Hans was responding to subtle and possibly involuntary cues given by his handler, Wilhelm von Osten. The "Clever Hans effect," also called the "observer effect," refers to unintentional cuing by a researcher (or other person) that influences the behavior of the subject — whether nonhuman or human — who is being tested. Some people claim that when dogs perform different tasks, such as counting or using tools, they are being given cues by humans. While this might be so in some instances, it doesn't explain the increasing number of these sorts of observations. *See also* **counting**.

clicker training. Often called "marker training." This type of training uses positive reinforcement and is based on operant conditioning. Using a clicker, a trainer or other person often can reinforce a desired behavior faster than if they provide food. By comparison, the "do as I do" (DAID) method, which depends on visual training, is more effective when training dogs to do object-related actions. *See also* **operant conditioning**.

cloning. Making a genetic copy of an animal. Although it's pricey, cloning services now offer the ability to clone beloved companion dogs who have passed away. However, while a cloned dog may look the same, they are a new animal who will have a different temperament or personality. Barbra Streisand, who created two clones of her deceased dog, noted, "You can clone the look of a dog, but you can't clone the soul." Cloning dogs is controversial for several reasons, but in part because there are so many existing shelter dogs who need forever homes.

cognitive ecology. The study of how animals process information where they live and have to adapt to local environments and conditions. While homed dogs might on occasion have to adapt to changing conditions, free-ranging and feral dogs have to be able to do this much more often. I like to think of a dog's home — along with the humans and possibly other animals who live there — as their niche to which they have to adapt.

cognitive ethology. The study of animal minds — what's in them and what animals know, think, and feel. The award-winning biologist Donald Griffin is often called "the father of cognitive ethology." I define cognitive ethology as the comparative, evolutionary, and ecological study of nonhuman animal minds, including thought processes, beliefs, rationality, information processing, and consciousness. Cognitive ethology is a branch of the science of ethology, which studies similar areas. *See also* **ethology**.

collars. Types of collars include the highly popular choke collars, which tighten when a dog pulls on a leash; shock collars, which are also called e-collars, that deliver an electric shock; and prong collars, which have spikes that dig into a dog's neck. There also are harnesses that fit over a dog's chest and gentle leaders that strap over a dog's muzzle. While some sort of device often is needed to control dogs and to keep them safe, the bottom line is that some collars can cause a good deal of physical and psychological harm. Dogs don't like to be choked, shocked, or pronged, and force-free alternatives should be used. *See also* **leashes**; **shock collars**.

color blindness. Dogs don't see the world in black and white, but they are what we would call "color-blind," meaning they have only two cones in their eyes, whereas humans typically have three. Technically, dogs are color-blind in the human sense of color-blind, since they can see a range of colors.

Based on a detailed analysis of what we know about color blindness in dogs, Stanley Coren notes, "Dogs act as if they are missing the cone which normally responds to longer wavelengths of light which we see as red. This means that dogs see the colors of the world as basically yellow, blue, and gray. They see the colors green, yellow, and orange as yellowish, and violet and blue as blue, while blue-green is seen as gray. The red-colored objects basically lose their hue and become quite dark, since the dog's eye is lacking the receptor to respond to red."

Ironically, the most popular colors for dog toys are red or bright orange-red, though as Coren notes, that's because people like these colors. Dogs can't see them, and they don't care if they have pretty painted nails, ribbons, or designer coats. *See also* **sight**.

Comfort Dog Project. A program in Uganda in which dogs who need a good home are rehabilitated and trained to help war trauma survivors. As the program states, the dogs' guardians "make a lifetime commitment to their dogs, live with and care for their dogs, and participate in a weekly training program. Upon graduation, the dog-guardian teams become project ambassadors — visiting villages and schools to: educate others about the importance of being kind to animals; teach others how to use positive reinforcement training techniques; and serve as testimony of the healing power of human-dog bonds."

commodifying dogs. Using dogs to make money. People profit from dogs in many ways, such as by forcing them to engage in dog fighting, breeding them to do well in dog shows, and breeding novelty dogs. One example is lilac dogs, who are bred to have a coat deformity that has a purple-ish tinge. Far too often breeding is done for fashion and what humans want, even when this causes physical problems that can harm dogs. *See also* **artificial selection**; **designer dogs**.

common sense for how we treat dogs. Concerning dogs, it's common sense that dogs don't like being beaten or scolded. They like feeling safe, secure, and loved. They like to play and enjoy it. That doesn't mean that *all* dogs like to play, which is another bit of common sense: Every individual dog is a unique being.

companion animal. A more positive term for *pet*, one that acknowledges that the well-being of dogs and humans are equally important.

comparative psychology. A branch of psychology that studies similarities and differences in behavior in humans and other animals. However, comparative psychology rarely focuses on the evolution of behavior patterns. *See also* **ethology**.

compassionate conservation. This rapidly growing international discipline is made up of a diverse group of researchers who believe that the life of every single *individual* matters. The four guiding principles of compassionate conservation are first do no harm, individuals matter, value all wildlife, and peaceful coexistence. While these principles might not necessarily apply directly to homed dogs, they apply to free-ranging and feral dogs, some of whom wind up interacting with wild animals, with whom they can coexist, cooperate, or compete. Compassionate conservation mandates that these dogs should be treated with respect and dignity, not as disposable pests. Indeed, many countries, such as Turkey and India, are granting free-ranging dogs protection from harm. During the early stages of the Covid pandemic, India's government declared feeding "streeties," as they're called, to be an essential service. *See also* **free-ranging dogs**; **precautionary principle**.

compassion fatigue. This refers to exhaustion from helping others. People who work in animal rescue and rehabilitation often suffer from this sort of burnout.

competition. Of course, dogs can engage in competition, or desire a common goal that cannot be shared, like possession of an object, food, or a place to rest. This can result in threatening behavior or even fighting.

composite signals. Signals comprised of a variety of sensory information. For instance, when evaluating another dog or situation, a dog might use smell, hearing, and sight — such as to consider another dog's body, posture, and gait — simultaneously or rapidly in succession. Composite signals are like a puzzle with each piece representing information a dog has to assemble into something meaningful.

In one study done as part of the Family Dog Project in Budapest, Hungary, researchers learned that dogs use information from different senses to locate toys in light and dark environments. They preferred to use vision but relied more on odor when lights were off.

A Cornell University study of twenty-three dogs using MRI scans showed connections between dogs' smell and vision — between their noses and occipital (visual) cortex — that allow them to integrate what they smell with what they see. One of the researchers said the research supports her clinical experiences with blind dogs, who function very well: "They can still play fetch and navigate their surroundings much better than humans with the same condition." This research shows how neuroscience and ethology can help us understand the behavior of dogs. *See also* **Family Dog Project**; **hearing**; **sight**; **smell**; **taste**; **touch**.

conditional probability. This refers to the likelihood of something happening after the occurrence of something previously happening. It's often phrased as, "If I do this, what is the likelihood you will do something?" Or, when it comes to dogs at play: "If I do a play bow, what is the likelihood you will play?"

conditioned response. The learned response to a previously neutral stimulus. *See also* **classical conditioning**; **unconditioned response**.

conflicts over dogs. Dogs can often get in the way of what their humans want to do or cause conflicts over how to care for the dog, such as when people disagree about whether a dog should be praised or reprimanded. My overall impression is that these sorts of conflicts are usually short-lived; a mutually acceptable solution can usually be found for most situations. However, I've heard of two instances where the riff became so heated that the couples split, one just for a short while and the other permanently. In both cases, people who knew the couples indicated that the disagreements weren't really about the dog; the conflicts had much deeper roots. This didn't surprise me and is worth being aware of.

consciousness. Dogs are conscious beings, but defining consciousness is tricky. Even those who study it find it very difficult and often disagree. Consciousness generally refers to how organisms experience things and how the brain generates these experiences. Simply put, it means being aware of what's happening inside and outside of you and making changes to accommodate what's happening. Very few if any people now try to argue that dogs and numerous other nonhumans aren't conscious, and their arguments aren't very convincing. By any definition, it's clear that dogs and other animals are conscious beings. *See also* **sentience**.

consent. I'm increasingly seeing the word *consent* used in popular and scientific literature on dogs. Basically, it is essential to take *the dog's* perspective on matters at hand and ensure that the dog agrees with what you want to do. *See also* **agency**.

conservation dogs. Dogs are sometimes used to solve different conservation problems, such as finding individuals of rare and endangered species. For instance, an English springer spaniel named Indy has helped to find rhino poachers and detect caches of rhino meat, called bushmeat, in South Africa.

conservation psychology. According to the Society for Environmental, Population, and Conservation Psychology, "Conservation psychology is the scientific study of the reciprocal relationships between humans and the rest of nature, with the goal of encouraging conservation of the natural world. This relatively new field is oriented toward conservation of ecosystems, conservation of resources, and quality of life issues for humans and other species." Free-ranging and feral dogs can become part of different ecosystems, and their quality of life and the possible harm they do need to be studied.

conspecific. A member of the same species.

context, studying dogs in. Dog behaviors do not occur in a vacuum, and it's critical to consider the context when studying dogs. Context provides critical information about who's involved, where they are, and what caused a dog to do whatever they're doing. For example, certain actions or behaviors — like bared teeth and growling — can mean different things in different contexts. These behaviors are not necessarily aggressive. The same can be said for mounting and humping. *See also* **research techniques**.

contactual behavior. Interactions involving body contact. For example, when one dog leans into another when standing or lying down.

contrafreeloading. When a dog or other animal would rather work for food than eat what is offered to them. The term was coined in 1963 by animal psychologist Glen Jensen.

cooperation. Cooperative hunting in wolves is quite common, but it's not known whether dogs would regularly cooperate if they had the chance. There are observations of packs of free-ranging dogs hunting together, but there haven't been any detailed studies of this behavior.

In one laboratory study, two dogs learned to work together to get a reward on the other side of a fence with two openings. Each had to stand in front of one opening in order to cross through and get food. In another part of the study, researchers learned that the dogs didn't monitor one another and concluded that each of the dogs was working for themselves. *See also* **competition**.

coprophagy. Eating feces. Coprophagy among dogs isn't as rare as one might think. In one study, 23 percent of respondents said they had seen their dog eating dog poop, and 16 percent saw it more than six times. In the study, coprophagy wasn't related to diet or age, fresh stools were preferred, and coprophagic dogs were reported to be "greedy eaters."

Dogs in Ethiopia have been observed to eat human feces, and this impulse may have played a role in the evolution of dogs. Hal Herzog came to that conclusion after reviewing some of the unsavory literature on the topic. Dog experts Brian Hare and Vanessa Woods say the same thing in their book *Survival of the Friendliest*: "Poop is central to the story of how dogs came into our lives." Available data show that Brian and Vanessa might be right on the mark, as distasteful as it sounds. In some locations, human feces may have been an important and nutritious meal for dogs.

copulatory tie. Aka coital lock. This happens during intercourse when the bulbus glandis of the male dog's penis swells inside the female reproductive tract. After the male inserts himself, the animals step over one another and assume a butt-to-butt position. Thus, the dogs are essentially locked together, butt to butt, for as few as five minutes or occasionally up to almost an hour. This is sometimes also called the coital tie, or just a tie.

core area. A research term that refers to the place where an individual spends around 50 percent of their time. The core area is a smaller area within an individual's larger home range or territory. *See also* **home range**; **territorial behavior**.

counterconditioning and desensitization. Counterconditioning refers to training a dog to change their emotional response so that it is different than their current reaction to a stimulus. For example, if your dog doesn't like unfamiliar people, you can use something they like, such as a special treat, to condition them to feel more comfortable around strangers.

Desensitization is also a form of conditioning. It means exposing your dog to something at a very low intensity at the beginning, and then slowly increasing the intensity. When counterconditioning and desensitization are used together, they can be very effective in changing a dog's reaction to situations they're afraid of or that result in aggression.

countermarking. When a dog pees over another dog's urine. This is also called marking over. *See also* **pissing matches**.

counting. Most people agree that dogs and other nonhumans don't count like we do, but rather they are able to estimate quantity and track low numbers. For example, I've watched wild coyotes move pups from one den to another and never leave one behind. I have no idea how they do it, and they seem to know how many have been moved even when more than one adult is moving them. Stanley Coren told me that dogs must have some counting ability because, in order to qualify in an advanced retriever trial, a dog must be able to count to three, and also remember where in the sequence each item belongs.

A few years back, a woman at a local dog park told me her dog Albert was an "Einsteinian genius" with highly evolved math skills. She said, "Albert counts treats and always goes to the larger number rather than to the larger pile." Cindy's claim might be a bit overexcited, but after a few demonstrations, Albert showed that he had a very strong sense of numbers.

Then there's Mellie, the math dog who seems to count and display other cognitive skills. I'm not quite sure what to make of what she's doing. Her human claims it's not due to the Clever Hans effect and cues that he is providing to Mellie.

When animals count or do math, it's said they're subitizing or have a sense of numerosity, or what's also called an "approximate number system" (ANS). As one research paper describes it, ANS is "a system for rapidly assessing the approximate number of items present in an array," and it "appears to be present both across the animal kingdom, and early in human development, with even newborn infants possessing the remarkable ability to discriminate stimuli based on numerosity."

Similarly, in his book *Can Fish Count?*, Brian Butterworth argues that many animals have a sense of numbers — their own types of mathematics — that helps them survive in their social and nonsocial worlds. For example, stingrays and cichlid fish can add and subtract, and there's no reason to think dogs can't also do this. *See also* **Clever Hans**; **numerosity**; **subitizing**.

Covid-19. Dogs and cats can get Covid-19, but infections occur mostly when they're around people who have been infected. In an unpublished study done in the Netherlands, a mobile veterinary clinic was sent to 196 homes where dogs and cats were living with humans who had tested positive for Covid-19 in the past two to two hundred days. Seven of 156 dogs (4.5 percent) and 6 of 154 cats (3.9 percent) had positive Covid tests, and 31 cats (20.1 percent) and 23 dogs (14.7 percent) had Covid antibodies. Pet-to-pet transmission wasn't detected nor was pet-to-human transmission.

crating. Putting a dog in a cage to constrain their movements is usually done to keep them out of trouble, but crating is not a substitute for caring and loving a dog. There are debates about the use of crates — how big they must be and the maximum time limit dogs should be crated. Of course, opinions go all over the place. In October 2021, I received an interesting email about the use of crates. The woman wrote, "Shouldn't we focus on teaching our dogs social skills rather than simply 'put them away' when they are inconvenient?" Yes, we should.

creativity. In her book *The Creative Lives of Animals*, Carol Gigliotti defines creativity as "a dynamic process in which novel and meaningful behaviors are generated by individuals with the possibility of affecting others at cultural, species, and evolutionary levels." Carol shows how important creativity — improvisation and invention, finding novel solutions to difficult problems — is to nonhumans in a wide variety of contexts, including expressing different emotions, playing, socially communicating with others, courting, mating, raising children, and designing and engineering one's home. Dogs display creativity when they're playing and trying to solve different problems. One remarkable example is how some stray dogs have learned to catch metro trains in Moscow, Russia.

critical period of development. This refers to the time in early life when a small amount of experience has the greatest effect on development and later behavior. Between birth and around four months, puppies acquire many of the social skills they'll need to be card-carrying dogs. People disagree on the precise timing of the critical period, and many people prefer to call it the "sensitive period." Dogs vary in how much socialization they need to be able to adapt well to the different situations in which they live.

Building on the classic work of John Paul Scott, John L. Fuller, and others, Dr. Carmelo L. Battaglia writes: "History is full of examples that demonstrate the importance of early life. Most focused on the kinds of experiences thought to affect early behavior and influence later development. The first year of life for a canine can be divided into three important time sensitive periods that overlap each other. The first is called the Neonatal or Primary Period (three to sixteen days). The second is called the Period of Socialization (four to fourteen weeks). The third is called the Enrichment Period (fourteen to fifty-two weeks). When combined they can produce amazing dogs. In humans the important period in early life is longer. It begins at birth and lasts through high school. Regardless of the species, early life experiences are known to influence later adult behavior."

During their first three to four months, dogs experience increasing independence that is critical to socialization — with all animals, including dogs and humans. Dog researcher Zazie Todd notes, "The sensitive period for socialization is a time when [dogs and cats] need lots of positive experiences with all kinds of people and other animals. During this time they will also habituate to anything they might meet in later life (different sounds, surfaces, etc.). If they are well socialized during the sensitive period, they are likely to develop into friendly, confident adult dogs and cats." *See also* **developmental stages**.

cross-species relationships. Friendships between individuals of different species, often called odd couples. Dogs form many such connections, including friendships with humans. There's even a very interesting story about a unique friendship between a dog and a fish.

Chino, a golden retriever who lived with Mary and Dan Heath in Medford, Oregon, and Falstaff, a fifteen-inch koi, had regular meetings for six years at the edge of the pond where Falstaff lived. Each day when Chino arrived, Falstaff swam to the surface, greeted him, and nibbled on Chino's paws. Falstaff did this repeatedly as Chino stared down with a curious and puzzled look on her face. Their close friendship was extraordinary and charming. When the Heaths moved, they went so far as to build a new fishpond so that Falstaff could join them. *See also* **friendship**.

crying. There's little to no evidence that dogs cry like humans do, but one study showed there was an increase in tear volume (caused by oxytocin) after dogs were reunited with their owners.

cultural traditions among free-ranging dogs. While cultural traditions have been found in wild populations of elephants, chimpanzees, dolphins, and other animals, we don't know much about free-ranging or feral dogs. Dog expert Roger Abrantes reports that among dogs in Italy, facial expressions, body language, barking, and howling can vary from region to region. Almost by definition, since they live among people and not with each other, homed dogs do not seem to have cultural traditions.

curiosity. Young animals, like puppies, are often more curious and exploratory than older animals. *See also* **neophilia and neophobia**.

Curly (Jerome Lester Horwitz). One of the Three Stooges who was known for being kind to stray dogs.

cynology. The study of dogs and members of the dog family, Canidae. *See also* **anthrozoology**.

cynomorphism. How dogs "see" or sense the world. *See also* **anthropomorphism**.

D

daily rhythms. The activity rhythms of many dogs — what they do and when and where — are highly controlled by humans in one way or another, and it's difficult to know what is "natural." Free-ranging and feral dogs show more variability in activity patterns than homed dogs — when, where, and how they eat, rest, and interact with other dogs and humans — but most of them are still indirectly or directly influenced by humans.

Dangerous Dog Act. A 1991 act of the UK parliament limiting or prohibiting different breeds or mixes of dogs. This act makes it criminal for any dog to be "dangerously out of control." It pays more attention to what a dog looks like rather than to their behavior. *See also* **breed specific legislation (BSL)**.

Darwin, Charles Robert. Darwin was one of the most important, if not the most important, contributors to the science of evolutionary theory. Darwin wrote on numerous topics, including domestication and artificial selection, natural selection, sexual selection, and many aspects of animal behavior, including morality. Darwin also put forth the principle of evolutionary continuity; specifically, that many differences among species are differences in degree rather than in kind. He often told very interesting stories about the cognitive, emotional, and moral lives of dogs. There's very little Darwin didn't ponder, and his influence in many different areas remains obvious and important. *See also* **antithesis, Darwin's principle of**; **domestication syndrome**; **evolution**.

data. Aka facts collected in research. The word *data* is plural, while *datum* refers to a single fact.

death and dying. Countless people wonder what dogs know about death and dying. Do dogs have a concept of death? Do they know that they and others will die? People on all sides have weighed in on this hotly debated topic. Some argue dogs don't know anything about death and dying, while others say they have a rich concept of death — of their own and others'. My view is that we simply don't know all that much right now, but we need to leave the door open to all possibilities. Some people think we make the concept of death and dying too complicated and this automatically excludes other animals. Other animals may or may not have a concept like ours, but death as a fact is universal.

I often wonder if dying has a unique odor or some sort of composite signal that dogs might recognize as denoting death. Perhaps there is a stimulus that causes stress. I've speculated that a composite signal made up of some unique combination of visual, auditory (for dying animals), and olfactory cues might tell an individual who is dying and others around them that something "new" and unique is happening — the process we call dying. After an animal dies, another composite signal might indicate that something else has happened — the event we call death. However, I'm not sure that this says much at all about what an individual actually knows about dying and death or the concept of death as we cash it out.

I look forward to further studies and discussions about nonhumans' concepts of dying and death because they also might tell us about many other aspects of what they think and feel in a wide variety of contexts. We also can learn about the other animals who interact with dying and dead individuals. As Susana Monsó suggests, opossums will "play dead" (a behavior called thanatosis) when coyotes are around, and even if this behavior is automatic, the display works because animals seem to have a hard wired aversion to death.

My cycling buddy Lawrence Bosch recently told me that when his dog Turbo passed away, the other five dogs in the house knew something was happening and cuddled up to him, something they hadn't done before. He told me that Turbo lived longer than they thought he would, apparently so he could be there for the other dogs. I've received many similar stories over the years, and they make me rethink just what dogs know. *See also* **mourning**.

debarking. Aka devocalizing, surgically removing a large portion of the larynx. Debarking is a cruel and painful procedure that is usually unnecessary, and numerous veterinarians won't do it. People often choose to do it when, in their opinion, a dog barks excessively, but of course there likely is a good reason why a dog barks. People just need to take the time to figure out what the dog is feeling and address the problem. Barking is a normal behavior, and it usually only becomes "excessive" by our standards. *See also* **abnormal behavior**; **barking**.

deceiving. Masking the truth and getting another dog to believe something that isn't true to take advantage of them. I agree with Stanley Coren, who notes that dogs have a theory of mind and will engage in deceptive behavior. I have seen it myself and been told numerous stories of dogs tricking humans and other dogs. Interestingly, while dogs tend to play fair, they will deceive other dogs and humans to get something they want, like food or a toy, or to pull a humorous prank.

Here's a story one of my friends and cycling partners sent to me.

Heather, who knows lots about dog behavior, told me that two of her dogs — a fifty-pound standard poodle named Jett and a fifteen-pound mini-poodle mix named Zoey — love to play with a squeaker. However, they don't play with a toy with a squeaker in it, but rather the squeaker itself.

Jett guts every squeaky toy he's given and then runs around with the squeaker. The two dogs take turns with the squeaker. Jett squeaks it for a while, and then when he puts it down, Zoey squeaks it for a while. They both want it, and I'm told it's the highest-value object in the house, other than possibly food.

One day, Jett stole the squeaker from Zoey and she stole it back a dozen times, after which Zoey took the toy to her favorite spot on the couch and snuggled down with it. Eventually, Zoey got distracted and jumped off the couch, leaving the squeaker toy behind. Jett immediately took it and started squeaking. Zoey tried to get it back from him in a game of tug-of-war.

When that failed, she found a discarded piece of paper on the floor. Zoey grabbed the paper and played with it right in front of Jett, tearing bits out of it and throwing it around. Jett saw her antics, discarded the toy, and went to grab the paper, which she immediately surrendered.

Zoey then grabbed the toy and jumped back onto her favorite spot on the couch with it. As Heather put it, "She tricked him right out of their treasured toy."

I don't know what Zoey was thinking as she consciously tricked Jett, but I've heard a similar version of this story many times. Two dogs — let's call them Harry and Mary — are eating side by side. One night, Mary finishes eating before Harry, and she runs to the front door barking, even though no one is there. Then when Harry follows her, Mary runs back to the food bowls and finishes what's left. Typically, this ploy only works a few times before the other dog figures it out, indicating something like, *You can't fool me anymore.*

Another story I heard involved Myron, a dog who loved to help his humans preclean dishes by jumping in the dishwasher and licking them. Myron's humans weren't especially happy about his dishwashing proclivities and tried to stop him, but Myron learned that if he could get the attention of one or both of his humans by barking near the front door or window, they would follow him to see what was up. Then he could race back to the dishwasher, jump in, and continue eating his dessert.

Of course, this ruse soon stopped working on Myron's humans, and once Myron "got it" and understood it wasn't working, he switched tactics. He slowly left the vicinity of the dishwasher without showing any interest in what was in there, lay down in another room, and whined. When his humans came to see what was up, Myron raced into the kitchen, climbed into the dishwasher, and began feasting once again. This scheme eventually stopped working, too.

The end of the story is perhaps the most amusing of all. Myron's humans relented and decided to allow him to feast in the dishwasher, but as they told me, he didn't seem to have as much fun knowing he wasn't fooling his humans. Nonetheless, I'm sure Myron appreciated being allowed to be a dishwasher foodie. *See also* **cheating**; **humor, sense of**.

declarative memory. Storing and recalling facts, ideas, concepts, and dates. In one 2014 study using the "do as I do" (DAID) training method, researchers found that dogs could imitate novel actions after 1.5 minutes and familiar actions after 0.4 to 10 minutes. The dogs' ability to encode and later recall an action and to imitate a novel behavior after some time led them to conclude that dogs display declarative memory.

declawing. Aka onychectomy. Removing a dog's claws remains legal in most of the United States. It's often done when claws scratch people or when they mar a floor, but filing down claws can usually work just fine. If claws become infected, see a veterinarian. A vet tech friend of mine once told me that a clawless dog is not a dog. They meant that dogs evolved claws because they serve a purpose in their lives — to grip surfaces and dig — and so were necessary.

decoding dogs. Trying to figure out what dogs are doing and why.

dedomestication. Undoing the effects of selective breeding. This is a form of reverse engineering in which people use selective breeding to create a more-original or more-wild version of a domestic species. I don't know anyone who is intentionally trying to dedomesticate dogs to make them closer to ancestral wolves. *See also* **domestication**; **feralization**.

defensive behavior. Actions dogs take to defend themselves can be aggressive, submissive, or passive. A dog might protect themselves by running away from a dangerous individual or by attacking that individual, particularly when there's no room to escape. As always, it's important to consider context when evaluating a dog's defensive behavior. *See also* **aggression**; **resident effect**.

delayed gratification. Dogs are quite capable of engaging in delayed gratification, or postponing an immediate reward in anticipation of getting something better in the future. A 2012 study entitled "Waiting for More" tested five dogs who all consistently exchanged lower-valued or less-preferred food for higher-valued or more-preferred food. All the dogs also learned to perform two and three exchanges in a row to get higher-quality and more food. Delayed gratification was also tested over different intervals of time — or how long a dog would keep one piece of food to exchange for a larger piece of food — and researchers found a good deal of variation. Periods ranged from ten seconds to ten minutes, but after forty seconds, the dogs who waited gave up earlier than researchers expected.

dementia. Like humans, dogs can suffer dementia. They can lose the ability to think or remember what needs to be done in a given situation. Hearing loss may predict a greater risk of dementia.

A few years ago, I received an email from my friend Rod, who wrote:

> You've met my pal Jack who celebrates his twelfth birthday next week. As of late, say the last couple months, Jack has awoken after

> maybe thirty minutes of seemingly sound sleep. He comes awake in a start, head and ears down, clambering quickly to run from whatever has terrified him in his dream. He goes a short distance and then stops, wide awake. This happens a few times a week and is not dependent on sleeping in a specific location. It had been suggested to give him some melatonin prior to bed to help his sleep pattern, but that does not seem to have much effect. I wondered if you have encountered anything similar. I always try to comfort him after the fact, but so wish there was something I could do to alleviate his terror before it occurs.

I immediately wrote back and said that perhaps Jack was suffering from a form of sundowner's syndrome, which is related to dementia. Rod was describing some classic signs of dementia that I've seen in other senior dogs, and I was relieved when Rod concluded that most likely Jack's behavior was caused by bad dreams. *See also* **dreaming**; **sundowner's syndrome**.

denning. When an animal prepares a place to have children and where the infants can be cared for. Some people think that homed dogs are denning when they dig incessantly, but I'm not sure this is so. Free-ranging and feral dogs dig dens just like their wild cousins.

derived activities. Behaviors that are used out of their original context. For example, a derived activity is when an adult dog exhibits infantile behavior or mounts another dog during an aggressive, nonsexual encounter. *See also* **emancipation**; **socio-infantile behavior**; **socio-sexual behavior**.

desensitization. *See* **counterconditioning and desensitization**.

desexing. *See* **neutering**.

designer dogs. A term for new combinations of breeds that people find appealing. Designer dogs are simply mixed-breed mutts, but they are often viewed and treated as fashionable accessories. They seem to have fewer health problems than purebreds, but there aren't any detailed studies of this. Wally Conron, the breeder who first crossed poodles and Labradors to develop the Labradoodle (called Cobberdogs in Australia) wishes he hadn't done so; they were his life's regret. Conron said, "I opened a Pandora's box and released a Frankenstein monster" that allows "unethical, ruthless people" to breed the dogs without any concern for the health of their offspring. *See also* **artificial selection**; **commodifying dogs**.

developmental stages. Here is a list of the typical stages of development that dogs go through from birth onward. The time periods are approximations because different dogs go through development differently.

- Stage 1: Neonatal period (0–2 weeks)
- Stage 2: Transitional period (2–4 weeks)
- Stage 3: Socialization period (3–12 weeks)
- Stage 4: Testing period (3–6 months)
- Stage 5: Adolescence (6–18 months)
- Fear periods
- Biting, nipping, and rough play

See also **critical period of development**.

diet. What diet is best for dogs? There are countless opinions on how and what to feed dogs, and it's one area in which people can exert control over their dog by deciding when, what, where, and perhaps with whom they eat. Many people are very concerned with different feeding plans. The BBC ran a program in 2022 called "How Not to Feed a Dog" that made it clear there is no one "right" way to feed dogs. Many different diets and meal plans work. Individual differences among dogs need to be considered.

Some people like to compare dogs to wolves when considering what sorts of food dogs should eat. However, this comparison doesn't represent dogs for who they are. Clearly, very few modern dogs exercise or engage in wolflike behavior patterns and activities, which require a high calorie intake. In addition, dogs and wolves may no longer have identical nutritional needs. For example, researchers recently uncovered an interesting genetic difference between dogs and wolves, namely, that dogs appear to have a greater ability to digest starches. The wolf genome has only two copies of the gene alpha-amylase 2B, which helps with processing starch in the pancreas, while dogs have somewhere between four and thirty copies of this gene. When it comes to diet, treating dogs like wolves doesn't make biological or nutritional sense.

Concerning how many calories a day a dog needs, the consensus is that most dogs need about twenty-five to thirty calories per pound per day to maintain their weight. That means, on average, a thirty-pound dog needs around eight hundred calories a day. But weight alone isn't the only thing to consider. Veterinarians typically use a measure of "maintenance energy requirement" to figure out what a specific dog needs in terms of calories, and then they factor in what they call "multipliers." That is, they consider whether a dog is neutered or intact, if they need to gain or lose weight, their age, and how hard they work and how much exercise they get. So, after considering individual differences, even dogs of the same weight will have different needs.

In *The Forever Dog*, authors Rodney Habib and Karen Becker present a flexible feeding plan that "focuses on diet and nutrition, movement, environmental exposures, and stress reduction, and can be tailored to the genetic predisposition of particular breeds or mixes." The authors discuss various types of food — including what the commercial manufacturers don't want us to know — and offer recipes, easy solutions, and tips for making sure our dogs obtain the nutrients they need. They also explore how external factors we often don't think about can greatly affect a dog's overall health and well-being, from everyday insults to the body and its physiology to the role our own lifestyles and our vets' choices play. Indeed, the health equation works both ways and can travel "up the leash."

The best advice is to tailor diet to each individual dog. Just like people, dogs differ in how much exercise they get and how they process different foods. For instance, most dogs can do well on a vegan diet, while many commercial foods aren't very good, and they aren't suited for all dogs. Further, like people, dogs are probably impacted emotionally by the foods they eat, due to the gut-brain axis, so pay attention to mood when addressing your dog's best diet.

Food should be more than a bowl of something on the ground, and many if not most dogs would rather feed from a bowl that is at neck level. Feeding time for dogs should be enjoyable. Some interesting data also show that some dogs pay attention to what others can hear and prefer to take food from containers that don't make noise when food is removed.

Finally, I'm a fan of the "clean food pet food revolution." For example, research published in 2017 by UCLA professor Gregory Okin showed that a quarter of all meat-derived calories in the United States are fed to pets, meaning that modern high–animal protein pet diets are now a major contributor to human-induced climate change.

All in all, there are many different views on what dogs' meal plans should and should not look like. The most important thing is to get as much information as you can and pay attention to what works best for your dog. Good intentions are not enough. Also, remember that food does not equal love — let your dog enjoy feeding and still know you love them when you're not giving them food. *See also* **gut-brain axis**; **obesity**; **vegan diets**.

dingo. A wild Australian dog. Many people think when dogs go wild, absent human intrusions into their lives, they will look like dingoes, medium-size canids perhaps predominately tan in color.

disabled dogs. Like humans, dogs can lose legs and suffer physical maladies that make it difficult to get around or survive on their own. Many of these dogs offer valuable lessons about survival and hope. Dogs with prostheses can do very well. One of my favorite dogs was Penelope, who lost control of her rear legs and did just fine romping around and trying to play being aided by a "rear wheel wagon," as her humans called it.

disease detection. Numerous studies have shown that trained dogs can use odors to detect many diseases, including lung, breast, ovarian, bladder, and prostate cancers and Covid-19. Dogs' detection of Covid can be as accurate as PCR tests, and they can detect long Covid. Dogs can also sniff out chronic wasting disease in deer and elk. *See also* **smell**.

disgust. Yes, as surprising as it sounds, dogs can be disgusted. Typically, they show aversions to certain odors and tastes, which is probably the source of an aversion to death. *See also* **death and dying**.

displacement behavior. An action used to displace stress that is unrelated to the cause of stress. For example, stressed animals often groom when they are unsure whether to approach or move away from potential conflict. When dogs are uncertain, they will often scratch themselves or drink water. Humans also engage in displacement behaviors when in socially stressful situations. *See also* **humping**.

displays. An action that sends a specific message. Dogs use displays to communicate what they're thinking or feeling to other dogs or even to other species who might understand the display. A well-known social display is the "play bow," which is used to ask other dogs to engage in play. *See also* **play bows**; **ritualization**.

do as I do (DAID) dog training. *See* **clicker training**.

docking. Removing all or part of an animal's tail. This painful procedure can cause changes in how a dog communicates with others. Unless there is a medical reason, there is no reason to dock a dog's tail for fashion. *See also* **tails**.

dogcentric. Making dogs the center of attention and taking their point of view. This is different than canine exceptionalism, which views dogs as special and better than other nonhuman animals. *See also* **canine exceptionalism**.

Dog Cognition Lab. A research group run by Alexandra Horowitz at Barnard College.

"dog days." A term for hot summer days when you lie around and do nothing.

"dog-eat-dog world." A term for ruthless self-interest or any highly competitive environment or situation.

"dogfight." A term for a hotly contested battle.

dog fighting. An inhumane bloodsport in which dogs are raised, trained, and forced to fight one another. Raising and training dogs to fight for sport, money, and entertainment is a felony offense in all fifty US states, but it is still legal in Honduras, Japan, and Albania.

dog-friendly cities. Lists are published every year ranking the best cities for dogs. Here are the highlights from the list compiled in 2022 by the Swiftist: The top three large cities (350,000+ people) were Portland, Oregon; Austin, Texas; and Tampa, Florida. The top three medium cities (200,000–350,000 people) were Boise, Idaho; Salt Lake City, Utah; and Orlando, Florida. The top three small cities (140,000–200,000 people) were Alexandria, Virginia; Knoxville, Tennessee; and Fort Lauderdale, Florida. Some states had no cities that ranked in the study. Ranking factors included number of dog parks and pet sitters; the number of dog-friendly trails, hotels, restaurants, and rentals; and the cost of dog insurance.

"doghouse, in the." A saying meaning that someone is banished out of annoyance, anger, or disapproval. That said, being in the doghouse isn't always bad. Some doghouses are plush and much nicer than many people's homes. One man spent forty-five hundred dollars on a special room for his dog.

dog-human relationships. Dog-human relationships vary from culture to culture. In some cultures, dogs are considered members of the family and the local community, whereas in other cultures dogs are considered "food animals" or dangerous and dirty. In Istanbul, people and stray dogs get along very well, and it has been illegal to euthanize or capture any stray dog in Turkey since 2004. Turkey's model provides an alternative, more-compassionate way of coexisting with a species that has evolved to live alongside us.

During the Covid-19 pandemic, the government of India declared that feeding stray dogs, whom they call "streeties," was an essential service, and political leaders appealed to people to step up and take responsibility to care for these animals. And a pack of stray dogs changed the life of an art teacher living in the First Nation fly-in community of Shamattawa, Manitoba (Canada), who used her writing and artwork to reflect the need for veterinary services and compassion for nonhumans and humans.

Globally, there is an increasing number of projects focusing on the humane management of these dogs.

Different cultures attribute different emotions to dogs, and looking at cultural differences is also a way to parse out what the word *domesticated* means. In *Domestication Gone Wild*, ethnographer Natasha Fijn describes her studies of the dog-human relationships in the Khangai Mountains of Mongolia and among the Yolngu in Aboriginal Australia. She wonders why Australian dingoes are classified as "wild" in zoological terms, while Mongolian dogs are classified as "domesticated," when both have been closely associated with humans.

There also are cultural effects on the dogs people choose to live with. Several members of the Leech Lake Band of Ojibwe in northern Minnesota are working to address animal neglect on their tribal lands — and in doing so, they are bringing their community closer to its spiritual roots.

In an essay called "Is a Love of Dogs Mostly a Matter of Where You Live," Hal Herzog concludes, "Our relationships with pets are more a matter of culture than genes, and under the right circumstances, our attitudes toward animals can rapidly change." Herzog found that wealthier nations often have less dog ownership than poorer nations, and religion can affect our relationships with dogs. Since some branches of Islam consider dogs "unclean" animals, it's perhaps not surprising that "there were nearly three times more dogs per one thousand people" in the non-Islamic nations Herzog studied than in primarily

Islamic countries. Herzog also found there are "dog nations" — India, South Korea, and the Philippines — and "cat nations" — Indonesia, Switzerland, Austria, and Turkey. *See also* **breed popularity**; **movies, dogs in**.

"dog is my copilot." A recoining of the phrase "God is my copilot" and the motto of *Bark* magazine. While this saying honors dogs as guides for living, there are of course reasons we shouldn't always emulate dogs, since dog-appropriate behavior is not always human-appropriate behavior.

dognapping. In early 2022, it was reported there was a large increase in dognappings. Lady Gaga offered a reward of $500,000 for the return of her dogs, and the thieves were caught when they tried to cash in.

Stanley Coren writes: "The dogs that have the highest value are French bulldogs and other purebreds or posh designer mixes. English bulldogs, Maltipoos, and small exotic breeds are also high on the list. Dobermans were really hot for a while since coats were being made from them. According to the Los Angeles Police Department, the dogs that are at most risk are French bulldogs (since they can fetch $7,000–$12,000), Goldendoodles (resale value $800–$3,000), and Pomeranians (resale value starts at $3,000, but if there is an unusual or rare coat color, such as a merle, they can net up to $15,000)."

Dognition. The name of the Duke Canine Cognition Center where researchers Brian Hare, Vanessa Wood, and their students conduct research on canine intelligence.

dog parks. Fenced areas where dogs can run free. Dog parks are rapidly growing in number and provide a place for dogs to move about freely, sniff to their nose's content, meet up with old friends and make new friends, and romp around with them. However, dog parks have become controversial for some folks, mainly based on misleading information, such as that dogs learn bad habits like jumping on people or that play fighting frequently escalates into serious fighting. As dog park expert Dr. Patrick Jackson notes, the criticisms of dog parks tend to reflect human concerns and inconvenience rather than concerns for dogs.

It seems pretty simple to me — if your dog likes to go to a dog park, take them. And if they don't, don't force them to go even if you like to go.

After I wrote an essay saying this, called "Let Your Dog Tell You If They Want to Go to a Dog Park," I received a lot of interesting comments. Here are a few:

> "Just wanted to say I appreciate your response to the recent *New York Times* article against dog parks at large. I live in a city that has very little park space dedicated to off-leash areas, and it's not helpful when respected media outlets make misleading and overly cautious cases against their existence. They really can provide wonderful and enriching experiences for a multitude of dogs. Sure, not every dog is park appropriate, and always watch your dog and intervene when needed and so on. Considering the high incidence of under-enriched and under-socialized frustrated dogs, scaring people away from parks instead of guiding them on how to use them wisely seems counterproductive."

> "Just like a playground where dozens of tiny humans and their associated grown-ups hang out, dog parks can be places where things go wrong. But from my experience, dog parks, and playgrounds for that matter, are positive and fun places to be. If there are prickly dogs (or people) at the dog park, I sometimes leave. Likewise, if my dog isn't enjoying herself anymore, we also leave. However, I always go back because my dogs enjoy it more often than not and so do I and so do most of the other dogs. Watching dogs have fun with one another at the dog park is, in fact, one of my great joys."

> "Imagine if every human who has ever had a normal but negative human interaction in a public space (like throwing my hands up when someone passed me and then slowed down yesterday) was told they could never go out in public again because it's too dangerous or upsetting. It's surreal! Sequestering a social carnivore because people find species-normal play and conflict resolution to be worrisome is — I am just out of words."

"Thousands of dogs have fun interactions in dog parks daily. But the flash of teeth or the sound of a growl even without injury to either dog is enough to send many people scurrying for home. We clearly have more work to do educating pet owners about normal dog-dog behavior."

"This sweeping condemnation of dog parks is inane and ill-informed."

"This rampant dog park bashing is totally uninformed."

"The dog park is the highlight of any day for my husky. He'll play with any dog, any way that they want to play, and getting into the park is about the only time I could trust him off-leash. The socialization is the best treat he could want."

dogphilia. An innate attraction to and love of dogs. People have told me I'm a "dogphiliac." The word is a play on *biophilia*, which is an innate connection to nature.

dogphobia. An innate fear and dislike of dogs.

dog racing. Dog racing, usually with greyhounds, is a cruel sport that causes thousands of racing dogs to be injured each year. The only states that still allow greyhound racing are Alabama, Arkansas, Iowa, Texas, and West Virginia. Connecticut, Kansas, Oregon, and Wisconsin do not have active racetracks but would allow it. Numerous organizations are devoted to rescuing and rehabilitating retired dogs.

"dog's life, it's a." A saying for someone enjoying the good life, as if all dogs do is lie around, get fed, and play with friends. Of course, that's not true.

dogs or cats, who is smarter. Many people like to speculate whether dogs are smarter than cats or vice versa. There is no debate: Neither is smarter than the other.

dog-tolerant versus dog-selective dogs. Dog-tolerant dogs are generally friendly to all dogs, though sometimes they are merely nonreactive and indifferent, whereas dog-selective dogs like some dogs but not others. The vast majority of dogs with whom I have shared my mountain home and the surrounding land have been dog-tolerant. All the other dogs living up there were most welcomed, but occasionally when there was a new canine neighbor, my and other dogs gently taught them the house rules, including who rested and slept where and who first got the ample treats I provided. Over many years, there was only one serious altercation that I saw. A new youngster came down to say hello, and she tried to play with some of the elders. When they'd had enough of her energy, they chased her off, nipping at her butt. The next day all was fine, and for many years, they all got along peacefully sharing space and food.

dogtopia. Aka a dog utopia, the ideal dogcentric world for dogs.

dog trade. In places where dogs are openly eaten, people are astounded and offended by the conditions in which dogs are kept, which are like other "food animals" such as cows, pigs, chickens, turkeys, and fishes.

dog training. *See* **training.**

DOGTV. A streaming service providing televised content for dogs. The purpose is to relieve boredom and stress for dogs. They claim, "We're an entertainment brand, a pet brand, and a wellness brand, all in one." While there is nothing necessarily wrong with a dogcentric TV channel, particularly if it soothes a dog, it's not a substitute for human companionship and love.

dolichocephalic. Long-headed dogs, including Afghans and greyhounds.

domesecration. David Nibert coined the term *domesecration* as an alternative to *domestication.* He defines domesecration as "a perversion of human ethics, the development of large-scale acts of violence, disastrous patterns of destruction, and growth-curbing epidemics of infectious disease." Dr. Sarah Bexell made me wonder about whether domestication, viewed this way, could be an example of nonhuman "collective trauma," a phenomenon usually only discussed with respect to humans.

domestic abuse and dogs. Dogs often become targets when domestic abuse occurs, and groups are working hard to protect them and other companion animals in these situations. Because of the personal nature of these incidents, it's difficult to collect accurate data, but dog abuse can reflect or lead to human abuse, and many people are interested in what is called "the link," namely, the correlation of dog and animal abuse with violence toward humans. *See also* **link, the**.

domestication. The process by which a wild species becomes a domestic species. Most people think that domestication is the result of humans exerting control over the reproductive activities of wild animals (or plants) until they become domesticated. For people who study domestication in detail, it's not so simple. Domestication can take many different forms, and there isn't a single explanation for this process.

It's generally estimated that for dogs, who had a common, now-extinct wolf ancestor, domestication began around fifteen to twenty thousand years ago. It's also possible that dogs arose from two populations of wolves, but what this relationship means for the actual origin of dogs as we know them today remains unclear.

In *How the Dog Became the Dog*, dog expert Mark Derr stresses that the way in which dogs became domesticated resulted from a human partnership that offered mutual benefits. Many others agree, although they don't give Mark the credit he deserves. It's also possible that humans hunting with dogs were more successful than those who hunted alone.

A similar argument is put forth by Ray Pierotti and Brandy Fogg in their excellent book *The First Domestication: How Wolves and Humans Coevolved*. They correctly point out that almost every other book that has been published about the domestication of wolves and their relationship to humans has been written mainly from a Western reductionist tradition that emphasizes competition and rivalry between nonhumans and humans, rather than from a viewpoint of cooperation and compatibility. They also show how important it is to bring in the views of indigenous people, whose knowledge and traditions should be taken seriously and recognized as valid ways to think about nature and biological questions. Pierotti and Fogg aptly summarize their view this way: "As long as humans considered themselves to be fellow predators... we lived comfortably with wolves. They were our companions, sharing both our hunts and our kills and living with us in a more or less equal sort of reciprocity."

Along with many others, Pierotti and Fogg dispute and are troubled by the dump-scavenging model of domestication put forth by Ray and Lorna Coppinger. This theory suggests that ancient human garbage dumps attracted wolves, and those wolves who scavenged dumps frequently became habituated to humans and eventually evolved into dogs. The dump-scavenging model makes little sense in terms of the timing of the dog's domestication or how the transition from wolf to dog actually occurred. *See also* **Darwin, Charles Robert**; **evolution**.

domestication syndrome. Charles Darwin's idea that because of human artificial selection for certain traits, domesticated animals show marked physical similarities. These traits include being smaller and having smaller teeth and brains than their wild ancestral relatives, along with drooping ears, curled tails, white-patched and variable coats, and a tendency to look young — cute — even as adults. It's been hypothesized that these unrelated traits are due to deficits in neural crest cells during embryonic development.

Dogs display significant diversity, so some breeds display some of the traits associated with the domestication syndrome, whereas others do not. As Dr. Christina Hansen Wheat notes, "For dogs, the issue is that we are trying to infer what happened when we domesticated the species at least 15,000 years ago by looking at the dogs we have today... but the dogs we have today are not likely to be representative of the early dogs our forefathers domesticated." *See also* **artificial selection**; **neoteny**; **paedomorphism**.

dominance. Dominance typically means controlling the behavior of another individual, and this does not have to involve physical contact. Dominant animals may enjoy more freedom to move about in their group, and some studies have shown they are the focus of attention of lower-ranking individuals.

Some people claim that dogs do not display dominance, but that isn't true. However, just because dogs can dominate one another, this does not mean we should dominate them in training. Nor do dogs necessarily try to dominate us. A human-dog relationship is not a contest for dominance, and it's OK to let dogs go out the door first, eat first, and win when they play tug-of-war. *See also* **hierarchy of social relationships**; **positive training**.

dreaming. Some people wonder whether dogs dream. I'm sure they do, and many people, including researchers, agree. There is no reason to think that dogs don't dream, particularly about the things that happened to them. It's likely dogs also can have bad dreams or nightmares, as well as a bad night's sleep, just like we do. There are numerous videos of sleeping dogs who clearly have something going on in their sleepy brains.

A few years ago, a woman named Annie wrote to me to say that she was sure her dog Aaron relived some of the previous day's activities, especially the bad encounters he had with other dogs or people. Aaron slept near Annie's side, and she said he didn't sleep as deeply or as well and spent more time twitching — running in place — and vocalizing the night after he had a bad day. Annie also said that after a bad night of sleep, Aaron was more edgy and unsettled the next morning. She asked me what I thought was going on. While I can't say for sure, there's no reason to think he wasn't having bad dreams.

The important message concerning dog's dreaming is that we know very little about what they dream about and why, and I hope to see more research on this topic. Their brains and neurotransmitters are much like our own. As David Peña-Guzmán suggests, they may be dreaming of "imaginary pursuits" or "reality simulations." *See also* **sleep**.

drooling. *See* **salivating.**

drug-detecting dogs. Dogs trained to find illegal drugs. *See also* **disease detection.**

dry marking. When a dog lifts a leg without peeing. Dry marking is usually done by male dogs. The dog might be trying to send a visual signal, such as, *I'm peeing — this is my territory.* They also might be trying to get another dog to use up all their pee. On occasion, male dogs will lift a leg and not urinate — they're faking it — and then they walk a few feet and immediately lift a leg and pee. Similar behavior has been observed among free-ranging dogs living outside of Rome by Simona Cafazzo and her colleagues. *See also* **scent marking.**

E

ear clipping. Cutting off some or all of the external flaps of a dog's ear. Also called ear cropping, this is sometimes done to make ears stand straight up in the name of fashion. Like tail docking, ear clipping is usually done for humans' sense of beauty rather than for a dog's well-being. Dogs need their ears and there's no need to clip them.

ears. Dogs' ears come in many shapes and sizes — long and short, floppy and stiff, and all combinations in between — and they are surprisingly mobile. In his book *Canine Terminology*, Australian veterinarian Harold Spira discusses more than twenty-five different ear types.

More than eighteen muscles control the pinna (or earflap) alone, which allows the nuanced movements that make dogs' ears so expressive and so good at picking up and locating sounds. The ear muscles allow dogs to turn their ears like a periscope to follow the direction of a sound. Dogs move their ears to facilitate hearing; every dog owner will recognize the "pricked ears" of a dog who is suddenly attentive. The up-and-open ears allow dogs to best capture sound. Ears are also used as part of visual signals. *See also* **hearing.**

e-collars. *See* **shock collars**.

ecological relevance. This term refers to how relevant a study is to the ways in which members of a species typically behave and live. For dogs, we would ask how relevant a study of captive dogs is when compared to the natural behavior of dogs — are we asking the dogs in the study to learn or do something they naturally do? Of course, it's difficult to say just what is a "natural life" for dogs, but for around 20 percent of the world's dogs, it's a human's home with all the attendant benefits. Nonetheless, when studying dogs, it's essential to design studies that ask questions that relate to how dogs typically live. Some people worry that when dogs in a lab study don't do something or fail a learning test, it's not because they can't learn what needs to be done, but rather they're bored or they're being deprived of the relevant stimulus that is needed to have them do something. Just because dogs don't do something in the lab doesn't mean they don't or can't do it when they're free-ranging — in the field — and vice versa. We must be careful of sweeping generalizations. *See also* **object permanence**.

electric fences. Also called invisible and wireless fences, electric fences — which deliver a shock of various intensities when touched — are widely used to contain dogs on private property or in defined areas. The upsides include keeping a dog on your property and keeping them safe or preventing them from becoming a neighborhood nuisance, while still allowing them to exercise and run free. Whereas the downsides include the dog getting shocked, and some dogs get frustrated when they can't chase down another dog, even playfully, when they can't pursue other animals, and when they can't exercise their noses when they're on a scent. Many trainers tell me they strongly discourage using electric fences because the same results can be achieved by positive force-free training, but some people don't want to invest the time and effort to train their dog so these fences aren't necessary. During the many decades I lived in the mountains, I never used any aversive training, my dogs rarely if ever roamed (because there were always ample treats for them near my house), and I never had any incidents with the mountain lions, black bears, red foxes, and other animals with whom they had to share space. But also, they never were free when no one was home.

eliminating. When a dog pees or poops. While peeing and pooping can be done to mark a territory or communicate with other dogs, most often dogs eliminate just because they have to go. *See also* **pissing matches**; **scent marking**.

emancipation. When an action from one context is incorporated or freed up to become part of another. This is a type of derived activity. For example, begging can become part of a greeting or indicate subordination. *See also* **derived activities**.

embarrassment. I'm not aware of any formal studies of embarrassment in dogs, but it wouldn't surprise me if dogs could feel shame. They're surely not embarrassed by putting their noses in forbidden places or humping other dogs or objects. A few times I've seen a dog stumble when they were chasing a ball or another dog, stop and look around as if trying to see if anyone saw what happened, and then continue chasing whatever or whoever they were after. Friends of mine and some primatologists have seen similar behavior and called it embarrassment, but I really don't know.

emotional contagion. When individuals share the same or similar emotional state, which often leads to similar behaviors. Dogs possess empathy and can feel and share the emotional state of others, including dogs, humans, and other species. These shared emotions can function like "social glue" and foster bonding. I always think that play is one of the most contagious behaviors. When most dogs see other dogs playing, they want to jump right in.

Not much is known about the underlying variables that influence how emotions are shared. A 2019 study published by Maki Katayama and her colleagues sheds some light on this dynamic. To track whether emotional contagion was present between humans and dogs, the researchers used heart-rate variability (HRV), which changes in seconds, as a measure of autonomic nervous system activity and "positive emotional states," since previous studies have shown that this is a reliable relationship. Ultimately, fourteen pairs of dogs and their humans were studied. In the experiment, the humans were exposed to stress in which they were criticized for making mistakes when performing verbal mental arithmetic. This was done silently — using a board displaying the message "It's an error. Repeat the calculation again." — so the dogs didn't know their humans were being criticized.

This study found that the dogs shared the stress of their humans, and the shared emotions were stronger (as measured by HRV) when the duration of the human-dog relationship was longer. In addition, female dogs were more sensitive than male dogs to their humans. These findings were later supported by another study using different methods.

Research also confirms that humans can sense and share the emotions of their dogs and companion animals. A Japanese research team led by Bingtau Su and her colleagues found that "more than half of the respondents reported that they could often or sometimes attribute primary emotions of joy (96.2 percent), surprise (85.9 percent), anger (80.6 percent), fear (75.7 percent), sadness (61.9 percent), and disgust (57.7 percent) and secondary emotions of compassion (73.1 percent) and jealousy (56.2 percent) to their companion animals and [the] emotions of joy and sadness were more frequently attributed to dogs than to cats."

The researchers also noted there are cultural and gender differences in how people relate to their companion dogs and cats and the emotions they attribute to them. They wrote, "In Japanese and Chinese culture, the feeling of compassion reflects the principle of benevolence, one of the five basic elements of Confucianism. Dogs and cats are regarded as sentient beings and as having the nature of compassion to all misfortunes. Japanese and Chinese people therefore tend to give more anthropomorphic descriptions of animal emotions than Western populations."

They noted that their results generally agreed with studies done in European countries, but differed from those in China. Concerning gender differences, they observe that women attributed more emotions than men, females showed a higher level of attachment to their companion animals, and people living with dogs showed more attachment than people living with cats. *See also* **allelomimetic behavior**; **empathy**.

emotional intelligence. The capacity to recognize and understand one's own emotions and the emotions of others and to use this information to guide one's behavior. Some people call this *socio-emotional intelligence*. This is important as we consider how to interact with our canine companions to appreciate their joys, fears, and other emotions, and to reduce frustration on both sides. Sometimes we get frustrated when our dogs don't "listen," and they likely get frustrated with us when we don't "speak" clearly or listen to them.

emotional support animal (ESA). Any animal, including dogs, trained to give support to people who have psychological needs. ESAs must have legal status and are not service dogs. While living with a companion animal might reduce anxiety or otherwise help a person, if the animal is not licensed, they are not recognized as an ESA.

A woman named Paige told me that she and her licensed emotional support dog Jake had finely tuned nervous systems and closely shared emotions. Jake could find other people with similar needs in a room full of people. Jake could even let Paige know when she was entering into a particular mood even before she knew it! There are some data that show that dogs can inform humans when they're angry and the humans don't realize it. I've also heard stories of dogs informing humans of a dangerous situation. However, one formal study showed that dogs usually communicate with us to request something, rather than to inform us of something. I look forward to more research in this area. *See also* **animal-assisted therapy (AAT)**; **service dogs**.

emotions. Plenty of research has clearly demonstrated that dogs and numerous other nonhuman species experience a wide variety of rich and deep emotions. This is now a strongly supported fact. The real question today is *why* have emotions evolved, not *whether* they have evolved. While there are some naysayers who still claim that dogs lack "real" emotions, few scientists and trainers take them seriously. One of my favorite quotes about animal emotions comes from renowned primatologist Frans de Waal, who said: "We like to see ourselves as special, but whatever the difference between humans and animals may be, it is unlikely to be found in the emotional domain."

Dogs and numerous other nonhuman animals are sentient, conscious, and emotional beings. An extensive database unquestionably shows this to be a bona fide scientific fact. Researchers and others who are interested in animal emotions fully realize that "their" emotions aren't necessarily identical to our own, nor are they the same across species. However, this doesn't mean nonhuman animals are emotionless.

For example, I've argued that there's chimpanzee joy, dog joy, and human joy, and elephant grief, gorilla grief, and magpie grief, and even among members of the same species, these feelings and how they're expressed may vary. However, there's little to no doubt about what the individuals are feeling when their behavior and the context in which it's observed are detailed. *See also* **consciousness**; **sentience**.

empathy. Dogs possess empathy, or the ability to understand or feel what someone else is feeling, whether a dog, human, or other animal. There are different types of empathy. Emilie Le Beau Lucchesi notes, "Affective empathy...is the ability to feel the perceived emotions or feelings of others, while cognitive empathy involves understanding the experiences of others and imagining their reality....Empathic concern, on the other hand, is the motivation to end another's suffering."

Empathic concern is another term for *compassion*, and in this way, empathy is a building block of morality. Here are some stories that exemplify empathy in dogs.

Renowned anthropologist and author Elizabeth Marshall Thomas once told me a story about a dog named Ruby who helped another dog, Wicket, cross a partly frozen stream. Wicket was afraid to cross on her own, and Ruby, who had already crossed the stream, went back to Wicket, greeted her, and after around ten unsuccessful attempts, convinced Wicket to follow her across the ice.

My friend Anne shared a story about her two beautiful malamutes, Tika and Kobuk. The couple had raised eight litters of puppies together and now were enjoying their retirement years. Kobuk was charming, energetic, and always demanded attention. He'd always let you know when he wanted his belly rubbed or his ears scratched. He also was quite vocal and howled his way into everyone's heart. Tika, Kobuk's mate, was quieter and pretty low-key. If anyone tried to rub Tika's ears or belly, Kobuk shoved his way in. Tika knew not to eat her food unless it was far away from Kobuk. If Tika happened to get in Kobuk's way when he headed to the door, she usually got knocked over as he charged past her.

Then one day a small lump appeared on Tika's leg, which was diagnosed as a malignant tumor. Overnight, Kobuk's behavior changed. He became subdued and wouldn't leave Tika's side. After Tika had to have her leg amputated and had trouble getting around, Kobuk stopped shoving her aside and stopped minding if she was allowed to get on the bed without him. He was clearly worried about her.

About two weeks after Tika's surgery, Kobuk woke Anne in the middle of the night the way he did when he needed to go outside. Tika was in another room, and Kobuk ran over to her. Anne got Tika up and took both dogs outside, but the dogs just lay down on the grass. Tika was whining softly, and Anne saw that Tika's belly was huge and swollen. Anne realized that Tika was going into shock, so she rushed her to the emergency animal clinic in Boulder. The veterinarian operated on her and was able to save her life.

If Kobuk hadn't fetched Anne, Tika almost certainly would have died. As Tika recovered her health, Kobuk again became the bossy dog he'd always been, even as Tika walked around on three legs. But Anne had witnessed their true relationship. Kobuk and Tika, a true old married couple, would always be there for each other, even if their personalities would never change. They were love dogs doing for each other what needed to be done.

Here's another heartwarming story. Two Jack Russell terriers were found, filthy and terrified, cowering on the main street of a small town. The dogs were friends, not mates. One was bleeding from both eyes; the other was standing guard, barking, and snapping at anyone who approached. They were taken to a veterinarian, who determined that the one terrier had been stabbed: both eyes had to be removed and the lids sewn up. Two days after the operation, Ben, as he had been named, was reunited with the other dog, Bill, in the local animal shelter. From that moment on, Bill acted as Ben's guide dog. With Ben holding on to the scruff of his neck, Bill walked him around the yard until he knew the lay of the land. After a TV crew captured this amazing performance, the two dogs found a marvelous home with an elderly couple who had an old female Jack Russell. With Bill's nudges and tugs, Ben quickly learned to negotiate the little house and garden. They slept curled up together and behaved, their humans said, "rather like a married couple."

And here's a story of my dog Jethro:

After I picked Jethro from the Boulder Humane Society and brought him to my mountain home, I knew he was a very special dog. He never chased the rabbits, squirrels, chipmunks, or deer who regularly visited. He often tried to approach them as if they were friends.

One day Jethro came to my front door, stared into my eyes, belched, and dropped a small, furry, saliva-covered ball out of his mouth. I wondered what in the world he'd brought back and discovered the wet ball of fur was a very young bunny.

Jethro continued to make direct eye contact with me as if he were saying, *Do something*. I picked up the bunny, placed her in a box, gave her water and celery, and figured she wouldn't survive the night, despite our efforts to keep her alive.

I was wrong. Jethro remained by her side and refused walks and meals until I pulled him away so he could heed nature's call. When I eventually released the bunny, Jethro followed her trail and continued to do so for months.

Over the years, Jethro approached rabbits as if they should be his friends, but they usually fled. He also rescued birds who flew into our windows and, on one occasion, a bird who'd been caught and dropped in front of my office by a local red fox. *See also* **emotional contagion**.

empathy fatigue. Aka burnout. This refers to how we can become overwhelmed by the suffering of others, whether humans or nonhumans. It can be easy for those who rescue animals or work in animal shelters to feel helpless and hopeless to do anything lasting to help animals in need.

empathy gap. This refers to when we recognize the emotional lives of certain animals with whom we're familiar, like dogs and companion animals, and deny them in other animals we don't know as well or whom we eat, experiment on, or use for entertainment. That said, while most people acknowledge the emotional lives of dogs, dogs are also served as food in certain countries, and they are used in horrific experiments and for entertainment.

Given the shared emotions between humans and dogs, dogs can be an effective gateway species to help bridge the empathy gap — some might say chasm — that can exist with other animals. Dogs have served human beings in various capacities for millennia, but they've also trained us to serve them. In this way, they've deepened our humanity by expanding our capacity for empathy.

encephalization quotient (EQ). A measure of relative brain size when compared with body size. For example, it's estimated that the EQ of humans is around 7.4–8, dolphins 5.3, chimpanzees 2.2–5, and dogs 1.2. This means that the brain of a human is around 7.4–8 times larger than one would expect for a mammal of the same average size (usually taken to be 150 pounds). Whereas a dog's brain is only around 1.2 times larger than one would expect for similar-size mammals.

EQ is often used as a way to compare relative intelligence among species of different sizes, on the assumption that a bigger brain relative to one's body (and thus a higher EQ) means an animal is smarter. But how these numbers translate into such claims isn't all that clear, and it's also not clear what comparisons of relative intelligence mean. I like to say dogs do what they need to do to be bona fide dogs, and dolphins do what they need to do to be card-carrying dolphins, so claims of relative intelligence are a bit fuzzy. Also, different species have evolved unique adaptations for dealing with changing environments, so it's difficult to say which species is "more intelligent."

end-of-life decisions. Aka quality-of-life decisions. Deciding when to euthanize a dog who's terminally ill or in interminable pain is very difficult, as it's very hard to evaluate the level of pain and suffering in another animal or to decide what quality of life is bearable for them. There is no established standard or method for evaluating the situation of an individual dog that will guarantee the correct decision. *See also* **euthanasia**.

enrichment. Improving an individual's quality of life by challenging them mentally. For instance, dogs often like to work for food even when it's easily available, and this provides enrichment when it's not done in an aversive or painful way. This could include asking them to practice trained techniques (like sitting) before being given food or asking them to look for and find food that's been hidden. I did this with my dogs by hiding tiny treats around my house in the mountains. There are different forms of enrichment, which include having plenty of toys and social interactions. It's important to consider your individual dog and what gets them going. *See also* **contrafreeloading**.

episodic memory. The long-term memory of specific past experiences. Dogs definitely exhibit this ability, such as when they keep track of food caches. *See also* **bookkeeping**.

escalating. Increasing the intensity or seriousness of ongoing behavior. For example, with dogs, gentle play can escalate into rough-and-tumble play fighting.

estrous. The time when female dogs are in heat and reproductively receptive.

ethogram. A descriptive list of all the actions performed by members of a given species. In research, an ethogram is like a menu of possible behaviors. This list can vary in size from a handful of different actions to more than a hundred, depending on the questions being asked. Typically, researchers do a completeness analysis of an ethogram in order to determine how many different behavior patterns members of a species perform and the probability of adding another action. For dogs, I learned that after I identified fifty different actions, the likelihood of adding another new behavior was extremely low.

ethology. The study of animal behavior. Basically, ethology boils down to the study of animal behavior (or what's also called character) and social organization from an evolutionary and biological perspective, while *cognitive ethology* is the study of animal minds.

Konrad Lorenz and Niko Tinbergen shared a Nobel Prize (along with bee language pioneering researcher Karl von Frisch) for helping found modern ethology. In his superb book *Patterns of Behavior*, Richard Burkhardt describes the wide-ranging interests of classical ethologists and provides "a richly textured reconstruction of ethology's transformation from a quiet backwater of natural history to the forefront of the biological sciences."

In his classic book *The Study of Instinct*, Tinbergen stresses that we must be concerned with external and internal causes of behavior, and he outlined four areas of inquiry, namely, evolution, adaptation, causation, and ontogeny (development). Ethologists have always thought that behavior is but one way in which animals speak to us. However, ethologists have had a tendency to ignore animal psyches, though this is not true for all across the board. In an essay entitled, "Amending Tinbergen: A Fifth Aim for Ethology," Gordon Burghardt added a fifth area he called "private experience" to Tinbergen's list.

Dale Jamieson and I wrote a paper called "On Aims and Methods of Cognitive Ethology," in which we showed just how fruitful and influential Tinbergen's work has been in the study of animal minds. Indeed, numerous ethologists have noted that we must learn about, and appreciate, animal minds, hence the enormous growth of the field of cognitive ethology. *See also* **cognitive ethology**; **comparative psychology**.

eustress. Positive stress. This is stress that is beneficial by taxing an individual.

euthanasia. Ending an individual's life painlessly when they are terminally ill or in interminable pain. This is also called mercy killing, humane death, or good death. Clearly, numerous ethical questions arise when making the decision to euthanize a dog or another nonhuman because humans have to decide when is the right time to do so and how to do it.

For more information on this issue, and help when making a decision, read the American Veterinary Medical Association's guide to animal euthanasia (see notes at markbekoff.com). I also highly recommend Jessica Pierce's book *The Last Walk: Reflections on Our Pets at the End of Their Lives*, as well as her *Psychology Today* column "All Dogs Go to Heaven." Opinions differ even among professionals about animal euthanasia — such as what constitutes the "right" time and whether it should be done for reasons other than a terminal illness or interminable pain. *See also* **end-of-life decisions**; **zoothanasia**.

evolution. Biological or genetic changes in a population over time. In the first edition of *On the Origin of Species*, Charles Darwin used the phrase *descent with modification* rather than the word *evolution*. People define evolution in numerous ways depending on the context, but the result of evolution is genetic variation among individuals in a population. Darwin also stressed evolutionary continuity, or the idea that differences among various species are differences in degree rather than differences in kind — different species are shades of gray rather than black and white.

exaggerated approach. A bouncy, frisky, and frolicking "loose" approach. Often called gamboling, dogs often behave this way to solicit play or friendly interactions.

exercise. Of course, homed dogs need lots of physical activity to keep their bodies and minds working well and to avoid being bored by the same old same old and becoming dangerously obese. As Anders Hallgren stresses, "Daily exercise is obligatory. Your own comfort must never be more important than a dog's needs!" *See also* **aerobic and anaerobic exercise**.

exploratory behavior. When a dog looks around to see what's happening. Information can be gathered by walking, looking, hearing, and sniffing, and it includes what another individual is doing, how they're feeling, and whether there is food nearby.

extrasensory perception (ESP). Aka a "sixth sense," knowing information that can't be gained through the senses or deduction. The term was coined by psychologist J. B. Rhine, and if ESP exists, some believe dogs possess it.

The most famous example is the research by award-winning scientist Rupert Sheldrake, who found that some dogs knew when their humans were coming home at least ten minutes in advance, even though the dog and the human were far out of range of visual, auditory, or olfactory cues.

His research was highly controversial. Some scientists accused him of fudging his data, and others wrote it off as "impossible" and pure nonsense. For one of his studies, I was asked to be a tie-breaking reviewer — two reviewers essentially thought the work was garbage, whereas two thought it was sound. I agreed that it was sound, and the paper was published. *See also* **animal communicators**.

extrovert. Similar to people, some dogs prefer to spend time with other individuals rather than being on their own. *See also* **introvert**.

eye blinking. Also called eye flashing, rapid blinking might be used by dogs to appease another individual and/or to signal to other dogs that one is relaxed. More research is needed to figure out why dogs blink their eyes when they do.

eyebrow lift. When dogs lift their eyebrows, most notably when making puppy dog eyes. Interestingly, a 2013 study comparing the differences in canine faces when they set sight on their owner versus on a stranger found that dogs generally raise their left eyebrow half a second after seeing their owner, whereas they pull back their left ear when meeting a stranger.

Research by Juliane Kaminski and her colleagues shows that domestication has altered the facial musculature of dogs so that they, but not wolves, have a unique muscle called AU101 that controls eyebrow lift. Kaminski and her colleagues note that "domestication transformed the facial muscle anatomy of dogs specifically for facial communication with humans. A muscle responsible for raising the inner eyebrow intensely is uniformly present in dogs but not in wolves." They discovered that dogs had a greater ability than wolves to raise the inner corner of their eyebrows without squinting due to the action of AU101.

Whether or not this allows dogs to communicate better with humans is an interesting idea that requires further research. It may be that the evolution of facial muscles also is related to the way in which dogs and wolves eat, since dogs get prepared foods and wolves have to kill, bite, and chew difficult-to-eat prey. *See also* **puppy dog eyes**.

F

face bumping. Aka nose bumping. Dogs will sometimes bump into the faces of dogs or humans as part of a greeting. It's not clear why they do this, but presumably it's to get a whiff of what another dog ate or perhaps is feeling, or possibly to spread scent. A pilot study by a student of mine showed that dogs who don't know each other face bump and sniff more than familiar dogs, as a way to get to know each other before they decide to play. *See also* **play**.

face licking. There are many reasons why a dog might lick a person's face, including greeting, appeasing, begging, or giving affection. As with many other behavior patterns, what it means depends on context — who the dog is and what's happening to and around them.

Dog researcher Stanley Coren conducted his own study to learn more about face licking. He tested three hypotheses: dogs lick people as an expression of affection; dogs lick people as a holdover from when they were wild wolves, signaling they want to eat; and licking is a residual from the affection felt by puppies when their mother groomed them by licking. Coren concluded that we don't know why dogs lick faces, and I agree. I feel certain there is more than one reason, depending on context. *See also* **lip licking**.

facial expressions. Dogs display many different facial expressions depending on the position of the ears, exposure of the teeth, wrinkling of the nose, and the shape of the eyes. Facial expressions are often parts of composite signals incorporating information from more than one area of the face along with vocalizations and odors. Among canids, the more-social species (wolves) have more facial expressions than the less-social species (coyotes and foxes). There hasn't been any research on this topic for different breeds or mixes of dogs, but it's reasonable to assume that dogs with normal-shaped faces and erect ears might display more facial expressions than other dogs. *See also* **composite signals**.

fairness. Dogs have a keen sense of right and wrong. This is seen most vividly when they play. While playing, dogs follow the "golden rules of play" and don't try to dominate, harm, mate with, or eat another dog. They play fair just like wolves and other animals.

Just about everyone who lives with a dog knows they can learn the house rules — and when they break one, their subsequent groveling is usually ingratiating enough to ensure quick forgiveness. But few people have stopped to ask why dogs possess a moral compass.

Morality, as Jessica Pierce and I define it in our book *Wild Justice: The Moral Lives of Animals*, is a suite of interrelated other-regarding behaviors that cultivate and regulate social interactions. These behaviors include altruism, tolerance, forgiveness, reciprocity, and fairness. In canids (including wolves, coyotes, dogs, and so on), all of these are readily evident in the egalitarian way they play, which teaches pups the rules of social engagement that allow their societies to succeed.

Play also builds trusting relationships among pack members, which enables divisions of labor, dominance hierarchies, and cooperation in hunting, raising young, and defending food and territory. Because their social organization closely resembles that of early humans (as anthropologists and other experts believe it existed), studying canid play may offer a glimpse of the moral code that allowed our ancestral societies to grow and flourish.

That said, from time to time people ask me if dogs *always* play fair. They tell me about times when play escalated into what *seemed* to be an aggressive encounter. I explain that this is extremely rare. In fact, a study called "Bark Parks" reported that fewer than 0.5 percent of play fights among dogs developed into conflict, and only half of these were clearly aggressive encounters. *See also* **golden rules of play**; **inequity aversion**; **play**.

Family Dog Project. This project was founded in 1994 by Vilmos Csányi, Ádám Miklósi, and József Topál in the Ethology Department at Eötvös Loránd University in Budapest, Hungary. Currently the largest dog research group in the world, it focuses on studying the behavioral and cognitive aspects of the dog-human relationship. The Family Dog Project has more than a hundred publications in peer-reviewed journals, including *Science*, *Current Biology*, and *Trends in Cognitive Sciences.*

feinting. During play, dogs will use deceptive, feinting moves — such as "fake left, go right" — to get another dog to chase the feinting dog.

feral. Animals living on their own. *See also* **free-ranging dogs**.

feralization. When a domesticated animal becomes desocialized from humans on their own or never becomes socialized. Feralization is not dedomestication or reverse engineering, since it only refers to changes within an *individual*, not a species, that causes them to behave like an untamed, nondomestic animal. *See also* **dedomestication**; **domestication**.

fertility. Some research shows that there has been a steady decrease in fertility in male dogs. In the UK there is a concern about the unregulated and unnatural breeding and production of brachycephalic breeds, including pugs and French bulldogs, for monetary incentives rather than for good health.

fetching. Running toward an object such as a tennis ball and bringing it back to a human.

fighting. Engaging in combat. Dogs will fight over food, a toy, or a place to rest or sleep. Most skirmishes are minor, with few or no serious injuries, other than perhaps to a dog's pride. Research on free-ranging and feral dogs would provide the best information about fighting patterns and whether fights are influenced by an individual's rank. This is an area of study in which many researchers are interested because that might be one reason why it is advantageous to be a high-ranking individual. That said, a study conducted by my students and me on the development of fighting patterns in young coyotes provides some insight and is an example of the kind of research that needs to be performed with dogs.

In our study of young coyotes, we analyzed 2,350 fights, and these showed that no major injuries were sustained by any of the infants, even in serious fights. There was no relationship between social rank and the proportion of fights that were initiated by either animal. Dominant animals were more likely than subordinate individuals to escalate first (perform the first unprovoked dangerous move) during short interactions and to escalate and then subsequently win short fights. We also found that the highest-ranking (alpha) individuals in litters did not fight the most, yet alpha individuals initiated 73 percent of the fights in which they partook and won 86 percent of the contests that they initiated. Both alpha and midranking animals initiated and then escalated the greatest proportion of time with individuals nearest in rank — those with whom they may have experienced the greatest difficulty in assessing relative social standing. All in all, our data suggested that individuals, especially in litters, were able to make prefight assessments but that they were not perfect with respect to this ability.

During-fight assessments appeared to be easier to make, using escalation to test an opponent. *See also* **aggression**.

fireworks. The general rule of thumb is to avoid exposing your dog to fireworks, even if they seem to like them. Two of my dogs seemed totally fine with them, but all the others, including their canine friends, were clearly upset by the unpredictable loud noises and flashes. The UK's RSPCA offers valuable advice for how to calm dogs during fireworks, including comforting them and staying with them when the noise and light show begins, finding an area where they feel safe, giving them their favorite treats and toys, and possibly using pheromone diffusers that spread calming scents.

fitness. In evolutionary terms, fitness refers to an individual's ability to have children who are reproductively active and who go on to have their own kids. In physiological terms, fitness means being able to accomplish certain feats because of cardiovascular capacity.

Five Freedoms. The Five Freedoms were presented in 1965 in an eighty-five-page British government study, "Report of the Technical Committee to Enquire into the Welfare of Animals Kept Under Intensive Livestock Husbandry Systems." This document, informally known as the Brambell Report, was a response to public outcry over the abusive treatment of animals within agricultural settings. The Five Freedoms can also be used to assess the well-being and lives of domestic dogs. Here are the Five Freedoms:

1. Freedom from hunger or thirst by ready access to fresh water and a diet to maintain full health and vigor.
2. Freedom from discomfort by providing an appropriate environment, including shelter and a comfortable resting area.
3. Freedom from pain, injury, or disease by prevention or rapid diagnosis and treatment.
4. Freedom to express (most) normal behavior by providing sufficient space, proper facilities, and company of the animal's own kind.

5. Freedom from fear and distress by ensuring conditions and treatment which avoid mental suffering.

   See also **Ten Freedoms for dogs**.

fixed action patterns (FAPs). Stereotyped actions that are released by particular stimuli (called "releasers") and performed even if the releaser is removed. A classic example is egg retrieval by different species of birds. Most people use the phrase "modal action pattern" (MAP) because many FAPs are not as stereotyped as they were thought to be. Play bows are easy to recognize and highly stereotyped and can be classified as MAPs. *See also* **modal action patterns (MAPs)**; **play bows**.

flehmen response. Aka a lip curl. Males and females do it. Male dogs exhibit a flehmen response when tasting a smell, often the urine of a female in heat. *See also* **vomeronasal organ (VNO)**.

flirting. Yes, dogs flirt. And as with humans, flirting can be for fun or can lead to courtship and mating. Flirting might entail sidling into another dog, sniffing their bodies (including hind ends), or following them here and there. Context is critical for determining whether flirting or something else is happening.

focal animal sampling. In this research technique, the observer watches one animal for a specified amount of time and records everything that animal does and the length of time they do it. *See also* **research techniques**.

food, human stress over. When people worry too much about what and how to feed their dog, this stress can itself impact a dog's welfare. I feel that sometimes people worry more about their dog's meal plans than the dogs themselves. Sometimes a person's relationship with food is mirrored in how they view and treat their dog — whether they think their dog is too skinny or too fat. My dogs had preferences for some foods but pretty much ate what I gave them, often what I was also eating at the moment. *See also* **diet**.

food disorders. Dogs can develop abnormal eating habits just like those seen in humans, including anorexia and bulimia. Two veterinarians along with a number of other people I know have suggested that dogs reflect their humans' attitudes toward food. These include how often and how much dogs are fed and whether dogs simply eat whatever is placed in front of them or are annoyingly picky.

food sharing. When dogs allow other dogs to eat food that is present. Sometimes dogs will even offer food.

force-free training. *See* **positive training**.

forepaw raising. A gesture dogs often use in greeting, as a submissive gesture, and when asking for something, pointing (hunting), and sparring. Forepaw raising can be a socio-infantile (derived) behavior. *See also* **derived activities**.

forgiveness. Some dogs seem to practice forgiveness when they play, just like some dogs seem to hold grudges. But we don't know to what extent or what exactly those concepts mean to dogs. *See also* **grudges**.

foxes. Small to medium-size mammals belonging to the dog family, Canidae. Unlike wolves, coyotes, and jackals, foxes cannot produce viable offspring with dogs.

frame-by-frame film analyses. Watching film of dog behavior over and over again to measure what an action looks like and how long it lasts. *See also* **play**; **research techniques**.

freedom. The ability of an individual animal to move around and do what they choose to do. Some research has shown that dominant wolves have more freedom to move around in their group than do lower-ranking wolves, who carefully watch where others are and what they're doing.

In terms of dogs who live with humans, giving dogs more freedom means allowing them to act out their genes and dogness. One way to help do this is to dispense with misleading myths about who dogs are and what they are supposed to do and feel about us. *See also* **agency**; **myths about dogs**.

free-ranging dogs. Dogs who move around unrestrained and freely on their own. Free-ranging or free-roaming dogs, sometimes called village dogs, are not necessarily homeless (like stray dogs), a point stressed by Dr. Andrew Rowan in his detailed studies of the abundance of dogs living in various conditions. There also are trade-offs, with home companion dogs getting a place to sleep, regular meals, and veterinary care, whereas free-ranging or village dogs typically do not. However, village dogs have more freedoms and aren't subjected to unrealistic social demands.

In addition, free-ranging dogs can impact soil chemistry in urban green spaces and disrupt ecosystems, and dogs foraging on carrion can be vectors for disease. However, barking dogs can also lessen predation by raccoons who fear the dogs, so free-ranging dogs can also have a positive effect in certain areas. All in all, free-ranging dogs can have negative effects on wildlife and biodiversity in some places, but in some areas they don't, so we must avoid overgeneralizations about their impacts. *See also* **stray dogs**; **wildlife, impact of dogs on**.

frenetic random activity periods (FRAPs). Often called "zoomies," this refers to when dogs run around frenetically with seemingly reckless abandon. *See also* **zoomies**.

friendship. Of course, dogs (and other animals) make friends. It's a myth that dogs are inherently our "best friend," but individual dogs do make best friends with other species of all kinds. These unexpected, surprising friendships are sometimes called "odd couples." Among all animals, some people argue that there is survival value in being friendly. *See also* **cross-species relationships**.

frustration. Dogs get upset when they can't get what they want, just like people do, whether that's a piece of food, a toy, a walk, another dog to play with, or someone's attention. A frustrated dog might pace, bark, or redirect their behavior. For example, a dog might stop trying to get a toy and pick something else to play with, or if their best friend — whether dog or human — won't play, they might try to get another dog or human to do so. *See also* **satisficing**.

fun. Researchers are seriously studying different aspects of fun, including why and how it evolved. The journal *Current Biology* celebrated its twenty-fifth birthday with a special issue on the biology of fun (and the fun of biology). The editors wrote, "In a collection of essays and review articles, the journal presents what we know about playfulness in dogs, dolphins, frogs, and octopuses. It provides insights on whether birds can have fun and how experiences in infancy affect a person's unique sense of humor." I was pleased to be part of this celebration because there is no doubt that "having fun" played a role in the evolution of play and other behaviors. *See also* **play**.

future thinking. Thinking about and anticipating what might happen in the future. Do dogs make plans? In their own way, of course they do.

G

gamboling. An exaggerated "loose" swagger. Dogs often gambol when play soliciting.

games. Dogs love to play games. By that I mean, they understand the difference between free play and games, which is that games have rules that must be followed — even if the "rules" are invented. In his book *The Grasshopper: Games, Life, and Utopia*, Bernard Suits defines a game as follows: "To play a game is to engage in activity directed towards bringing about a specific state of affairs, using only means permitted by rules, where the rules prohibit more efficient in favor of less efficient means, and where such rules are accepted just because they make possible such activity." This matches the "golden rules of play" that dogs always abide by, and the "state of affairs," as Suits calls it, is the maintenance of the game because all participants agree to the rules. *See also* **golden rules of play; play; tug-of-war**.

game theory. Mathematical models used to study patterns of social relationships to learn whether humans or nonhumans are making logical decisions. To the best of my knowledge, game theory hasn't been used to study dogs. However, Lee Dugatkin and I used game theory to study winner and loser effects in young coyotes using real data. We found clear winner and loser effects that were rank-related. Highest-ranking (alpha) coyotes showed winner effects, lowest-ranking (omega) individuals showed loser effects, whereas there were no winner or loser effects for middle-ranking animals. It would be interesting to know whether dogs and wolves show the same patterns.

gender bias. Stanley Coren notes that people have a gender bias with unknown dogs, who are usually referred to as male. He writes, "To the extent that this data demonstrates that there is an implicit stereotype toward assuming that unfamiliar dogs are male, it probably explains why most people, when they interact with an unfamiliar dog on the street, are more likely to say: 'Hello boy' rather than 'Hello girl.'" I have also noticed this tendency, which doesn't apply to cats, and like Coren, I'm not clear why people seem biased to assume a dog they don't know is male.

generosity. Dogs exhibit generosity, or kind and unselfish behavior, when they engage in food sharing, or when they show concern and care for individuals who are injured or need special attention. Further, one study found that some dogs prefer generous rather than selfish humans, a choice that could benefit them in gaining access to food or other resources.

gesturing. Visibly moving part of the body indicating something a dog wants to communicate. *See also* **referential signaling**.

gifting a dog. Giving dogs or other animals as gifts is a bad idea. Of course, asking a person if they would like a dog before gifting them one takes the surprise and pleasure out of doing so, but gifting without asking should be strongly discouraged. *See also* **adopting a dog**.

global positioning system (GPS). A satellite-enabled device used for tracking animals, including free-ranging dogs.

goal-directed behavior. A play bow is a type of goal-directed behavior, since the goal is to engage in play with another dog. A dog returning to a place where they once found food is similar. These actions also represent future thinking. *See also* **future thinking**.

"going to the dogs." A saying that means going from a good or tolerable situation to a worse situation.

golden rules of play. Dogs observe fair play when playing with one another, which requires them to stick to mutually agreed upon codes of conduct. In essence, these codes boil down to the "golden rule" we all learn as children: "Do unto others as you would have them do unto you."

For dogs, the golden rules of play include the following:

1. **Ask first and communicate clearly.** Many nonhumans announce that they want to play and not fight or mate. Canids punctuate play sequences using a play bow to solicit play, crouching on their forelimbs while standing on their hindleg. Bows are used almost exclusively during play and are highly stereotyped — that is, they always look the same — so the message "Come play with me" or "I still want to play" is clear. Play bows are honest signals, a sign of trust. Even when an individiual follows a play bow with seemingly aggressive actions, such as baring teeth, growling, or biting, their companions demonstrate submission or avoidance only around 15 percent of the time. This suggests they trust the bow's message that whatever follows is meant in fun. Trust in one another's honest communication is vital for fair play and a smoothly functioning social group.
2. **Mind your manners.** Animals consider their play partners' abilities

and engage in self-handicapping and role reversing to create and maintain equal footing. For instance, a coyote might not bite their play partner as hard as they can, handicapping themselves to keep things fair. And a dominant pack member might perform a role reversal, rolling over on their back (a sign of submission that they would never offer during real aggression) to let their lower-status play partner take a turn at "winning."

3. **Admit when you are wrong.** Even when everyone wants to keep things fair, play can sometimes get out of hand. When an animal misbehaves or accidentally hurts their play partner, they typically apologize, just like a human would. After an intense bite, a bow sends the message, *Sorry I bit you so hard — this is still play regardless of what I just did. Don't leave; I'll play fair.* For play to continue, the other individual must forgive the wrongdoing. And forgiveness is almost always offered; understanding and tolerance are abundant during play as well as in daily pack life. Dogs often apologize and ask for forgiveness.
4. **Be honest.** An apology, like an invitation to play, must be sincere. Individuals who continue to play unfairly or send dishonest signals often quickly find themselves ostracized. This has far greater consequences than simply reduced playtime. For example, my long-term field research shows that juvenile coyotes who do not play fair often end up leaving their pack and are up to four times more likely to die than those individuals who remain with others. There are substantial risks associated with dispersal by young coyotes, and violating social norms established during play is not good for perpetuating one's genes.

See also **fairness**; **play**; **play bows**; **self-handicapping**.

goodbye, saying. When leaving a dog, it's a good idea to say goodbye. Pilot data show that petting or talking to some dogs can make the absence of their humans easier. In 2018, I wrote an essay about this entitled "Should You Say Goodbye to Your Dog Before You Leave?," and here are some of the comments I received from readers:

> "Why in the world would anyone not say goodbye to their dog? Do they do the same with humans?"
>
> "I don't make a big deal when I leave my dog, but I always say the same thing when I leave. 'I'll be back,' and when I return I say, 'I'm back.'"
>
> "Always has just seemed like the natural thing to do."
>
> "Well yeah!!!! I have certain things I say to my Lab depending upon how long I'll be out the door. They are smart. They know."
>
> "I can't imagine that there are many dogs who would prefer that their owner leave without doing or saying something to them."

"good dog" / "bad dog." It's natural for us to praise and scold dogs whenever they do something that we like or dislike. But I recommend rethinking and avoiding these labels or phrases, since they reflect our perspective and prejudices. From a dog's perspective, they usually only do things that are perfectly dog appropriate. Many times, people say "bad dog" when a dog does something that pleases the dog but not the person, and "good dog" when a dog does something that pleases the person but that isn't necessarily truly expressing "good dogness." For example, "good dogness" could include sniffing the crotches and butts of humans.

grass eating. There is no one-size-fits-all answer to why dogs eat grass. Many people feel it is because of some nutritional or bacterial deficiency, and in fact, grass might add roughage to a dog's meal plan and help in digestion and defecation. Others think dogs do this when they are bored, anxious, upset, or trying to get our attention. There is no evidence that dogs eat grass to vomit. If a dog is eating a lot of grass and it seems to be abnormal, visit a veterinarian to confirm whether there is a health issue.

greed. A good number of people ask me if I think dogs are greedy. Sometimes dogs collect and hoard things just for fun, or what seems like greed might be showing off, but it's difficult to know for sure. *See also* **hoarding**.

greeting. Dogs use different behaviors to greet other dogs, including joyfully approaching, face sniffing or licking, body and butt sniffing, and play soliciting. Also, the type of approach — whether it is rapid, slow, or exhibiting approach-withdrawal — can be a good indicator of the dog's mood. It's not clear whether dogs or other nonhumans ever say goodbye.

Elephant expert Joyce Poole once told me: "Here in Norway, trainers like to tell us: 'Don't allow your dog to greet strange dogs. People don't greet strangers so why should your dog?' I always tell them — in Africa strangers always greet one another and so do dogs, if given the chance. Of course, some just cruise along with a plan in mind — way too busy for anyone else."

Greyfriars Bobby. After his guardian, John Gray, died in Edinburgh, Scotland, Greyfriars Bobby, a Skye terrier, became famous for sitting at his human's grave for fourteen years until Bobby himself died on January 14, 1872. He has since been immortalized in a statue, a book, and several movies.

grieving after losing a dog. The death of a companion dog is a serious loss. In many homes, dogs are not simply "pets" but part of the family group. So take the resulting grief seriously and seek out whatever support and counseling might help. In her book *Sacred Sendoffs*, Reverend Sarah Bowen offers great advice for how to honor animal companions and manage our emotions when we lose an animal we love.

grieving by dogs. *See* **death and dying**; **mourning**.

groining. When a dog sticks a nose into someone's crotch. I coined this term in *Canine Confidential* because of the nonstop groining by a dog I called "Gus the groiner." His human told me he had been a "groiner" since he could walk and meet dogs and humans on his own. Many dogs I know find groins to be especially attractive, including those of humans, and I wonder if dogs feel frustrated when their noses are yanked away from these rich sources of odor — just because we find these olfactory delights inappropriate. After all, a dog is merely trying to learn as much as they can about who a person is and perhaps what they're feeling, and this is how they do it.

Some years ago, a woman asked for my advice about this. She had been trying to break her dog from nosing in and around people's private parts, and she was considering giving up her dog, since she couldn't stop her from doing it. I humbly and nicely suggested that she reconsider her attitude about this perfectly dog-appropriate behavior rather than give up her dog, which would be incredibly traumatic for the dog. Instead, she should find a user-friendly trainer who could help them both along. This is a prime example of failing to take the dog's point of view. *See also* **abnormal behavior**.

grooming by dogs. Dogs clean and groom themselves, and when a dog is doing it to another individual, it's called social grooming. Social grooming may be involved in developing, solidifying, and maintaining social bonds and may be used during reconciliation.

grooming by humans. Numerous people choose to have their dogs groomed professionally, rather than doing it at home. I hadn't thought much about what can be involved when a dog goes to a groomer — traveling to a facility; being caged before the procedure; being left alone with a groomer; being touched and restrained during the treatment; being exposed to multisensory overload; being shampooed, trimmed in vulnerable places, dried, and perfumed; and perhaps having their nails cut and painted. Then I read Stephanie Zikmann's book *The Magic of Holistic Grooming: A No-Nonsense Guide to Pawsitively Grooming Your Dog with Less Stress*, and I interviewed her for my *Psychology Today* column.

Understandably, many people want their dogs to "look good" and use professional groomers. A major problem is that grooming, like training, is an unregulated, anything-goes industry. Depending on the personality of the dog, being groomed can be enjoyable or highly traumatic, since grooming a dog isn't as emotionally benign as it seems. It can be done mindfully as long as the dog consents and their point of view is given the highest priority. If they like it, fine; if they don't, don't do it. Grooming is essentially an invasion of a dog's personal space, body, and freedom, but it still can be done in cooperative ways. If the dog agrees to be groomed, it can be a pleasant experience. The grooming environment has many hidden and not-so-hidden layers. It can be noisy, smelly, and full of potential stressors, which could lead to sensory overload and increase a dog's stress and anxiety.

ground scratching. When dogs use their paws to scratch the ground, this might be because they are relieved or excited. It also might be a visual mark or signal telling other dogs something like, *I just peed (or pooped) here.*

When other dogs are around, ground scratching can work as a visual display for other dogs. In one of my studies of free-running dogs, I found that ground scratching is more likely to occur when other dogs are physically present. The ground scratching usually occurred after a dog had done a raised-leg display, with or without urination, and it can occur after defecation.

growling. A low guttural sound in a dog's throat. Growling isn't as simple as it seems, and it's difficult to pin down a single reason why dogs growl. It is usually a warning to another dog or a human and signals something they are upset about. Growling is entirely appropriate dog behavior.

One of the dogs I rescued years ago growled when another dog or a person, including myself, came near him when he was eating or playing with food. I was able to teach him not to growl on most occasions, especially when I was the human intruding on "his" food. Over time, his growls became less intense and, on occasion, almost inaudible. I came to realize that growling was his way of saying, *Please leave me alone*, or *This is my food, and I need it.* Most likely, he reacted this way because of how he was treated (or mistreated) when he was young and on his own, and perhaps he had to find and defend food before he went to the local humane society, where I found him.

He never did anything more than growl, and I would tell other people to leave him alone when he was around food. That worked very well — there never was any aggression, and all he did was growl a few times and then stop. Other dogs also learned very rapidly to leave him alone when he was around his food. This growling did not indicate a failed relationship, but rather we had a very deep and enduring friendship for many years.

Another dog I rescued didn't like people to touch his front feet, so once again, I honored that and told other people not to try to touch his front feet. There never was a problem, even if he growled to show how he felt about it. I've heard numerous similar stories from many people about situations in which their otherwise friendly dog would occasionally growl, and there was no problem at all.

A 2017 study by Hungarian researchers showed we're pretty good at assigning context and emotional state to different growls, and that women are better than men at doing so.

grudges. Anecdotal evidence is that some dogs, perhaps all dogs, can hold grudges, but we don't have enough research to say for certain yes or no.

A few years ago, I received this email: "Yesterday, at my local dog park, I said that my dog, Tommy, holds grudges, but other people told me I'm wrong — that it's all about me and my reading into the situations, rather than about Tommy, and that dogs don't hold grudges." This email made me want to learn more, so I asked twenty "dog people" I know whether they thought dogs hold grudges. They were evenly split — ten yes and ten maybe or no — and each of their stories was compelling.

Of course, a lot hangs on how one defines the word *grudge*. It can mean feeling resentment or ill will toward another individual such that you want bad things to happen to that person. This can include a desire for some type of retaliation or score settling. But holding a grudge can also simply mean feeling someone can't be trusted because of something done in the past, and further, if the other person apologizes, and seeks forgiveness or reconciliation, the grudge can be let go.

Here's another story someone wrote to me:

A few days ago, Henry had a tussle with Irving. Irving stole Henry's tennis ball, and when Henry tried to get it back, Irving growled at him and made it clear the ball was now his. The very next day, Henry got to the dog park first, and when Irving showed and was on the other side of the swinging fence door, Henry made it clear that Irving wasn't welcome. He followed Irving as he paced back and forth, as if he was blocking him from coming in. I have no idea what Henry was thinking, but it seemed as if he held a grudge against Irving and didn't want him to be there and join in the fun.

Do dogs hold grudges? I think it's entirely reasonable to think they do, but we really don't know how or what that means to them.

guard dogs. Dogs used to protect wild animals (such as penguins and marsupials in Australia), food animals or livestock, businesses, and homes. There is some evidence that dogs used to protect animals raised for food might also help change farmers' attitudes toward predators such as wolves, since the guard dogs prevent predators from killing the animals.

guardian. Some people prefer the term *guardian* instead of *owner*, since "owning a dog" speaks about dogs as if they're property or an object. Meanwhile, *guardian* embodies a caretaker role for a living being.

guilt. Do dogs feel guilty? And do they act guilty with us when they know they've done something we've told them or trained them not to do? These are extremely interesting questions that generate a lot of debate, but we still haven't confirmed definitively whether dogs feel guilt. However, I was glad when Dr. Frans de Waal titled one of his essays "Guilt, Jealousy, Empathy: Your Dog Has the Same Emotions You Do." While we still don't know whether dogs feel guilt, I'm sure that when the proper research is done, we'll learn they do, just as they probably possess all the other emotions we seem to recognize in them.

Confusion over whether dogs feel guilt has arisen in part because of rampant misinterpretation of Alexandra Horowitz's research, especially in popular media. This was fed by an essay written by William Brennan in *The Atlantic*, who wrote: "According to Alexandra Horowitz, a dog-cognition expert at Barnard College, what we perceive as a dog's guilty look is no sign of guilt at all." However, this misunderstood the focus and conclusions of Horowitz's study, which she published in an essay titled "Disambiguating the 'Guilty Look': Salient Prompts to a Familiar Dog Behavior." In her research, Horowitz focused on whether or not humans can detect guilt in dogs, not whether dogs actually feel guilt. She discovered that we are not very good at *reading* guilt, but this does *not* mean dogs can't or don't feel guilt.

When I asked Horowitz to comment on this, she wrote:

> Spot on, on "guilt." Thanks so much for alerting me to and correcting the ubiquitous error about my study, some years back, which found that dogs showed more "guilty look" when a person scolded or was about to scold them, not when the dog actually disobeyed the person's request not to eat a treat. Clearly what the results indicated was that the "guilty look" did not most often arise when a dog was actually "guilty."
>
> My study was decidedly NOT about whether dogs "feel guilt" or not. (Indeed, I'd love to know...but this behavior didn't turn out to indicate yay or nay.) I would feel dreadful if people then thought the case was closed on dogs (not) feeling guilt, which is definitely not the case. Many secondary sources got this right, but it must require reading the study to appreciate exactly what I did.

There are other misrepresentations of what we know about guilt in dogs. For example, in an article in the *Telegraph*, Susan Hazel, a veterinary scientist at the University of Adelaide, once wrongly claimed, "There have been a number of studies, and it's pretty clear that dogs don't feel or display guilt. It's not the way their brains work." As far as I can determine, and I've asked other researchers, there are no studies that show that "dogs don't feel or display guilt," and there have been no neuroimaging studies of dogs' brains that focus on guilt.

It's extremely important to get things right. There's no reason why dogs shouldn't be able to feel guilt, as do other mammals, but we need further research — such as the way Gregory Berns and his colleagues have used fMRIs to study jealousy in dogs — to learn more about guilt.

guilty look. Most guardians have seen their dogs display a "guilty look," when the dog cowers, possibly showing the whites of their eyes, and perhaps also yawning or lip licking. Further, many feel that dogs must know they have done something wrong because their dog shows the "guilty look" prior to the person discovering the misdeed and scolding them. Personally, I thought I was pretty good at knowing when a few of my dogs did something they knew I wouldn't like. However, Alexandra Horowitz has done research that shows that dogs will adopt this look even if they haven't done something wrong because they anticipate being scolded. *See also* **guilt**.

gut-brain axis. The term for the relationship between intestinal microbiota — the gut biome — and one's emotions. The gut-brain axis exists in humans, and there is no reason to think that this dynamic doesn't also apply to dogs and other mammals. Some people call the gut the "second brain." Daniela Olivero, an Italian veterinarian, has verified that epileptic dogs can greatly improve their condition by changing their diet (to a ketogenic diet). *See also* **diet**.

H

hackles. The term for the hairs that run along a dog's back, hackles rise involuntarily when a dog is angry, alarmed, excited, or frightened. Piloerection, when the erectile hairs stand up, is sometimes called "hair up."

hallucinating. In September 2012, I had the good fortune of having lunch with neurologist and best-selling writer Oliver Sacks. His book *Hallucinations* had just been published, and he asked me if I thought animals hallucinate. I said yes, there's no reason to think they don't, and we had a most lovely chat. Given the similarities between the brains of dogs and humans, since we can hallucinate, dogs probably can, too.

happiness. Dogs definitely feel happiness. The real question is, how do we recognize happiness in dogs when they (and we) feel it? Dogs display their emotions in many different ways, and it's important to carefully watch them and to pay close attention to the whole dog — from the tip of their nose to the end of their tail. We must also keep the context in mind in order to accurately understand what a dog is feeling and what they're trying to communicate. Happy dogs generally look very relaxed — their gait is springy, their tails loosely wag back and forth, their eyes are wide open, and it often looks like they're smiling. Many people often say you can easily tell when a dog is happy and when they're not. I agree. Happy dogs put out a good deal of contagious positive energy. Their happiness is easy to see and feel. I can't tell you how many people tell me their dog's happiness is contagious and how it gets them out of a funk. Likewise, when a canine companion is having a tough day, we feel and empathize with that mood, too.

We're most likely to have a happy dog if we do our best to listen to them and honor what they want and need at any given moment. However, as I often advise people, there are few, if any, one-size-fits-all explanations. Some people say, "Well, the last two dogs I had were really happy when I did this, but my new dog isn't. What's wrong with the dog?" There's nothing wrong. Their current dog is just different than their previous dogs. People are the same way. If your dog seems unhappy, experiment with changing your behavior and seeing what has the most positive effect on them.

head shaking. Shaking the head from side to side usually occurs when a dog is delivering a bite to increase its intensity.

head tilting. There's no shortage of opinions on why dogs tilt their head to the side or from one side to the other. Most likely, there are multiple reasons. Dogs might be simply stretching their necks or trying to locate where and how far away something is. They might be concentrating in order to process incoming information. As always, when trying to figure out why a dog is doing something, it's essential to pay close attention to context, to as many variables as possible, and to consider their body posture, gait, and other cues.

hearing. Dogs have far more sensitive hearing than humans and can detect much quieter sounds. Their sense of hearing is about four times as sensitive as ours, so what we hear at twenty feet, a dog can hear at about eighty feet. They also hear a lot of things we don't because they can hear higher-frequency sounds. From available data, scientists suggest that dogs hear in frequencies as high as 67,000 cycles per second (also called hertz), while humans hear frequencies up to 64,000 cycles per second. This means there are some sounds that are inaudible to us but quite available to our dogs. For example, they can hear the high-pitched chirping of mice running around inside the walls or in the woodpile. Also, some of the electronics in our homes emit constant high-frequency sounds we don't notice but which can be distressing to dogs.

Dogs need to be protected from auditory overload and sensory pollution in general, so they can use their senses as they're meant to be used. We must pay close attention to all the sounds we expose dogs to and do what we can to protect their long-term health. There is evidence that many dogs fear loud sounds, particularly older dogs. Stanley Coren reports in one study that "83 percent of the dogs had shown fear in response to fireworks, 66 percent to thunderstorms, 26 percent to gunshots, 24 percent to cars backfiring, and 12 percent to loud noises on the television. That means that, on average, around half (49 percent) of the dogs had clearly shown fearfulness to some form of loud noise at least once."

Among the least-sensitive dogs to loud noise are Labrador retrievers, cocker spaniels, springer spaniels, German and Belgian shepherds, basset hounds, dalmatians, bulldogs, poodles, malamutes, Siberian huskies, and Samoyeds. In terms of hearing, one important way to improve your dog's life is to silence their dog tag, which can interfere with their keen sense of hearing. *See also* **ears**; **tags**.

heat detection. Researchers have recently discovered a new ability for a dog's nose: It can detect heat. As science writer Virginia Morell describes it, "Dogs' noses just got a bit more amazing. Not only are they up to 100 million times more sensitive than ours, but they can also sense weak thermal radiation — the body heat of mammalian prey, a new study reveals. The finding helps explain how canines with impaired sight, hearing, or smell can still hunt successfully." While we know just how sensitive dogs' noses truly are, the ability to sense heat hasn't previously been shown in carnivores.

This was presented in a paper by Anna Bálint and her colleagues titled "Dogs Can Sense Weak Thermal Radiation." Scientists at Lund University in Sweden and Eötvös Loránd University in Budapest were involved in the research. Using double-blind experiments, three dogs were able to distinguish between objects radiating different amounts of heat, including one warm object that approximated the surface temperature of a furry mammal. In another study at Eötvös Loránd University, the brains of thirteen awake dogs were studied using neuroimaging as the dogs were exposed to objects giving off various amounts of heat. The results showed that the warm stimulus caused activity in the part of the brain that receives input from dogs' noses, which responded more to the warm object than to a neutral object.

After reading about this amazing discovery, Heddie Leger sent me a note about her dog Hope, whom she calls "congenitally blind, deaf, cognitively delayed, and olfactory sensory deprived."

> However, I can say without question life is an adventure to behold each time we go for a walk.
>
> The world for Hope is experienced through different senses, such as touch, vibration, thermal waves, and wind currents. She may not see, but she knows there is something there and goes forth with unquestionable confidence to experience all the wonders of the world. Her favorite game is finding the kitty cat, who she will play with for hours, as our barn cat engages in a game of cat and mouse with her. However, the cat is the mouse who hides, and Hope finds her. Then they dance together with glee. This occurs for hours outside amongst the trees with Hope on a long thirty-foot lead, and the

> barn cat finding new places to hide for Hope to seek and find her. I recently read a study on how she does this with thermal radiation sensory abilities. Hope allows me to experience nature in an entirely different frame of reference, always mindful of keeping her safe from harm.
>
> With a dog like Hope it becomes even more important, as she would unabashedly run off the side of a cliff or into traffic with abandon. She is 100 percent of the time an at-risk being. That is the life I accepted when I invited her into my life journey. I live with no regrets as she brings intense joy and laughter at any given moment. She loves all other species and finds joy in just being. I often wonder what the world would be like if each of us could attain that level of enjoyment in experiencing life.
>
> Now three years old, her passion in life is to run. She is not given to chewing, or is attracted to very many toys, but she does love to run, so we run. There are many dogs who love to run. The difference is I have to guide her with no cues to indicate direction, stopping, and a myriad of other communications to keep her safe. This leads me to experience the reality that communication with any species is more than just the sounds we make. As humans, we consider communication to be mostly verbal. While this is for the most part true, there is so much more that creates true communication than words. With a dog like Hope, I have learned to sharpen those subtle communications that do not involve verbal cues.

It seems inevitable that future research will show that we've only discovered the tip of the "nasal iceberg" of dogs and their sensory organs. *See also* **noses; smell.**

hedonic treadmill. This term refers to the temporary emotional lift a person experiences after doing something fun or exciting, like getting a dog. In his essay "Puzzling Relationship between Pet-Keeping and Happiness," psychologist Hal Herzog summarizes what we know about this dynamic. Herzog notes,

> In her book *The Happy Dog Owner*, the University of Liverpool anthrozoologist Carri Westgarth suggests that a phenomenon called hedonic adaptation (also called, the hedonic treadmill) may be to

blame. Hedonic adaptation is the tendency for humans to return to a stable baseline level after they experience either a major positive or negative event. That's why the happiness you get from, say, buying a new guitar, or in the case of college professors, getting tenure, wears off, usually surprisingly quickly. Dr. Westgarth thinks the same thing applies to getting a pet. After the initial buzz you get from your new kitten or rescue dog, your life gradually goes back to normal. The upside of hedonic adaptation is that happiness levels tend to return to normal after bad things happen, for example, when your pet dies.

Further, Herzog did a detailed analysis of thirteen studies done in five countries and found that not a single study concluded that, as a group, pet owners were any happier than non–pet owners. Surprisingly, in a follow-up study, people with strong attachments to their companion animal showed higher levels of depression and loneliness and didn't perceive positive experiences as well as people who were less attached or who didn't live with a companion animal.

Herzog wrote, "Does the inverse connection between pet attachment and well-being only occur during crises such as a pandemic lockdown?" My daughter Katie, who is intensely attached to her goldendoodle, Moose, thinks so. When I sent the study to her, she wrote back, "I'm not surprised by the results. Covid meant spending more time with our pets than is typical. This leads to intense, even detrimental, connections, which makes having life-affirming events like travel or even a night out with friends more difficult." *See also* **"pet effect paradox."**

helicopter parenting. Many people micromanage the behavior of their dogs in the same way parents try to micromanage the lives of their kids. To me, "helicopter parenting" of dogs expresses itself when the amount of correction and scolding a dog receives overwhelms the amount of praising.

Over the course of several years, I collected data on patterns of scolding and praising. I looked at three hundred instances in which people talked to or yelled at their own or someone else's dog. This included corrections like "No! Don't do that!" or "Stop that!" and statements of approval or praise like “Good dog” or “That’s OK.” My best estimate is that I sampled between seventy-five to a hundred different people.

The results of this pilot study were very clear. I discovered that dogs were reprimanded almost five times more than they were praised. On 248 out of 300 occasions (82.7 percent), scolding was recorded, whereas during 52 out of 300 times (17.3 percent) praising was recorded. Meanwhile, only 3 of those 52 expressions of praise (5.8 percent) were spontaneous positive messages, that is, praise given when the dog wasn’t doing anything other than just walking around or hanging out.

I often find myself saying “good dog” just to be nice, for no apparent reason, or when dogs are themselves being nice, whether to other dogs or to a human — such as when dogs are playing fairly and allowing all participants to frolic and have fun. On several occasions, people have asked me why I’ve praised a dog, thinking that perhaps they had missed something. I explain that I feel it’s OK to give praise, be nice, show affection, and love dogs for just being themselves. Like kids, dogs shouldn’t have to “earn” our love. Some people tell me that they had never thought of it this way and admit they don’t offer praise just to be nice or when their dog is “behaving appropriately.” *See also* **“good dog” / “bad dog.”**

heterosis. Hybrid vigor due to outbreeding, when dogs of two different breeds or mixes (who aren’t truly hybrids) mate and have children.

hide-and-seek. Over the course of thousands of hours watching dogs, I’ve seen dogs playing what seemed to be hide-and-seek among themselves a few times. Then a few years ago, a woman sent me an email with a video of two dogs who seemed to be intentionally taking turns hiding from each other while the other looked. I hope someone studies this in more depth because it says a lot about dog intentions and what’s happening in their brains.

hierarchy of dog needs. A few years ago, I read about Linda Michaels’s hierarchy of dog needs, which is a variation of Maslow’s “hierarchy of needs," a psychological theory developed in the 1940s by Abraham Maslow. Saul McLeod writes that Maslow's hierarchy is "a five-tier model of human needs, often depicted as hierarchical levels within a pyramid. From the bottom of the hierarchy upwards, the needs are: physiological (food and clothing), safety (job security), love and belonging needs (friendship), esteem, and self-actualization. Needs lower down in the hierarchy must be satisfied before individuals can attend to needs higher up."

I was very impressed with Michaels's adaptation of this hierarchy to apply it to dogs, as follows: (1) biological needs, such as proper nutrition, fresh water, safety, indoor shelter, and sufficient air, sleep, grooming, and vet care; (2) emotional needs — security, love, trust, consistency, and benevolent leadership; (3) social needs — bonding with people and dogs, and playtime; (4) force-free training needs; and (5) cognitive needs — adequate stimulation to provide choice and novelty and thereby facilitate problem-solving skills. Her overall approach emphasizes level 4 via a "positive training" approach to working with dogs and their humans. As Michaels notes, the hierarchy of dog needs "is supported by scientific evidence and makes no apologies for embracing protective ethics concerning our beloved dogs. The No Shock, No Prong, No Choke logo is loud and clear." *See also* **affective dog behavior (ABD)**.

hierarchy of social relationships. A hierarchy delineates social relationships (or social dominance) on a scale from high-ranking to low-ranking. There are different ways of measuring and describing these sorts of relationships, and groups of dogs have been observed to demonstrate them all. This is colloquially called a "pecking order" because of a study by Norwegian researcher Thorleif Schjelderup-Ebbe, who observed that hens pecked one another to maintain their social hierarchy.

Overall, hierarchies are considered either linear or nonlinear. For example, imagine there are four dogs involved: a linear hierarchy means 1 dominates 2, 3, and 4; 2 dominates 3 and 4; and 3 dominates 4. A nonlinear hierarchy could mean something like 1 dominates 2 and 3;

2 dominates 3; 3 dominates 4; and 4 dominates 1 and 2. When there are nonlinear hierarchies, social interactions can become more complex and less predictable, and this makes studying them more difficult but much more interesting. *See also* **dominance**; **Landau's index**; **linear hierarchy**.

"hightail it out of here." A saying that means rapidly clearing out or hotfooting it away from some type of trouble.

hip slamming. Dogs will sometimes intentionally bump or slam their hip into another dog. Depending on the context, this could be part of a greeting or play or it can be an aggressive interaction. The bump can range from a simple nudge to a genuine slam that can lift a dog off the ground.

hoarding. Some dogs seem to have an urge to collect things. Years ago, some friends of mine had a dog, Rafa, who collected toys and placed them in a corner — including his own toys, those belonging to other dogs, and some of his human guardians. My friends couldn't get Rafa to break the habit, so after a while they let him do it because he seemed to enjoy it! Frankly, I have no idea what was going on in Rafa's head other than perhaps he saw it as a form of play. He didn't seem greedy, he didn't defend the toys, nor did he exclude others from retrieving them. He simply seemed to enjoy collecting them and dumping them in a corner. *See also* **greed**.

holistic veterinary medicine. This includes using both conventional and alternative methods to treat nonhuman clients, and the dog, or other nonhuman, is viewed and treated as an integrated whole system — mind, body, and spirit. While drugs may be used, changes in lifestyle may be favored in certain situations, and surgery is usually only considered as a last resort. The American Holistic Veterinary Medical Association (AHVMA) is a group of veterinarians and allies who are elevating the veterinary profession through innovation, education, and advocacy of integrative medicine. *See also* **veterinary medicine**.

home alone, leaving dogs. Dogs are often left home alone for some period of time during the day, but when they are alone for too long, it can cause anxiety and even trauma for the dog. How long is too long? There's no easy answer. Some people say it's OK for people to be gone from thirty minutes to two hours, but leaving dogs for more than two to four hours is ill-advised. I tend to agree with these estimates, but a lot depends on the personality of the dog, how they're feeling, their relationship with their humans, and where they're left. Like people, some dogs handle solitude better than others. *See also* **separation anxiety**.

homed dogs. This term is used for dogs who have a stable home environment where they reliably get food, a bed, veterinary care, and hopefully lots of love. Meanwhile, the term *intensively homed dogs* is sometimes used for dogs who have few if any freedoms because their humans control just about all aspects of their lives.

homelessness and dogs. Homeless people often have dogs as companions, which can sometimes be controversial. Some people think these dogs suffer a lot of abuse, but my experience with the dogs of homeless and formerly homeless people is that they are treated very well — surely as well as many homed dogs. In Multnomah County, Oregon, most cruelty complaints again homeless pet owners are baseless. Some homeless shelters are beginning to see the importance of making room for people with companion animals.

A UK study concluded, "Major emergent themes included participants' descriptions of their pets as kin; the responsibility they felt toward their pet; and anticipatory grief when contemplating a future without their companion animal. Importantly, the analysis also suggests the importance of a mutual rescue narrative, whereby pet owners felt that they had rescued their dogs from a negative situation, and vice versa."

homeopathic veterinary medicine. According to VCA Animal Hospitals, "The underlying basis of homeopathy is the principle that 'like cures like,' or that a substance that is capable, in toxic doses, of producing a set of symptoms is also capable, in much lower doses, of curing the same set of symptoms regardless of their perceived cause." Dogs, cats, ruminants (hoofed grazing or browsing mammals), and birds have been treated in this way. Only veterinarians trained in homeopathy should practice this form of medicine. It remains a controversial area, but I've been told by a number of traditional veterinarians that they have used it successfully.

home range. This refers to the area where an animal spends most of their time but doesn't defend the space, which can be shared with other animals. Free-ranging and feral dogs have home ranges, but it's not especially meaningful for dogs who spend most of their time in homes. *See also* **core area**; **territorial behavior**.

homing behavior. Dogs display amazing homing abilities, and there are some very interesting stories of long-distance homing, but it's not clear what cues they use. Some suggest that dogs use scent or the earth's electromagnetic field. The classic story is about a dog named Bobbie who disappeared during a car trip in 1924 and six months later found his way home, traveling on foot from Indiana to Oregon, a trip of around twenty-five hundred miles.

On a smaller scale, I've witnessed this myself. Some years back, my friends visited my mountain home with their dog Kodak, who had only been there once before. Kodak enjoyed romping around with my dog Jethro, but during dinner, Kodak disappeared. We looked all over and called for him, but he didn't respond. We figured Kodak, a city dog, had gotten lost. Three hours later, when he hadn't returned, my friend had to go home, and I went out looking for Kodak two more times that night, along with Jethro, but we had to be careful because of some local mountain lions and black bears. When we couldn't find him, all we could do was wait and see if he came back in the morning.

Kodak still hadn't shown up the next day, but when I left the house later that morning, there was Kodak sprawled out on the dirt road right next to my car. I was thrilled to see him and checked him out.

All he had were sore feet; he was fine but thoroughly exhausted. As I later learned from someone who'd seen him, Kodak had walked pretty much straight uphill to a tiny town called Gold Hill around nine miles from my house, which made a roundtrip of eighteen miles through very rugged, unfamiliar terrain. I have no idea why he went up there or why he returned or how he accomplished this journey. Did he chase a deer, or was he avoiding a mountain lion, or did he simply get lost? And how did he find his way back to my home, one he barely knew, when there were countless alternative paths he could have followed? *See also* **pooping along Earth's magnetic field**.

honest signals. Actions that reflect an animal's true intentions. They could be play signals, threat displays, or invitations to roam here and there. *See also* **golden rules of play; play; play bows**.

hospice care. End-of-life care for those with a terminal illness. For dogs and other companions animals, the goal of hospice care is to provide compassionate care so that the individual may live as fully and comfortably as possible; vets also help a dog's humans. The International Association for Animal Hospice and Palliative Care helps people find hospice care for companion animals. *See also* **end-of-life decisions**.

howling. Little is known about the long, loud sound dogs make that we call howling. Since it can evoke sad soulful overtones, it suggests the dog is lonely or upset and perhaps telling others where they are and seeking contact. It's also possible that dogs, like coyotes and wolves, howl to tell others they've located something, even if they're not feeling lonely.

hugging. It's a myth that dogs don't like being hugged. Some do and some don't — so if your dog likes to be hugged, hug them. If they don't, don't. In general in the animal kingdom, hugging is common and meaningful; it's calming and shows affection. *See also* **petting; touch**.

human-animal interaction (HAI). A phrase that refers to any sort of relationship or interaction between a human and a nonhuman animal.

The study of human-animal interactions has developed into a very important and global field of study. *See also* **anthrozoology**; **conservation psychology**.

human-directed social behavior. In dogs, this means contact focusing on humans that can include physical interactions and eye contact and that has strong heritability. Heritability is a measure of the amount of variation in a trait that can be attributed to genetic variation.

human gaze, dogs following. Following someone's gaze is a form of perspective taking; that is, one is literally trying to see what someone else is seeing. Different breeds of dogs show differences in following human gazing, and more research is needed to determine how widespread this is.

There have been many studies to determine if dogs and wolves differ in their ability to follow the human gaze. The results range widely and depend on the tests involved, the conditions under which the wolves were reared, the age of dogs, and training. It's difficult to know if and how the process of domestication played a role in differences between wolves and dogs, although many people argue there is a connection. Results suggest that, although the domestication process may have shaped the dog's human-directed communicative abilities, the later selection for specific types of work might also have had a significant impact on their emergence. One study has shown that wolves and dogs bond similarly to humans when they are hand-raised. *See also* **perspective taking**.

human health and fitness, dogs' impact on. Many people feel that living with a dog keeps them healthy and fit. Certainly, the need to walk a dog several times a day can keep people from being too sedentary. However, there are few data that actually speak to this relationship. A study of Japanese dog owners showed that people living with a dog or who had lived with a dog (but not a cat) had lower risks of disabilities as they age. Gender, age, income, smoking, diet, and heart disease didn't play a factor in this relationship. That said, there was no benefit if dogs weren't walked or if the people didn't take another form of exercise. In contrast to this study, Hal Herzog offers data that show that pet owners are not better off than non–pet owners. *See also* **hedonic treadmill**; **"pet effect paradox."**

human pointing, comprehension of. Following human pointing, like following the human gaze, is a form of perspective taking. While there are a large number of pointing and gazing studies, they are extremely difficult to summarize. Many of the studies focus on trying to compare the relative abilities of dogs and wolves, in part to determine how much domestication might have influenced this in dogs. Yet I find these studies too messy to offer precise predictions along the lines of "Dogs do this" or "Wolves do or don't do that." How dogs and wolves behave in studies is related to how they're raised, trained, and tested, and these factors can vary widely. In the notes at marcbekoff.com, I provide two papers that are well worth reading for their summary overviews of this topic: "Free-Ranging Dogs Are Capable of Utilizing Complex Pointing Cues" and "Comprehension of Human Pointing Gestures in Young Human-Reared Wolves (*Canis lupus*) and Dogs (*Canis familiaris*)."

In the latter study, the researchers wrote: "Comparing the wolves to naive pet dogs of the same age revealed that during several months of formal training wolves can reach the level of dogs in their success of following momentary distal pointing in parallel with improving their readiness to form eye contact with a human experimenter. We assume that the high variability in the wolves' communicative behavior might have provided a basis for selection during the course of domestication of the dog."

Some research suggests that infant dogs are more attracted to humans than are infant wolves raised by humans, and that young dogs use human gestures and make more eye contact than young wolves. Dog researcher Juliane Kaminski refers to dogs as "human whisperers" because of their unique socio-cognitive skills, which aren't observed in other species.

Researchers Brian Hare and Michael Tomasello suggest that some of these skills, such as following human pointing, arose during the course of domestication as the individuals on the way to becoming dogs changed how they dealt with fear and aggression toward humans. This is a very reasonable suggestion, but it's still not clear precisely why dogs have the unique skills they have when compared to wolves and other undomesticated animals.

In "The New Science of Canine Cognition," Jennifer Burks summarizes the research on canine cognition that was conducted from 1998 to 2015. She begins by asking the questions: "How much do dogs understand about human cues?" "What is responsible for the dog's ability to do this (age, breed, training, domestication)?" And, "If this is a learned ability, when do dogs learn this ability?" Burks concludes, "Over the last two decades scientists have been debating the origin of the domestic dog's social skills with regards to their human companions. Researchers agree that the domestic dog has an uncanny ability to both interpret and utilize human-given cues, and they agree that domestication has played a part in the evolution of this skill. Unfortunately, though, that's about all they agree on; the issue is still debatable and requires more research. However, evidence appears to be skewed in favor of the Two Stage Hypothesis over the Domestication Hypothesis. Evidence that human-raised wolves, with no history of domestication can outperform domestic, pet dogs in the ubiquitous object choice by human cue task cannot and should not be overlooked."

I agree with Burks. We should be careful about generalizing. Even with more research, precise species-wide generalizations will be difficult to make.

human selection. *See* **artificial selection**.

humor, sense of. People often ask me if dogs and other animals have a sense of humor. I'm pretty sure that dogs and many other animals do, but I go back and forth on which other animals have the cognitive capacity for humor. Stanley Coren also thinks dogs have a sense of humor, though he notes there are likely breed differences in addition to individual differences among dogs. If a nonhuman animal displays a sense of humor, it reveals a lot about what they know about what's happening around them.

In his classic book *The Descent of Man and Selection in Relation to Sex*, Charles Darwin writes: "Dogs show what may be fairly called a sense of humor, as distinct from mere play; if a bit of stick or other such object be thrown to one, he will often carry it away for a short distance; and then squatting down with it on the ground close before him, will wait until his master comes quite close to take it away. The dog will then seize it and rush away in triumph, repeating the same maneuver, and evidently enjoying the practical joke."

Having a sense of humor means that an individual knows whatever they're doing has an effect on others, and although they themselves might enjoy whatever they're doing, the reaction of the human (and perhaps nonhuman) observer is also a goal and keeps them doing what they're doing. Having a sense of humor might confirm that animals have a theory of mind.

While I'm always careful to say that I don't really know if dogs and other animals have a sense of humor and enjoy comedy, since there are few formal, ethological studies on this topic, the anecdotal evidence is pretty overwhelming. For example, my companion Jethro not only was a savvy food thief but also quite a jokester. He'd run around with his favorite stuffed animal, a rabbit, in his mouth, shaking it from side to side and often looking at the people who were around to see what effect this had on them. When they laughed while he was doing this, he seemed to do it more and more. When they weren't paying attention to him, he would stop running around or he would bark, look to see if they were watching him, and continue running here and there with his stuffed toy.

Or consider Benson the burper. My friend Marije terEllen tells me that Benson, a Bernese mountain dog, likes to come up to her, face to face, look her in the eyes, and burp. He seems to get a kick out of doing it and doesn't burp at other times. Is this his way of saying "hello" or "I love you"? Or is he just having a good old time doing it to his human? Marije also insists that Benson is not mimicking her or her daughter Arianne.

I've also come across numerous examples of other species who act like stand-up comedians and jokesters, including horses, moon bears (aka Asian black bears), a scarlet macaw, and more. Humor may be more widespread among nonhuman animals than we think.

Elsewhere (in the "deceiving" entry), I tell the story of Myron, a dog who loved to lick dirty dishes in the dishwasher. While this story mainly shows how Myron learned to trick his humans so he could get at the dishes, it also indicates his sense of humor. For Myron, fooling his humans seemed to be part of the fun, and he became much more subdued once his humans decided to stop caring and ignored him. *See also* **deceiving**; **theory of mind**.

humping. When a dog mounts another dog from the side or from behind or mounts a human's leg and thrusts with their hips. Mounting and humping are two dog-appropriate behaviors that many people find offensive. There isn't a single reason why dogs do it.

Males and females do it to same-sex and opposite-sex individuals (and same-sex humping doesn't mean a dog is gay). Dogs do it in order to mate, but they also do it in other contexts outside of trying to mate. In these cases, to understand why, it's important to consider context, including who's the initiator and who's the recipient and when and where it's happening. Humping can be an expression of interest in mating, dominance, or play, or a dog may just wind up in that position and some reflex gets triggered. I wonder if on occasion some dogs hump simply because they can. When this happens, you can turn away, pretend it isn't happening, or giggle nervously and let them be dogs. You also can watch and record what happens before and after mounting and humping. This can tell you more about the behavior itself. This technique can help you determine when a behavior needs to be managed and when it's just fine.

Mounting could also be what ethologists call a displacement behavior, meaning that it's a by-product of conflicted emotions. For some dogs, a new visitor to the house could elicit a mixture of excitement and stress that could trigger a dog to start humping. Or, just like we might flip on the TV when we're bored, some dogs might develop the habit of mounting during downtime, getting better acquainted with a pillow. Mounting is also very common during play, sometimes as an attention-getter, an affiliative behavior, or when a dog is overexcited. I've seen dogs going "berserk," enjoying their zoomies, running here and there, and mounting and humping a friend and then a ball.

A few years ago, at a local dog park, a man told me an interesting story about his dog Reggie: "My dog Reggie, a male, is a humper — anything and anyone — water bowl, beach ball, other dogs from different orientations, and human legs. I can't say why and surely I can't provide an overall explanation. He just likes to do it, and if another dog or a human rejects him, he sort of shrugs and tries again with someone else. I don't allow him to do it to me, and I say no, but that doesn't work in other situations. When he's rejected, he just slides off and goes elsewhere." *See also* **displacement behavior**; **mounting**.

hybrid. The offspring of two animals of different species, such as a mule (a hybrid of a donkey and a horse). The offspring of wolf-dog, coyote-dog, or wolf-coyote matings are hybrids, but mixed-breed dogs, often called mutts or mongrels, aren't really hybrids. *See also* **breed**; **designer dogs**.

I

idiosyncratic behavior. Like people, dogs display large individual differences in behavior and personality, often quirky. A dog named Pete would always run into a local dog park, twirl around and bark, sit and scratch his neck, run back to his human, and only then seek out his friends. Pete was rescued from a local shelter, and Marianne, his human, told me he did this from day one when she brought him home.

One of my dogs would always turn around and run into the kitchen when he knew he was going on a walk, rather than run straight to the door. I have no idea why he performed this quirky behavior, but he must have had a good reason. I couldn't get him to simply run directly to the door, so after a few months I gave up. He continued to do it for the rest of his life, and I hear similar stories from numerous people about their canine companions.

Iditarod. This famous sled-dog competition commemorates the role that sled dogs played in settling Alaska. It's held annually in early March and goes a thousand miles from Willow to Nome (after a ceremonial start in Anchorage). There are two routes, a northern route that's used in even-numbered years and a southern route that's used in odd-numbered years.

It's a rough trip for dogs and humans, and there are many welfare concerns for the dogs. At least 150 dogs have died during the running of the Iditarod, and in 2022 an enraged moose injured four dogs on a training run. Also in 2022, more than two hundred dogs were pulled from the race, a dog went missing, a musher was apparently forced out of the race because his dogs were in poor condition, and several big companies pulled their sponsorship. Three mushers also were punished by Iditarod officials for caring about their dogs and sheltering them during a fierce windstorm.

imprinting. Early exposure to a stimulus can establish a close attachment to, and future preferences for, members of a species, food, or where the individual was born or lives. Nobel Prize–winning ethologist Konrad Lorenz popularized imprinting because of his work with newborn (precocial) ducks and geese, including some who thought Lorenz was a parent. Early exposure to different stimuli can override genetics, and the birds would follow any object with which they had contact early in life. Puppies also imprint, especially on their mothers and littermates. Imprinting can explain why it seems like some dogs innately recognize and prefer dogs of their own breed when they're simply preferring dogs who look, sound, or smell like those with whom they were reared. If and after they go to another home, puppies will usually imprint on their new humans and perhaps the location where they wind up. Dog researcher Zazie Todd also notes that there's a "fear imprinting stage" from around eight to ten weeks of age when puppies are most vulnerable to trauma. *See also* **breed recognition among dogs**.

inbreeding. Mating by genetically related individuals. Many dog breeds are highly inbred because money-hungry breeders are selecting for the distinctive traits that represent the breed. However, inbreeding is related to increases in disease and costs for health care.

One 2021 report said, "The average inbreeding based on genetic analysis across 227 breeds was close to 25 percent, or the equivalent of sharing the same genetic material with a full sibling. These are levels considered well above what would be safe for either humans or wild animal populations. In humans, high levels of inbreeding (3–6 percent) have been associated with increased prevalence of complex diseases as well as other conditions."

inbreeding depression. This term refers to the reduction in fertility — decreased variation in genetic makeup — in the children of parents who are genetically related.

inequity aversion. A preference for fairness and equality in animals. This trait was important in the evolution of cooperation. A review of inequity aversion in dogs concluded, "Domestic dogs represent an interesting case as, unlike many primates, they do not respond negatively to inequity in reward quality but do, however, respond negatively to being unrewarded in the presence of a rewarded partner." Researchers call this a *primitive* form of inequity aversion. Wolves respond in the same way, so this does not seem to be a result of domestication. More research needs to be done on this important topic. *See also* **fairness**.

infantile behavior. Aka et-epimeletic behavior. Childish behaviors associated with young dogs or other animals include suckling, nursing, whining, begging, temper tantrums, and the inguinal response. *See also* **inguinal response**; **neonatal behavior**.

information theory. A measure of the degree of complexity of a system of communication. The amount of information is measured in units called bits. This is not necessarily applied to dogs, but I often wonder how much information is contained in various dog behaviors and whether it changes over time as dogs have more social experience and get to know one another. For example, when two unfamiliar dogs meet and want to play, is there more information in a play signal, such as the play bow, when they are introducing themselves to one another, and is there less once they get to know one another and don't have to be as formal?

inguinal presentation. When a dog rolls over onto their back and spreads their legs. This is the same position dogs assume when their mother licks them to stimulate them to urinate. It may signal submission or something like, *Please stop what you're doing to me.* It's a nonthreatening and passive behavior.

inguinal response. A light touch to the inguinal or groin area that results in an animal moving the leg on that side outward. Dogs and wolves display this response, but young coyotes have a lower threshold for eliciting it. It's not clear what it's good for, but research on coyotes shows it might be useful for terminating an aggressive interaction, since even a light touch of the area with another individual's tail leads to the stimulated dog lying still on their back. Humans can also elicit it by slightly touching a dog's inguinal region. When a female licks her young children in that area, it stimulates them to pee or poop reflexively before they have self-control, and this might be the origin of this response.

inhibitory control. The ability to stop the urge to do something, especially negative behaviors, but sometimes dogs get wired when they're intensely playing and zooming here and there with reckless abandon and need to tone it down for their own and other's good. In dogs, the level of inhibitory control varies among individuals, and it also varies by situation or activity. A comprehensive study performed on dogs showed that there were three components that explained variation across behaviors that needed to be inhibited — persistency, compulsivity, and decision speed — and "no unique measurement for inhibitory control exists in dogs, but tests rather measure different aspects of this ability." In addition, dogs and wolves differed in inhibition tasks, and the role of domestication, if any, remains unclear.

These are important results because it means that there are no simple answers for how to get dogs to stop doing certain things, and each dog needs to be considered for their individuality and their unique personalities. Age and sex don't seem to play any significant role.

inmates and dogs. Many jails and prisons have dog-training programs that overall are good for the dogs and the humans who work in them. The nonjudgmental dogs benefit from the close contact and care they receive, and the inmates learn to be responsible for the well-being and quality of life of another individual.

innate behavior. Inborn, hardwired, instinctual actions that don't require learning. Examples include running away from danger or approaching a friendly individual. These behaviors can be modified over time, so learning can play a role in how they're used in different contexts.

innenwelt. A term used by ethologists to refer to an individual's inner world and subjective experiences. *See also* **umwelt**.

inner lives. Aka hidden lives, private lives, or secret lives. These terms refer to what's happening in the heads, minds, and hearts of dogs. That is, they refer to a dog's cognitive and emotional self — their thoughts and feelings. Of course, these aren't directly observable but they can be inferred through careful observation of dog behavior. Someone even once asked me if dogs have secrets they don't want to share, and I thought that was a great question, but how will we ever know?

instantaneous sampling. Recording behavior at fixed intervals, such as every few minutes. During research, this is easier to do than trying to write down everything a dog does. However, a lot of information can be lost because this method doesn't measure frequency or rates of occurrence. *See also* **research techniques**.

intelligence. The ability to flexibly and intentionally deal with different situations, both based on one's own past experiences and by observing others. Many people like to think their dog is exceptionally intelligent — often because their dog seems to know and learn things other dogs don't — but one study showed that time spent with a dog is more important than how psychologically close one feels toward their dog in their perceptions of how intelligent a dog is.

It's useful to think of intelligence as adaptation — or the ability to adjust and deal with different circumstances. In our book *Wild Justice*, Jessica Pierce and I stress that intelligence is not a universal and measurable entity, but rather is context-specific. Cross-species comparisons or even within-species comparisons are fraught with difficulty because members of different species do what they need to do to be card-carrying members of their species, and even among individuals of the same species there are marked differences.

There is some evidence that larger dogs are smarter than smaller dogs, and grumpy dogs are better learners than dogs who are content, but much more information is needed before these become rules of thumb. Some people say that dogs are as intelligent as two-year-old humans, but I honestly don't know what that means because dogs and humans are very different mammals. *See also* **dogs or cats, who is smarter**.

intimidating. Doing something that makes an individual uncomfortable, timid, or fearful. With humans, some dogs can be intimidated by threats and by rapidly running head-on at a dog.

introvert. Similar to people, some dogs choose to spend more time alone rather than with others, during which they may recuperate and energize on their own. *See also* **extrovert**.

investigative behavior. Information gathering. In dogs, this includes nosing, sniffing, circling, and being attracted to new situations. *See also* **neophilia and neophobia**.

J

jackals. Members of the dog family (Canidae) and related to dogs, coyotes, and wolves. There are three species of jackals — golden, side-striped, and black-backed — and they're about the size of coyotes. In many ways they are coyotes' equivalent in the ecosystems in which they live, and they, like coyotes and wolves, also can interbreed with dogs and produce viable young.

Jacobsen's organ. *See* **vomeronasal organ (VNO)**.

jaw wrestling. When dogs spar with their jaws without vigorously biting down. Sometimes dogs will growl when they are jaw wrestling, and people can mistake jaw wrestling with serious fighting. As always, consider the context to discern what's happening. *See also* **biting**.

jealousy. Studies show that dogs experience jealousy. That is, they can feel belittled and ignored and don't like being dissed. An important neuroimaging study by Peter Cook and his colleagues called "Jealousy in Dogs?" showed that dogs displayed jealousy (snapping, getting between the owner and an object) when owners showed affection to a stuffed dog, though the dogs *didn't* do this when humans showed affection to nonsocial objects. This research showed that the same part of a dog's brain (the amygdala) lit up in the same situations and ways that a human brain does when we're feeling jealous.

joy. Feelings of pleasure and happiness can be contagious, and they help to bond dogs together by working like "social glue." Joy can also facilitate dog-human bonding. *See also* **emotional contagion**.

juvenilization. *See* **paedomorphism**.

K

kin selection. A form of natural selection that favors positive or beneficial behavior directed toward kin who share different percentages of the animal's genes. The measure of genetic relatedness is called the coefficient of relatedness, r. For parent-child and sibling-sibling relationships r = ½. I'm not aware of any studies of kin selection in dogs, but it wouldn't surprise me if patterns of kin selection observed in wild canids — the preferential treatment of related individuals — also were displayed in free-ranging and feral dogs.

kissing. Whether dogs or other animals truly kiss is hotly debated because, while it looks as if dogs are kissing one another, it's difficult to know their motivation. I've been told by many people that their dogs kiss one another especially after they've been apart.

kneading. When pups paw mom's nipples to get more milk.

knowledge translation gap. This is the discrepancy between what is known and how animals are treated based on what we know. In terms of animals in general, the knowledge translation gap refers to how tons of scientific research shows that nonhuman animals are sentient beings and yet people still doubt this and cause intentional harm in order to serve human society and needs. On a broad scale, it means that what we now know about animal cognition and emotion needs to be translated into human attitudes and practices that acknowledge and respect the inner lives of animals. This is closely related to the precautionary principle. One example for dogs would be using what we know about how deeply emotional they are and banning puppy mills and invasive research. A good but depressing antiscientific example of the knowledge translation gap is found in the wording of the federal Animal Welfare Act, which explicitly excludes rats and mice from the taxonomic kingdom Animalia. That is, they are defined as "not animals" so they won't be covered by the Animal Welfare Act in scientific research. *See also* **precautionary principle**.

L

lactating. Females producing milk for their children. In dogs, lactation lasts for around ten weeks.

Laika. The first dog in space. Laika means "barker" in Russian and replaced the dog's actual name, Koryaks, since she barked a lot. Laika was launched in Sputnik 2 in 1957, and she both died in space and suffered throughout her flight, as she overheated and was cramped, frightened, and probably hungry.

Landau's index. This is a mathematical test to measure whether a social hierarchy is linear. The index, designated by the letter *h*, varies from 1, which indicates perfect linearity, to 0, which indicates perfect nonlinearity. Dogs, like their wild relatives, including coyotes and wolves, form linear and nonlinear social hierarchies. *See also* **hierarchy of social relationships**.

language recognition. Dogs recognize human speech and can learn the meaning of specific words, but can they recognize different human languages? According to a 2021 study of dogs using brain scans, they can. Researcher Attila Andics summarized their results this way: "This study showed for the first time that a nonhuman brain can distinguish between two languages. It is exciting because it reveals that the capacity to learn about the regularities of a language is not uniquely human. Still, we do not know whether this capacity is dogs' specialty or general among nonhuman species. Indeed, it is possible that the brain changes, from the tens of thousands of years that dogs have been living with humans, have made them better language listeners, but this is not necessarily the case. Future studies will have to find this out."

laughing. Do dogs laugh? Most people who study dogs agree that dogs don't laugh like us. However, dogs emit a sound — the play pant — that is a laughter-like, breathy vocalization they emit when playing. It's possible laughing evolved in mammals from this type of panting or forceful exhalation. Hyenas seem to laugh, and rats also laugh and like being tickled.

Studies by researcher Patricia Simonet at Sierra Nevada College (now the University of Nevada, Reno at Lake Tahoe), has explored laughter sounds in dogs. Her team used a parabolic microphone that allowed them to record dogs at a distance while playing. Simonet said, "To an untrained human ear, it sounds much like a pant, 'hhuh, hhuh.'" However, she found that the exhalation bursts contained a broader range of frequencies than regular dog panting. Also, when fifteen puppies heard the sound, they joyfully romped around, showing that these same sounds could calm other dogs. Clearly, a lot of interesting research needs to be done to learn more about whether, why, and when dogs laugh. *See also* **play panting**.

leadership. Research has shown that, among dogs, group decisions indicating one dog is a leader and others are followers are strongly influenced by dominance rank. That is, the lead dog often directs the group. This has an important practical application. As a report on this study said, "The researchers hope that this way of studying dogs could help to create optimal pairings of dogs used for important tasks such as search-and-rescue operations. The method could determine how well certain dogs work together, putting together those with the highest compatibility." This would be a win-win for dogs and humans and how they work together. Leadership within dog groups can change, and this helps us to understand how dynamic social relationships can be over time. *See also* **hierarchy of social relationships**.

learned helplessness. Accepting that a given situation can't be changed and giving up, even when escape or change is possible. Humans experience this, and we know dogs do, too, because of a study on learned helplessness in them and other nonhumans. Unfortunately, the study's methods were reprehensible because it used shocks on a grid from which the dogs couldn't escape until they gave up even trying to do so. This sort of research should never have been permitted.

learning. I view learning as a form of adaptation. That is, dogs adapt to the many different situations they face and then use this information in the future, showing improved performance in specific and more generalized situations. In dog training, dogs are being taught to adapt to what humans want them to do and to use this information in the future.

An interesting question is whether, and how, dominance rank influences how dogs learn. One study focusing on this concluded: "Perceived dominance rank in its own group has a strong effect on social learning in dogs, but this effect seems to depend also on the demonstrator species [dog or human]. This finding reveals an intricate organization of the social structure in multi-dog households, which can contribute to individual differences existing among dogs." *See also* **adaptability**; **intelligence**; **training**.

leashes. There are various types of leashes (a tether attached to a dog's collar or harness), ranging from those that are a few feet long to retractable leashes that allow a dog to explore a wider range. It's difficult to say which one is best; it very much depends on the best way to control a dog without harming them. Without leashes, dogs wouldn't be able to go many places with us, and used well, they give dogs access to their world and can be a critically important freedom enhancer. However, when used poorly, the leash can become a source of severe physical and sensory deprivation and harm. We need to be responsive to what's happening on both ends of the leash. A walk should involve ongoing negotiations and mutual tolerance between dog and human, erring on the dog's side whenever possible. There's no reason not to allow dogs, who are often cooped up for hours on end, the luxury of exercising their bodies, minds, and hearts.

In general, we mediate and control access to the physical and social worlds of our dogs quite a bit. We decide when, where, and for how long dogs get to be outside each day, and by using the physical constraints of collars and leashes, we control the speed, direction, and range of a dog's movements. Using a leash, we can impact what and how long dogs sniff, where they pee and poop, and who they interact with. These things inhibit a dog's freedoms, and when dogs are yanked here and there, or pulled on a leash suddenly and forcefully, these devices can be physically harmful.

Lead pulling is a welfare concern. In the United Kingdom, being pulled is the second-leading cause (after dog bites) of nonfatal dog-related injuries. When their lead is pulled, dogs can be injured and can experience stress, fear, and anxiety. This weakens the relationship between a dog and their human, and when unresolved, it can lead to relinquishment.

A leash-tension monitor that measures pull direction and force is now available and is considered to be a "robust and valid approach in exploring the real-world scenario of human-dog interactions when walking on a leash. It measures the leash tension and, most importantly, detects the direction of pulling." Using this haptic device can help people learn to control how hard to pull their dog and to allow dogs as much freedom as possible.

Our goal should be to use leashes to facilitate access to a wide variety of positive physical and social experiences and to allow our dogs to experience their own sense of agency. Dogs should be leashed more for their safety than for our convenience. Ultimately, a leash is simply a tool, a kind of umbilical cord between human and dog that can be used well or poorly. *See also* **collars**; **walking the dog**.

legal status. Globally, dogs and other nonhuman animals are legally considered to be things or property. Thinking of dogs as "owned" things is harmful and a double cross on these amazing beings. Although homed dogs live highly restrictive lives, they still aren't mere objects, but rather conscious beings with subjective lives. In June 2022, Tennessee passed a law making it illegal to harm police dogs, and it would be nice if *all* dogs could be legally protected from harm. *See also* **personhood**.

LEGS dog training. This positive, force-free, and very effective method of teaching is championed by dog trainer Kim Brophey in her book *Meet Your Dog*. The acronym LEGS stands for learning, environment, genetics, and self. *See also* **training**.

licking wounds. An animal licking their wounds is a natural, soothing response to injury, and it's helpful, since saliva can kill certain bacteria and promote healing. However, if a dog is wounded, seek veterinary care, if possible, because saliva can also increase the risk of infection and spread to a wound, making it worse.

life expectancy. Average life expectancy varies greatly in dogs. One study showed that French bulldogs have the shortest life expectancy, 4.53 years; and Jack Russell terriers have the longest life expectancy, 12.72 years. However, individual dogs can sometimes live much longer lives; a beagle was once reported to live for twenty-seven years, and in 2023, the world's oldest dog — a purebred Portuguese Rafeiro do Alentejo named Bobi — was revealed to be thirty years old. Note that the term *life span* refers to the maximum number of years a dog can live, while *life expectancy* is the average number of years.

Many people would like their dogs to live longer, healthier lives. The best way to help them is to give them plenty of exercise, don't overfeed them, enrich their lives, give some extra love, and give them regular veterinary checkups. Studies are also being conducted to see if a drug called rapamycin, an antibiotic used to treat human transplant patients, can help improve canine health, but as of this writing, we don't know, and there are side effects. Check out the Dog Aging Project for advice on how to give dogs longer and healthier lives.

life-history strategy. A life-history strategy, as defined by biologist Stephen Stearns, is "a set of co-adapted traits designed, by natural selection, to solve particular ecological problems." The life history of an organism is how it grows, survives, and reproduces throughout its lifetime. Some examples of life-history traits are litter or brood size, age at reproductive maturity, reproductive life span, body size, and diet. When biologists conduct life-history studies their goal is to understand how organisms balance the competing energetic costs of survival, growth, and reproduction — what biologists refer to as evolutionary trade-offs.

Traditionally, biologists don't study the life-history strategies of dogs or other domesticated animals because these animals are often considered "artifacts"; they were influenced by human selection and didn't evolve trade-offs among life-history traits solely through natural selection. Nonetheless, dogs and other domesticated animals do have life histories, they have made necessary trade-offs, and they are worthy of study. The life-history strategies of dogs reflect the ways in which humans have deliberately manipulated trade-offs among different variables to suit human interests; they also reflect the fact that humans don't exert as much control as we think.

linear hierarchy. A social hierarchy in which everyone in a group is dominated by higher-ranking group members and, in turn, high-ranking individuals dominate lower-ranking individuals. Dominance hierarchies influence the social dynamics of groups. *See also* **hierarchy of social relationships**; **Landau's index**.

link, the. The term *the link* refers to the relationship between human violence toward nonhumans, often started in childhood, and violence toward humans. A 2013 study found that 43 percent of those people who committed school massacres also committed acts of cruelty to animals. Dogs frequently are the targets of human violence. *See also* **domestic abuse and dogs**.

lip curling. A lip curl, when a dog bares their teeth, means something like, *Leave me alone, go away*. It's not accompanied by snarling and not necessarily an aggressive act, but rather a threat or a warning that a dog wants to be left alone. *See also* **snarling**.

lip licking. Also called air licking, mouth licking, and tongue flicking. There isn't one reason why dogs lick their lips; as always, context is important to evaluate. It can be used to indicate submission or to appease another dog. An appeasement behavior inhibits or reduces the aggressive behavior of a social partner. Or lip licking can be a sign of stress, worry, fear, or anxiety. Dogs also lick their lips to remove food or water.

Natalia Albuquerque and her colleagues conducted a study comparing the responses of dogs to happy and angry human and dog facial expressions. They found that dogs engaged in lip licking in response to angry expressions, which indicated low-level stress. Dogs were more likely to lip-lick when they saw an angry human face, but they did not do so when they heard angry human voices. This emphasizes the importance of visual cues with dogs. The study suggests that dogs may have evolved their sensitivity to human facial expression to facilitate interactions with us. *See also* **calming signals**.

literature, dogs in. Dogs have appeared in literature since Homer's *Odyssey*, where Odysseus's dog Argos is the only one who recognizes the hero's return. Two of the most famous fictional dogs — Lassie and Toto — began life in novels, and other imaginary and mostly beloved dogs include Tock from *The Phantom Tollbooth*, Cujo from Stephen King's horror novel, Winn-Dixie from *Because of Winn-Dixie*, and Fang, Hagrid's giant hound from the Harry Potter series.

On occasion, dogs also appear in poetry, usually with deep affection, such as this two-liner by Ogden Nash:

> The truth I do not stretch or shove
> When I state that the dog is full of love.

A discussion of the complex symbolism of dogs in literature and myth notes, "Perhaps the two most important and prominent qualities which dogs have symbolised in literature and myth down the ages are *vigilance* and *loyalty*...with many religions and myths linking the dog to death, hell, and the Underworld." *See also* **movies, dogs in**.

litter size. For dogs, the average litter size is around six, while the range is one to twelve. However, the number can vary widely from a single puppy to as many as twenty-four. On average, the sex ratio of litters is usually close to 1:1 (females to males), but the sex ratio can be influenced by the age of the parents. For beagles, Stanley Coren writes, "roughly speaking, for each increasing year of the dam's age beyond the age of two, the percentage of males in the litter is expected to increase by 15 percent." It's not clear why this happens, but it might be due to the chemical composition of vaginal fluids in older females.

locomotor play. Aka running around, often frantically. This can involve dogs chasing one another or a dog just having fun on their own. *See also* **frenetic random activity periods (FRAPs)**; **zoomies**.

long-distance identification. People are constantly telling me that their dog can "read" — visually identify — other dogs from afar and seem to be able to make reliable, long-distance assessments about whether another dog is familiar or unfamiliar and even what they're feeling, such as if they are friendly, want to play, or are saying back off. I've seen this myself and heard many stories, but we know next to nothing about this mysterious cognitive capacity, which cannot be fully accounted for by a dog's sense of smell, sight, or hearing. People tell me things like: "Joe recognizes another dog from afar and knows if they want to play or not and if they might be aggressive." Or, "Jasmine 'sees' other dogs from more than two hundred feet away and either tucks her tail as if she's submitting or runs toward them so she can play with them. She doesn't do this to any other animals and seems to know that whoever is out there is a dog and whether they're unfriendly or friendly."

In other words, dogs seem to be able to recognize another dog, and assess their mood, when they are too far away to smell, see, or hear clearly or well, unless the other dog was barking. It's possible that some composite of signals might form some sort of "dog gestalt" that helps them discriminate "dog" from afar, including their mood, but we don't have any data that support this possibility despite many people telling me they're sure their dog can do this.

Some people suggest that gait might be the key variable. Perhaps dogs can recognize by the way another dog walks that they are a dog and how they feel, but again, we don't know.

One way to study this ability would be to use a "robotic" dog. By adjusting its body morphology, and its tail, ears, and gait, this might shed some light on how dogs recognize other dogs from afar and which variables are most important. Where there's a will, there's a way, and there are good reasons to pursue these investigations. *See also* **composite signals**.

lost dog syndrome. Dave Pauli coined this term to describe the state of mind of dogs who are lost. He also offers advice for how to interact with and capture lost dogs. Here are his three "lessons learned":

1. Do not pursue a lost dog — instead, take the pressure off them and drop treats and walk/drive away.
2. Let them anchor to a protected spot and feed at a bait site that provides them a safe eating location.
3. Recapture is not a sprint but a marathon. Work on the individual dog's timeline and celebrate every time the dog decides to relax near you or accepts bait you toss to it.

Pauli stresses that "these dogs want to return to their former coexistence with humans. They are just too scared and confused to know how to make it happen."

love. When people wonder whether dogs are capable of loving, my answer is an emphatic *yes*. If you define love as a long-term commitment — meaning individuals seek one another out when they're apart, they're happy when they're reunited, they protect one another, they feed one another, they raise their children together — then of course nonhuman animals love each other. There's really good evidence that oxytocin stimulates positive affect and connection. It feels good to be in positive relationships, whether you're a dog or a person.

lumping data. *See* **splitting and lumping data**.

lying, dogs recognizing. Dogs can tell when humans are lying to them and being deceptive, and they can differentiate honest mistakes from outright lies. I would love to know how they do it. For example, are they using visual or olfactory cues or a composite signal combining information from these or other indicators we are unaware of? Or perhaps do they simply remember what humans have done, and they are saying something like, *Hey, you're lying to me, and I don't believe you! See also* **bluffing**; **deceiving**.

M

mammals. A group of vertebrates who have mammary glands that produce milk for feeding their children. Mammals are also defined by having a neocortex (an area of their brain), hair or fur, and three middle ear bones. Dogs and humans are both mammals.

management in dog training. This refers to changing a dog's environment to solve a problem with the dog's behavior, such as trying to calm a fearful dog by talking softly to them or offering a hug, or changing a garbage pail to thwart a dog who steals food. Many of my dogs were master thieves, and one figured out how to open a garbage pail that was supposed to be dog proof! Afterward, I read the fine print, and the product actually said it was 99 percent dog proof. Interestingly, she was the only dog who saw me put the lid on and turn a small knob. I honestly have no idea if she learned as she watched me or if she simply fiddled around until the knob loosened.

maternal effects. A female's offspring are influenced by her behavior and social rank. There isn't a genetic basis for this phenomenon. Maternal effects have been observed in insects, amphibians, reptiles, birds, and mammals, including wild rats, mice, deer, sheep, pinnipeds, and nonhuman primates. However, this hasn't been studied in free-ranging dogs.

mating preferences. For dogs, we really don't know much about mating preferences because so much is controlled and forced upon the potential mates by humans, but as more studies are conducted on free-ranging dogs, who mate without human interference, we will learn if they establish mating preferences as do their wild relatives and other nonhumans. *See also* **assortative mating**.

matrix of social interactions. A table used by researchers that lists different options for patterns of social interactions. As part of learning about your own dog — as well as doing citizen science and becoming an ethologist — consider creating your own matrix of social interactions. Here's how it works: Focus on a single social behavior, like play, and use the matrix to track the patterns of interactions. The matrix below is an example for the different possibilities for who begins an interaction and who is the focus of the initiator among dogs and humans. The four possibilities are (1) dog initiates / dog receives, (2) dog initiates / human receives, (3) human initiates / dog receives, and (4) human initiates / human receives. If you only want to track patterns among dogs, or dogs and other animals, simply change the categories.

	RECEIVER	
INITIATOR	Dog	Human
Dog	1	2
Human	3	4

A sample matrix of social interactions

Then, at a dog park or other place with humans and dogs, watch for and write down each play encounter and assign it a number. Do this for a set period of time or for as long as you want. It's important to note that often, when watching dogs or other animals, the different sorts of interactions become rapidly blurred. Sometimes it's simply impossible to figure out who initiated and who ended an encounter, and when there are more than two dogs, or a dog and a human, it can become a nightmare very fast. Nonetheless, we still can learn a lot from parsing out the different types of interactions using this simple matrix.

You can make matrices for all sorts of interactions. It's a simple and fun exercise through which you'll learn a lot about your dog's personality. For example, are they more of a leader or a follower, a player or a loner? What types of interactions do they initiate, and what sorts of encounters don't they especially like and try to avoid? You also can discover if they prefer some dogs rather than others, if they're having a good or bad day, how their behavior changes over time with familiar and unfamiliar dogs and humans in different social and physical contexts, and whether you and your dog agree or disagree on what you're asking them to do. The list of things you can learn is long, depending on your interests. That's what makes watching dogs so exciting! *See also* **research techniques**.

mental maps. A mental representation of the areas in which a person or animal lives or travels.

mercy killing. *See* **euthanasia**.

mesocephalic. Dog breeds — such as golden retrievers and beagles — with skulls in between dolichocephalic (long-headed dogs) and brachycephalic (broad-headed dogs). *See also* **brachycephalic**; **dolichocephalic**.

metacognition. Thinking about thinking. Metacognition can help people understand their own learning processes. We don't know if dogs and other nonhumans engage in metacognition, but I'd like to know. It wouldn't be surprising to learn that they do because part of being a social animal means understanding what we ourselves and others are thinking. *See also* **theory of mind**.

metacommunication. Communication about communication. Dogs engage in metacommunication as they establish a relationship. For example, if Harry does a play bow directed to Michelle, they both understand that Harry wants to play, and Michelle can decide whether she wants to. Anthropologist, linguist, and social scientist Gregory Bateson first put forth this concept. Actions such as play bows are called metasignals. *See also* **play bows**.

midlife crisis. Do dogs experience anxiety when they realize they aren't as young as they used to be? Some think that dogs do — but it's not known if animals other than humans truly experience these sorts of events.

military dogs. Since ancient times, dogs have been trained and used to carry out military missions, and this continues today. Still, it's a controversial topic. Some people argue it's OK to use dogs in this way, even though they might get harmed or killed, and others are against using dogs in this way. *See also* **bomb-sniffing dogs**.

minding dogs. In my book *Minding Animals*, I use the phrase "minding animals" to refer to two things: (1) the fact that dogs and other nonhumans have active minds, and (2) the need to care for them — to mind them — when they need our help.

mirror recognition. The "mirror test" is a method for researching self-recognition in nonhuman animals. The standard procedure is to place a mark, such as a red dot, on the forehead of an individual when they don't know it's there, then place them in front of a mirror and see if they point or make movements toward the dot. In other words, when they see themselves, do they behave as if asking, *Is that me in the mirror?*

However, for many animals, self-recognition might depend on odors or sounds rather than on visual cues. Dogs typically fail the mirror test, but they show some indication that they know their own urine. They respond differently when they come upon their own urine than when they sniff the urine of other dogs. However, I've been told some interesting, citizen-scientist stories suggesting that some dogs might know they are seeing themselves when looking in a mirror.

When I was talking to a group of students at a class in January 2017, Arianna told a story about her dog Honey.

> One day a few years ago, Honey had been lying with me on my bed. I was wearing these truly awful purple fuzzy socks, and she got some fuzz on her forehead at some point. It was adorable. After a little bit of this, she caught a glance of herself in my mirror and almost immediately reacted. She batted at the fuzz with her front paws until it caught,

> then sat on my stomach until I pulled the fuzz off her paw. Then she went back to the foot of the bed for a few more hours. Honey was really upset but calmed down as soon as she saw the purple was off.. I always just thought of it as a cute, dopey dog story, but I really hope that it will help out your research!

Arianna's story is the best I've heard about a dog paying attention to something on their forehead after seeing it in a mirror. Honey hadn't been observed paying any attention to herself in the mirror previously. This observation comes very close to the more formal, red-dot mirror recognition studies that have been done on nonhuman primates, dolphins, orcas, elephants, birds, and fish.

I hope that Adrianna's observations of Honey motivate people to look for similar behavior in their dogs and for researchers to develop more formal tests that can be used on a wide variety of animals who rely on different sensory modalities. There still is so much more to learn about whether dogs and other animals know "that's me." It's very exciting to learn about the taxonomy of self in nonhuman animals.

Concerning how dogs might use a mirror, researchers Megumi Fukuzawa and Ayano Hasha have shown that some dogs can learn to use mirrors to locate a food reward, though another study showed that dogs weren't very good at using a mirror to find hidden food. *See also* **olfactory recognition**; **self-recognition**.

mislabeling behavior. Mistaking what a dog behavior means. This can occur when a person is not dog literate or fluent in dog, and when someone fails to take context into account. For example, standing over, barking, humping, or growling can mean different things in different situations, ranging from being playful to being assertive or aggressive.

mixed messages. Dogs sometimes send out signals that seem to contradict one another, such as when growling, tail wagging, and bowing at the same time. This composite signal could mean the dog is pissed off, and the bow is simply a stretch. Or depending on the intensity of the growl and how the tail is waving, it could simply mean "let's play."

Mixed messages are confusing to dogs and to us, so always consider context to figure out what a dog really wants to say. *See also* **composite signals**; **play**.

mobbing. When a group of animals band together and approach another individual.

mock fighting. Any rough-and-tumble play fighting. Mock fights are often mistaken for real fighting, and they rarely escalate to serious fighting. Research by Melissa Shyan and her colleagues shows that fewer than 0.5 percent of play fights in dogs developed into conflict, and only half of these were clearly aggressive encounters.

modal action patterns (MAPs). The typical or most common behavioral pattern expressed in response to a stimulus (called a releaser). In classical ethology, the term *fixed action pattern (FAP)* was used to describe behavioral responses, but this term obscures the variation in behavior typically seen within and between individuals. George Barlow, an ethologist who studied fishes, put forth this important idea. Play bows are modal action patterns; they are stereotyped and recognizable, but they're not performed exactly the same each time they're used. *See also* **fixed action patterns (FAPs)**; **play bows**.

mongrel. A mixed-breed dog. *See also* **breed**.

morality in dogs. In the simplest terms, morality refers to social guidelines concerning what is right and wrong or good and bad in our behavior with others. During play, dogs exhibit fairness and follow egalitarian codes of conduct with each other, which is a form of morality. *See also* **fairness**; **golden rules of play**.

moral policing. Do dogs play "moral police" with other dogs? I honestly don't know, but several people have written to me about dogs who watch other dogs play and then break things up when play gets too rough or they sense an ensuing fight. A few have described dogs who routinely break up fights. Personally, I've only seen what I would interpret as dogs breaking up rough-and-tumble play or serious fights on a few occasions, but I can't say why they did it with any certainty. Rather than a sense of justice or morality, perhaps these dogs were jealous of dogs who were playing and wanted to jump in and have a good time, or maybe they were trying to protect a friend. *See also* **fairness**.

Morgan's Canon. A principle for explaining animal behavior coined by British psychologist Conwy Lloyd Morgan. He writes: "In no case is an animal activity to be interpreted in terms of higher psychological processes if it can be fairly interpreted in terms of processes which stand lower in the scale of psychological evolution and development." Basically, in practice, this boils down to explaining behavior as reflexes or conditioned responses and not considering whether cognitive or mental processing is involved. Morgan's Canon was proposed to avoid the pitfalls of anthropomorphism and the use of anecdotes. Those who think that dogs don't think or feel very much, if at all, use it to offer reductionist, mechanistic stimulus-response explanations of behavior. But this can obscure what is going on in a dog's head and heart as they think through a situation and decide: *Should I play with this dog, threaten or fight with them, or hightail it out of here? See also* **Occam's razor**.

mounting. Many people use the terms *mounting* and *humping* interchangeably, but sometimes a dog will mount another dog or someone's leg and not thrust their hips. Males and females will mount members of either sex, and what it means depends on the context — who's the initiator and who's the recipient and where it's happening. Mounting might express interest in mating, dominance, or play, or some reflex might get triggered. *See also* **humping**.

mourning. Dogs grieve and mourn, but it's not clear what they understand. They seem to treat seriously ill and injured individuals differently from how they treat dying and dead individuals. One study showed that dogs who had lost a canine companion showed changes in behavior after the death. They played less, ate less, sought more attention, and slept more. Since this study depended on the use of online questionnaires, there are concerns about the reliability of the reports. Nonetheless, dogs showed behavioral changes at the loss of a canine housemate that related to how friendly the dogs were to one another.

Lots of nonhuman animals display grief and mourning. In *The Last Lions of Africa*, Anthony Ham wrote about the lion Jericho, whose close friend Cecil was killed by a trophy hunter. Ham writes: "It is dangerous to ascribe human emotions to animals, but if you don't believe that animals are capable of emotion, consider this: for nights after his partner was shot and later killed, Jericho roamed the forest, roaring, calling for his friend."

People have sometimes asked me if dogs and other animals might grieve too long or if they would benefit from closure, such as we experience in a wake or funeral. I have no idea, nor is it clear how this could be studied. My impression is that, especially in the wild, nonhumans grieve only up to a point, and then the daily demands of life need attention. I saw this in a pack of wild coyotes in which a mother disappeared, leaving her children and spouse alone. The remaining pack members looked for her for a while and then stopped because they had to do what was needed to survive without her. *See also* **death and dying**.

mouthing. Light chewing. *See also* **jaw wrestling**.

mouth licking. *See* **lip licking**.

movement notation. Aka movement choreography. Using methods developed for analyzing dancing by humans, movement notation displays how animals move their bodies.

movies, dogs in. Dogs have appeared in numerous movies. In a list of one hundred of the most iconic film dogs, the top three are Asta in *The Thin Man*, Lassie in *Lassie Come Home*, and Toto in *The Wizard of Oz*. Then again, for a time, no dog was more famous than Rin Tin Tin, a German shepherd who received votes for Best Actor during the 1929 Academy Awards. Other notable Hollywood canines are the Saint Bernard Beethoven, Old Yeller, and Buddy, a basketball-playing pooch who launched the ridiculous *Air Bud* franchise.

From the perspective of dog-human interactions, dogs in movies also impact the popularity of breeds in what's been dubbed "the dog movie star effect." Hal Herzog called this a "social contagion" — how a famous dog can create huge shifts in that breed's popularity. This occurred with dalmatians after Disney's animated film *One Hundred and One Dalmatians* came out, and also with rough collies after Lassie hit the big screen. Herzog concluded that not only is the dog movie star effect real, but the effects can be surprisingly long-lasting and large. Of course, the bigger the film, and the more people who see it, the bigger the impact, but he also noted that the dog movie star effect appears to be declining more recently. *See also* **breed popularity**.

multiple sires. Aka multiple fathers. In dogs (as well as wolves), it is possible for there to be more than one father for dogs of the same litter.

"musical dogs." A term for when dogs are moved often from home to home, such as when a dog is abandoned, then sent to a shelter, then brought to a new home.

musical preferences. Many people tell me that their dog prefers this or that type of music, ranging from rock and roll to classical piano to opera. Some say that their dog seems to recognize a song from just hearing a note or two. Humans can do this, too, particularly with pop songs they heard during their adolescence. Anticipating what's coming next in a song can activate the brain's reward system, and I wonder if this is so for dogs who have musical preferences.

mutt. A mixed-breed dog. *See also* **breed**.

muzzle. The part of a dog's face that includes the nose and mouth.

muzzle biting. Dogs often use muzzle biting to quiet down pups or other individuals, since it makes them less active and more passive.

myths about dogs. False beliefs and ideas about dogs abound in popular culture — about who dogs are and what they always or never do. While some make for catchy phrases, like "dogs are our best friends," these misrepresentations are harmful, since they mislead us about the real nature of dogs. Here are some of the myths I hope this book helps correct:

- There is a universal, prototype dog.
- Dogs are our best friends.
- Dogs are unconditional lovers.
- Dogs only need food and a warm safe bed and place to rest.
- Dogs don't display dominance.
- Dogs don't feel guilt.
- Dogs live in the present.
- Dogs don't like to be hugged.
- Dogs shouldn't sleep in bedrooms or beds.
- It's OK to give dogs as gifts.
- Dogs are trying to dominate us when we play tug-of-war.
- Peeing is always scent marking.
- Dogs know another dog is the same breed.
- Dogs don't dream.
- All dog parks are bad.

N

naming dogs. I've never quite understood how people choose the names they give their dogs or other companion animals. Some people have told me they chose a name even before they got a dog, and when they finally adopted a dog, the name didn't fit, like a Great Dane named Tiny and a beagle named Brutus.

Zazie Todd and Kristi Benson provide good guidance in a YouTube video entitled "Pets' Names: How to Choose Them, How We Use Them, and How to Change Them." While I think many dogs know their names, sometimes my dogs responded to other names spoken with the same intonation. I never changed the name of a rescued dog, but when I've asked people who have, they don't think their dog had any sort of identity crisis. Most people with whom I've talked think that the name of a dog says more about their human than the dog.

narcolepsy. Dogs can be narcoleptic, or have difficulty staying awake during daytime. But this isn't all that unusual or problematic because their wild relatives can rest up to around 90 percent of a day depending on what's happening. Of course, if this seems to indicate that a dog isn't feeling well, see a veterinarian.

natal dispersal. Leaving the place where an individual was born. Of course, this doesn't apply to homed dogs, but some free-ranging or feral dogs do leave the place where they were born, just as do their wild relatives. When an individual leaves, it is not necessarily because they are forced out by other group members; rather, they may leave of their own accord because they're unable to form social bonds with other group members. It may be because they're avoided because they don't play fair and are assumed to be cheaters, or because they themselves avoid others. This is called the "social cohesion" hypothesis.

Knowledge of the behavioral interactions that occur before dispersal may provide a key to understanding dispersal patterns. Research shows that individuals who have the most difficulty interacting with littermates will not develop strong social ties with their siblings and will be the most likely individuals to disperse of their own accord. This hypothesis is testable by collecting data on the social interaction patterns of individual littermates throughout early development and during dispersal. In this way, the importance of a heretofore neglected factor in dispersal — namely, the relationship between the behavioral antecedents of dispersal and which individuals disperse at what age, and in what manner — can be assessed.

National Pet Month. May.

natural death. People wonder what a "natural" death for domestic dogs is. For homed dogs with good home care, it would be euthanasia when they're interminably ill or suffering from interminable pain. For free-ranging or feral dogs, it would be peacefully dying of old age.

natural selection. Obviously, the domestic dog is the result of artificial selection (or selective breeding), and it will be interesting to see what will happen if, or when, free-ranging or feral dogs return to a process of natural selection. This is something Jessica Pierce and I consider in our book *A Dog's World.*

This entry summarizes natural selection among wild animals. I find this definition by *National Geographic* to be as good as they get:

> Natural selection is the process through which populations of living organisms adapt and change. Individuals in a population are naturally variable, meaning that they are all different in some ways. This variation means that some individuals have traits better suited to the environment than others. Individuals with adaptive traits — traits that give them some advantage — are more likely to survive and reproduce. These individuals then pass the adaptive traits on to their offspring. Over time, these advantageous traits become more common in the population. Through this process of natural selection, favorable traits are transmitted through generations.

Biologists generally categorize different forms of natural selection as stabilizing, directional, or disruptive/diversifying. *Stabilizing selection* is the most common form of natural selection, and it refers to "a type of natural selection in which genetic diversity decreases and the population mean stabilizes on a particular trait value." That is, selection settles on an average value that most individuals display, such as for size, speed, or color, for example. Dog breeders generally practice artificial stabilizing selection when they try to produce dogs to satisfy rigorous breed standards.

Directional selection is selection away from the average values to extremes for different traits. For example, selection that favors smushed or long faces; running speed that is slower or faster than others; color that is duller or brighter; or extremes in weight. There are very few examples of directional selection in nature.

Finally, *disruptive or diversifying selection* occurs when extreme behavioral or physical traits — like running slowly or rapidly, or being very large or very small — are advantageous over what would be considered the intermediate or average ranges for the animal. For free-ranging dogs or feral dogs, differences in running speed or size could both be advantageous or disadvantageous depending on where they're living, the nature of their diets, and who else is around with whom they would cooperate or compete. *See also* **artificial selection**; **domestication**.

neonatal behavior. Behavior expressed around and soon after birth. When used by adults, these behaviors are called derived activities. *See also* **derived activities; infantile behavior**.

neophilia and neophobia. Neophilia is attraction to novelty or new situations, and neophobia is fear of novelty.

neoteny. A delay in the physiological or behavioral development of an animal, as well as the retention of juvenile traits into adulthood. For example, puppies have the cute "puppy dog" look, floppy ears, and round forehead that can get others to care for them. *See also* **domestication syndrome**; **paedomorphism**.

neuroimaging. Aka functional Magnetic Resonance Imaging (fMRI). Neuroimaging measures small changes in blood flow that occur when the brain is active. It provides a window into dogs' minds by being able to see the changes that occur in the brain as dogs experience various emotions, and we can compare this brain activity with what happens in ourselves and other animals.

In an interview with neuroscientist Gregory Berns about the use of fMRI to study the inner lives of dogs and other animals, he told me: "For many years, academics have tended to avoid the question of the subjective experience of a nonhuman animal because it has generally been thought to be unanswerable. This has allowed scientists to side-step the moral question of whether it is OK to use animals in medical research. When we see similar brain processes occurring in these animals, it becomes harder to ignore. And it isn't just dogs: Every week, I read about discoveries on the sophisticated cognitive abilities of other animals. Certainly, they aren't automatons, like Descartes thought."

neutering. Removing sex organs to make individuals sterile; also called desexing and "fixing." Neutering is often recommended in the United States for two reasons: to avoid unwanted pregnancies and to make dogs less aggressive. However, there is much debate about whether neutering dogs is necessary in either case. While desexing renders dogs sterile and unable to produce children, there's no consensus on whether it actually makes individuals less aggressive or less likely to roam.

We must take responsibility for the dogs for whose existence we are responsible, and we need to come to terms with the fact that neutering them far too often is more for us than for them. Neutering is not a panacea for fixing behavioral problems such as aggressiveness, and it is important to note that neutering doesn't have any clear effect on trainability. In her book *Run, Spot, Run: The Ethics of Keeping Pets*, Jessica Pierce offers more discussion about these and other similar ethical issues. She writes, "Spay/neuter is the mantra of veterinarians, the nation's humane organizations, and the majority of animal activists."

In a *New York Times* essay titled, "Dogs Are Not Here for Our Convenience," Alexandra Horowitz notes that castrating dogs isn't standard operating procedure in Europe. She writes, "Until recently, it was illegal to desex a dog in Norway. Only 7 percent of Swedish dogs are desexed (compared with more than 80 percent in the United States). Switzerland has a clause in its Animal Protection Act honoring the 'dignity of the animal,' and forbidding any pain, suffering, or harm, such as would be incurred by desexing. Yet none of these countries has a problem with excessive stray dogs." Horowitz also shows how fixing dogs not only changes their anatomy but also their behavior and susceptibility to contracting various diseases.

I've conducted many workshops on the cognitive and emotional lives of dogs throughout Europe, and I've always been impressed by how many intact dogs, male and female, can easily get along with one another even when they first meet. On two occasions I wasn't sure what to expect when I was told by my hosts that most, if not all, of the dogs I would meet weren't fixed. Frankly, I was somewhat surprised and pleased by how well they all got along. On one occasion there were more than fifty dogs, and aside from a very few brief minor scuffles, none of whom were especially assertive or aggressive, everything was pretty calm. My narrow views based on what I'd been told on this side of the Atlantic weren't supported, and I was thrilled to experience this lesson up close and personal. *See also* **castrating**; **spaying**.

no-kill shelters. A term for animal shelters where killing residents is not an option and never done.

normalizing dog behavior. This refers to thinking there is some sort of prototype "normal" or "universal" dog who can be used as an example for *all* dogs. Research shows there is no universal or prototype dog. Believing the various myths that all dogs do this or that leads people to believe that there must be something wrong with their dog if they don't do these things. *See also* **myths about dogs**.

nose fatigue. A "tired" nose that is habituated to an odor.

noses. As Frank Rosell's book *Secrets of the Snout* summarizes it: "With 300 million receptors to our mere 5 million, a dog's nose is estimated to be between 100,000 and 100 million times more sensitive than a human's." In fact, there is a lot of variability in the sensitivity of dogs' noses. Claims that a dog's nose is more sensitive than a human nose by some specific ratio isn't always very accurate. Nonetheless, dogs' noses are far more sensitive than ours, in part because the section of a dog's brain related to processing smells is almost seven times larger than ours. Dogs' noses are amazing organs that are virtual works of art.

The dog's fantastic sense of smell can be explained by the fact that dogs don't exhale when sniffing a faint scent. This enables the dog to sniff faint odors without disturbing or destroying them. Dogs have a winglike flap in each nostril that determines the direction of the airstream in and out of the nose. When the dog inhales, an opening above and beside this flap allows air to pass through. When the dog exhales, this opening closes and the air comes out below and beside this flap through another opening, enabling the dog to increase its collection of odors. As a result, the warm air that is exhaled flows backward and away from the odor being sniffed, preventing them from mixing. Dogs also use their nostrils differently according to the nature of the scent. During behavioral trials, when dogs sniffed at unfamiliar smells that were not dangerous, first they used the right nostril and then switched to the left nostril to sniff at the odors again. Once they had become familiar with the smell, the left side of the brain took over. When they sniffed sweat odors from veterinarians who worked at a kennel, they used only the right nostril. In short, the left and right sides of the brain take in different kinds of information. The right side of the brain is associated with intense feelings, such as aggression, flight behavior, and fear. For most dogs, a veterinarian is a frightening person.

It's a very exciting time to study and learn about how other animals sense the world. This information tells us more about the choices they make, how distinct their sensory capacities are from one another's, and how foreign they are from ours. *See also* **heat detection**; **olfactory recognition**; **smell**.

nosing. Sniffing when greeting and checking out another dog, a human, or nature.

numerosity. Aka number sense. This refers to the ability to assess the quantity of items without actually counting them. An interesting example comes from research on free-ranging dogs living outside of Rome. Roberto Bonanni and his colleagues discovered that free-ranging dogs living in small packs in a suburban environment are able to assess the number of opponents during intergroup conflicts with other dogs. *See also* **counting**; **subitizing**.

O

obesity. Obesity, being very fat or overweight, is a major health threat for numerous homed dogs. Some call it a global crisis, even an epidemic. The bottom line is that far too many dogs are overfed, many commercial foods aren't very good, and they aren't suited for all dogs.

Different breeds are not significantly more prone to being obese. Rather, overweight dogs show similar personality traits displayed by overweight humans, such as impulsivity. Further, feeding dogs as if they're wolves could be part of the problem. A *New York Times* article entitled, "Do Wild Dogs Sleep as Much as Your Pets?" states, "When wolves are active, they are really active. On a daily basis, wolves burn about 70 percent more calories compared to typical animals of similar size. The researchers note that while hunting, wolves may burn calories at 10 to 20 times the rate they do while resting." Dogs aren't wolves, they aren't marginally as active as wolves, and feeding them as if they're wolves is a misguided practice. *See also* **diet**.

object permanence. Knowing something still exists even when it can't be seen. Object permanence is an ecologically relevant measure of dog cognition, since dogs and other animals must be able to track objects when they disappear from sight. Dogs have done well in some studies of object permanence, but like in other research on dog cognition, results vary from lab to lab depending on who the dogs are and the tests that are used.

I've seen object permanence among dogs at dog parks and on hiking trails. One day when I was at a local dog park, three dogs were playing fetch when one of their humans was throwing a tennis ball. On a few occasions, the ball rolled behind a rock. While one of the dogs stopped in his tracks and began looking, unsure where the ball went, two of the dogs didn't break stride and ran to the opposite end of the rock. Invariably, one picked it up on the run and returned to the human, dropped it at her feet, and immediately turned around waiting for it to be airborne once again. I've also seen similar scenes among wild coyotes when playing what looked to be hide-and-seek. *See also* **ecological relevance**.

Occam's razor. This term refers to choosing the simplest explanation for some phenomenon, including behavior. Many people think it was originally stated by William of Ockham in the early 1300s; however, others had argued for the "keep it simple" rule before him. Like

Morgan's Canon, in practice, this concept is often used as a rationale for explaining behavior patterns as conditioned reflexes, while ignoring or denying that animals actually think and have feelings that influence what they do. *See also* **Morgan's Canon**.

odor preferences. Not much is known about the odors that dogs prefer. In my experience, there are widespread individual differences. One study showed that dogs interacted the most with scents of blueberry, blackberry, mint, rose, lavender, and linalool, which is a terpene alcohol found in flowers and spice plants and is used in soaps, detergents, and shampoos. From time to time I offered different sorts of scents to my dogs and their canine friends, and I couldn't detect any real preferences — other than the more disgusting or putrid I thought a particular odor was, the more attention they paid to it. Of course, my labeling an odor is far different from theirs, so what I thought was putrid, they thought was attractive and vice versa. On a number of occasions my dogs would roll in a deer carcass and parade around proudly as if they were the predators who killed the deer. They would try to rub it on me, and I couldn't get away from them fast enough, but their dog friends seemed to want to hang out with them and savor the odors. *See also* **rolling in stinky stuff**.

olfactory recognition. Recognizing another individual or oneself using odor cues. I and other researchers have long been interested in the question, "Do dogs know themselves by what their urine smells like?"

Years ago, I did what has come to be called the "yellow snow" experiment. While taking Jethro on his daily walk, I did a study of his sniffing and urination patterns. To learn about the role of urine in eliciting sniffing and urinating, I moved urine-saturated snow ("yellow snow") from place to place during five winters to compare Jethro's responses to his own and other dog's urine. Immediately after Jethro or other known males or females urinated on snow, I scooped up a small clump of the yellow snow in gloves and moved it to different locations. For some reason, passersby thought I was strange and generally left me alone, but one wrote a letter to the editor of the local paper inquiring who this "nutball" was. Usually, when I explained to people what I was doing, they were very interested and wanted to know more.

Moving yellow snow was a useful and novel method for discovering that Jethro spent less time sniffing his own urine than that of other males or females. Other researchers have also noted that male dogs (and coyotes and wolves) spend more time sniffing the urine from other males compared to their own urine. Dogs also usually spend more time sniffing urine from females in heat compared to urine from males or reproductively inactive females.

When Jethro arrived at displaced urine, he infrequently urinated over or sniffed and then immediately urinated over ("scent marked") his own urine, but he sniffed and then immediately scent marked the displaced urine significantly more when it was from other males than when it was from females. Also, while his interest in his own urine waned with time, it remained relatively constant for other individuals' urine. Does this mean that Jethro recognized himself? I'm not sure. I concluded that Jethro clearly had some sense of "self," a sense of "mine-ness," but not necessarily of "I-ness," and it's not surprising that odor played a large role. Mirror recognition is not the only show in town for learning about what animals know about themselves, especially for animals who aren't dominated by visual input.

Other researchers have refined the "yellow snow" methodology, and more work needs to be done in this area. In her book *Being a Dog: Following the Dog into a World of Smell*, Alexandra Horowitz writes about the results of a more systematic study of self-recognition with dogs in her cognition laboratory. She notes that the dogs "peed only on other dogs' containers, not their own. They saw themselves." *See also* **mirror recognition**; **self-recognition**; **yellow snow**.

One Health Initiative. This program stresses that we must be concerned with the well-being of all humans, nonhumans, and ecosystems. If we harm one, we harm them all. Some people think that One Health doesn't go far enough because nonhumans are often valued for the sake of humans, and they argue that other animals should have their own right to health.

one-zero sampling. Recording when a behavior does and does not occur during a set amount of time. This method doesn't yield much information, but often it's the only way to learn some of what animals are doing when they can't be seen regularly or in which it's difficult to reliably identify individuals over time. *See also* **research techniques**.

onychectomy. Aka declawing. Dogs are rarely declawed unless there is a health issue, such as an infection or a severe injury. Declawing for other reasons should be strongly discouraged.

operant conditioning. Also called instrumental conditioning. Operant conditioning occurs when the consequences of doing something — whether it is rewarded or punished — influences the likelihood of doing it again. B. F. Skinner championed this method of learning. *See also* **clicker training**.

overmarking. This refers to dogs peeing or occasionally pooping over the pee or poop of another dog, which is often done to mask its odor. *See also* **pissing matches**.

oxytocin. A neurotransmitter often called the "love hormone." Levels of oxytocin often correlate with positive feelings and social attachment. Petting a dog increases oxytocin in both the human and the dog, and dogs who gaze at their humans longer show higher levels of oxytocin than dogs who don't gaze as long. Much more research is needed, but one study found that service dogs with placid temperaments had significantly higher levels of oxytocin in their blood than non-service dogs.

P

pacing. Just as we do, dogs pace for various reasons. Pacing can indicate stress or discomfort, or it may just mean a dog is stretching, looking for something or someone, or is antsy and aimlessly wandering around.

pack formation. Free-ranging and feral dogs form groups that work like wolf and coyote packs, and so too will posthuman dogs after we're gone. Packs are typically composed of a mated pair, their children from the most recent or an earlier litter, and some individuals who join who are not genetically related (or thought not to be). Group members work together to obtain and defend their territory (home), to get and defend food, and to raise youngsters (called cooperative breeding). It's misleading for humans to think they're "the leader of their dog pack" and to dominate dogs, as leadership among dogs is often maintained by nonaggressive or nonassertive actions. *See also* **alpha dog**; **dominance**.

paedomorphism. The retention of juvenile characteristics as an adult. *See also* **domestication syndrome**; **neoteny**; **puppy dog eyes**.

painting. Do dogs paint? Some apparently do — usually by holding a brush in their mouth, but also by using their own paint-covered paws. I have no idea what the dogs are thinking or feeling. One "dog-Vinci" can be seen in the YouTube video "Talented Painting Dog."

pair bond. A relationship between a reproductively active male and female. With dogs, this may include flirting, courtship, and mating, and pair bonds can last for years through many mating cycles.

pandemic puppies. Puppies born and adopted during the Covid-19 pandemic. During 2020 and 2021, as more people worked from home, dog adoptions rose. It's estimated that around 20 percent of American households adopted a companion animal during the pandemic, but they turned out to be mixed blessings. Many people were faced with radical changes in their schedules, and not only were there deep concerns about the well-being of their new pets, but a lot of pandemic dogs were subsequently abandoned. *See also* **adopting a dog**.

panting. Short quick breaths or being out of breath. Panting may mean a dog is hot, stressed, or exhausted and simply blowing off steam.

pasta. Dogs who like pasta can eat it because they have the alpha-amylase gene. This enzyme is found mainly in saliva and pancreatic fluid and converts starch and glycogen into simple sugars.

Pavlov, Ivan. A Russian physiologist. Pavlov was known for his research on classical conditioning, showing among other things that dogs salivate when expecting food. *See also* **classical conditioning**.

pawing. Feeling or scraping with a paw. Sometimes face pawing is used to appease or pacify.

paw licking. Also called paw chewing. This can indicate a lot of different things — allergies, soreness due to an irritant, poor gut health, poor dog food and nutritional deficiencies, stress, or none of the above. If paw licking seems excessive and the dog seems upset or out of sorts, see a veterinarian.

peeing. Dogs urinate both to simply empty their bladders (elimination) and to intentionally mark a particular spot and communicate with other dogs. Since urine can have a negative effect on soil chemistry, people need to be careful about where they allow dogs to pee. *See also* **pee-mail**; **scent marking**.

peeing and the size of a dog. A paper called "Urine Marking in Male Domestic Dogs: Honest or Dishonest?" described research that found that small dogs try to exaggerate their size when peeing. Previous research showed that small dogs urinate more than large dogs, perhaps indicating a preference for scent marking over direct interactions that could be risky. The researchers hypothesized that small male dogs would benefit more than large male dogs from exaggerating their size, and so they predicted small dogs would raise their legs higher (or at a higher angle) in proportion to their size than larger males in order to leave higher urine marks. Indeed, small dogs did just that, meaning they were being dishonest and exaggerating their size. Does this mean small dogs have a "little dog complex"?

Who'd have thought that small dogs might intentionally make

themselves "look" bigger by peeing at unexpected heights? There really is so much to learn about dogs.

pee-mail. A deposit of pee that communicates to other dogs. Pee can contain all sorts of information about who was there, how they were feeling, whether a female is in heat, and where the dog was heading. *See also* **scent marking.**

personality. Individual dogs have unique personalities, but breeds, taken as a whole, do not. Dog-human relationships have their own unique personalities as well.

Dogs display what are called the "big five" personality traits: extraversion/energy, agreeableness/affection, conscientiousness, neuroticism, and openness/intelligence. The results of one study showed that more extroverted, open, and conscientious dogs tended to be more dominant, whereas friendlier, more agreeable dogs usually rank lower. Additionally, in multidog households, older dogs are usually dominant.

Psychologist Michael Matthews studied dog personalities and learned that some of the twenty-four character traits described by positive psychologists for humans may also apply to dogs, including bravery, persistence, leadership, love, social intelligence, self-regulation, gratitude, a sense of humor, and jealousy.

While many people seem to think that dogs are always "up" and ready to bound around without a care in the word, this really isn't so. Anyone who's rescued a dog with a history of abuse, or spends time around a variety of dogs, knows some dogs are "uppers" and some are "downers." A very interesting and important 2014 study entitled "Canine Sense and Sensibility" shows clearly that not only might personality affect the way dogs see the world and how they behave, but also how positive or negative their current mood is. As one of the researchers noted, "The remarkable power of this [research] is the opportunity to essentially ask a dog 'How are you feeling?' and get an answer. It could be used to monitor their welfare in any environment, to assess how effective enrichment activities might be in improving welfare, and pinpoint exactly what a dog finds emotionally distressing." *See also* **breedism**; **character traits**.

personhood. A legal status granted only to humans. Led by lawyer Steven Wise and the Nonhuman Rights Project, an increasing number of people would like to grant the legal protections of personhood to certain nonhuman animals, including dogs.

Generally, the criteria for "personhood" include being conscious of one's surroundings, being able to reason, being able to experience various emotions, having a sense of self, adjusting to changing situations, and performing various cognitive and intellectual tasks. While most human beings fulfill these criteria, not all do. Some humans, such as young infants and seriously psychologically challenged adults, fail to exhibit one or more of these abilities, and yet they're also rightfully considered to be persons under the law.

What about animal beings, such as my late companion dog Jethro? He was very active, could feed and groom himself, was very emotional, and even cared for injured animals. Jethro was as autonomous as a dog could be. Yet many people wouldn't feel comfortable calling Jethro or other nonhuman animals a "person." This irreverence is a prime example of just what's wrong with academic musings! *See also* **agency**; **legal status**.

perspective taking. Can dogs take the perspective of another dog or a human and understand what they're thinking or feeling? That is, do they possess a theory of mind? Some people argue that dogs don't have the cognitive capacities for this, whereas others argue they do, at least in a rudimentary way. My view is dogs can understand the perspective of other dogs and humans, but confirming this requires more studies and data from free-ranging dogs. One study showed that dogs knew when humans could see them taking food near a barrier, and they took more when the human experimenter couldn't see them. *See also* **human gaze, dogs following**; **theory of mind**.

pet. The common term for a domesticated animal kept by humans for companionship, entertainment, or support. Some feel the term *companion animal* is more respectful of animals than *pet*.

"pet effect paradox." The "pet effect" is the claim that getting a companion animal automatically improves a person's life — emotionally, mentally, and physically. While there is research that provides evidence of a "pet effect" in some ways and to some degree, this isn't universally true. Thus, as researcher Hal Herzog puts it, the "pet effect paradox" occurs when "what we want to believe about pets does not always jibe with the results of empirical research."

For instance, Herzog carefully summarized the results of a large study that focused on the effects of living with a pet, including dogs. He writes, "After statistically adjusting for demographic and socioeconomic differences, there was *no evidence that pet owners were physically or psychologically better off* than people who did not have a companion animal in their lives.... Neither dog nor cat ownership was associated with the participants' general health status [and] depression was twice as common in pet owners as nonowners. This was true of both dog owners and cat owners."

While some people believe their lives are vastly improved by having a dog, some people don't, and that doesn't mean there is something wrong with the person or the dog. Companion animals are not feel-good pills, every relationship is different, and the animal's experience matters, too. So it's best not to adopt companion animals solely to improve one's mental health, since the well-being of everyone, dogs and people, matters. *See also* **hedonic treadmill**.

pet holocaust. At the start of World War II, fear over food shortages led the British government to recommend killing pet dogs and cats, which led to 750,000 dogs and cats being put down in Britain.

PETS Act. In the United States, the Pets Evacuation and Transportation Standards (PETS) Act authorizes FEMA to provide rescue, care, shelter, and essential needs for individuals with household pets and service animals, and to the household pets and animals themselves following a major disaster or emergency.

petting. Aka patting, stroking, or otherwise touching a dog. Not only do most homed dogs enjoy being petted, so do free-ranging dogs. However, not all dogs like being petted, or not all the time, so if a dog doesn't want to be touched, don't do it. *See also* **hugging**; **oxytocin**.

pheromones. Secretions, usually smelly chemicals, that are used to communicate various messages and emotional states. *See also* **allomones**; **scent marking**.

pica. An eating disorder in which an individual eats nonfood items. Dogs, as well as people, suffer from this condition, which can include eating toxic items that may be viewed as food, such as lead-based paint, drywall, and so on.

piloerection. *See* **hackles**.

pissing matches. A more colloquial term for countermarking, overmarking, or marking over, when a dog pees over another dog's urine. Pissing matches are a form of canine conversation, but we don't know what the dogs are really talking about.

I've seen hundreds if not thousands of pissing matches during the enormous amount of time I've spent at dog parks and watching dogs pass one another on leash. While most pissing matches take place outdoors, this is not always the case.

A few years ago, my cycling teammate John Talley and his wife Tyla told me about an ongoing pissing match between their two dogs, Rigby and Bodie. Bodie is Rigby's father, but Rigby joined the Talley household first. Once Rigby was nicely settled in, Bodie arrived, and soon after, Bodie started peeing in the house. Even though Rigby was already house-trained, once Bodie started peeing inside, Rigby did, too. Plus, it turns out that Rigby always has to have the last pee, and he will pee right in front of Tyla. No shame there!

In addition, Bodie will ground scratch after peeing, and this has become part of their ongoing pissing contest. Tyla told me that Rigby never ground scratched before Bodie came along, and now Rigby does it regularly, even if Bodie isn't around.

Is this a territorial battle? Is Bodie just doing what dogs do in a new habitat, and is Rigby, into whose home Bodie intruded, just "defending" his place? I honestly don't know. Scent-marking expert Anne Lisberg notes, and I agree, that it's a testament to dogs' social skills that so many dogs are thrown together at our whim, and they are able to work out sharing space in a home without resorting to pissing matches or duking it out. What might be most remarkable is how rare the Rigby-Bodie countermarking contest really is! *See also* **peeing**; **pee-mail**.

play. There are different forms of play, such as social, object, and self-play. Examples of self-play include tail chasing, throwing a rag or ball into the air and catching it, and using a tool to move an object; even chewing can be playful. Throwing a rag is also an example of object play, which becomes social when it involves tug-of-war or playing catch with a person who throws a ball or Frisbee. Social play among dogs is an activity directed toward another individual in which actions from different contexts — fighting, preying, mating — are used in different forms and sequences.

Individual dogs have different play styles and play differently, and I've seen dogs work out their differences and play seamlessly because each dog knows what the other wants to do and how they like to play. Play is both serious business and a lot of fun. Play is also all about improvisation. Play looks like a messy behavior, and it can be. It's inherently variable, using a hodgepodge of actions from various other contexts. In other words, every dog improvises in their own way, and as I've said many times, play makes messes of our prescriptive theories of why dogs do this or that when they romp around with their friends.

John Byers and I have defined play as "all motor activity performed postnatally that appears to have no obvious immediate benefits for the player, in which the motor patterns resembling those used in serious functional contexts may be used in modified forms. The motor acts constituting play have some or all of the following structural features:

exaggeration of movements, repetition of motor acts, and fragmentation or disordering of sequences of motor acts." Some actions also are not performed for the same amount of time during play or as vigorously as they are when animals are not playing.

In *The Genesis of Animal Play*, Gordon Burghardt defines play as follows: "Play is repeated behavior that is incompletely functional in the context or at the age in which it is performed and is initiated voluntarily when the animal or person is in a relaxed or low-stress setting."

These definitions center on what animals *do* when they play; in other words, they identify the structure of the behaviors that define play — what they look like and how they're assembled — rather than focusing on the possible functions of play. So why do dogs play? Why has it evolved and what's it good for? There are several reasons why dogs (and other animals) play. They include *socialization*, or forming social bonds; *physical training*, such as developing bones, tendons, muscles, and joints; *cognitive training*; and training for the unexpected because play offers a diversity of forms in which sequences of behavior are highly variable. Play can also be thought of as "brain food," in that it stimulates various parts of the brain.

I often say, animals who play together stay together, and this seems to be generally so for social carnivores. Possible functions of play are not mutually exclusive, and it's unlikely that there's one reason dogs and other animals play.

Play also is fun. Most dogs love to play and will seek it out and keep playing until they drop — and then play immediately once again. If something is important to do for survival and if it's fun, it's more likely that it will be retained in the animal's behavioral repertoire. If it's not fun, then it won't be sought out.

That said, some dogs don't like to play very much, just as there are individual play styles — some dogs like to chase others or be chased, some like to wrestle, and some like everything. When you play with your dog, let them choose how to have fun with you.

In September 2021, I received an interesting email from someone after reading *Canine Confidential*. They wrote:

In *Canine Confidential*, you talk so much about how dogs play. My dog hardly ever plays. Should I worry about it? He'll play with his toys maybe once a week for a couple minutes. He is really aloof when other dogs want to play. Unless it is a specific shih tzu from the neighborhood he sees every couple of months. Then it's like he doesn't know what to do. Is there anything I can do to help him?

Of course, I can't really address specific dogs or specific issues without seeing what's happening in person — or "in dog." But in theory, there is nothing at all "wrong" with a dog who is uninterested in play. This could be related to their development from when they were puppies, a bad play experience, their age, and so on. I've known some dogs who weren't players and had great lives. So long as the dog is an otherwise happy hound, there is nothing to worry about.

Age definitely impacts how much dogs play. Youngsters usually play more than older dogs, but adults will play when they can and are free to blow off steam, such as when they don't have to care for youngsters or get and defend food or space. Wild adult coyotes and wolves also play when they can, but far less frequently than youngsters.

When dogs play, they can send out mixed signals, and that is why it's essential to know about the *context* in which different actions are used. When my students and I study play, we analyze single movie frames one at a time (called frame-by-frame film analysis) to get the details we need about what the dogs are doing — the actions they perform, how long they last, and how vigorously they're playing.

People often ask me how well dogs read one another when large groups are running around like they're in a daze. While no one has carefully studied this yet, it seems as if they do it pretty well. Research of dogs during play and other contexts finds low levels of escalation and the rapid-fire exchange of signals — those cocktails of composite signals — contain a lot of information about what is happening and what is likely to happen.

Some of our data show two somewhat different conclusions. One is that group size doesn't seem to be a factor in the extremely rare occasions when play escalates into fighting or aggression. There is no real difference comparing groups of two, three, four, five, or more dogs.

Yet we've also noticed that play in large groups breaks down more rapidly than play in smaller groups. This happens not because play escalates into aggression but, rather, because the dogs can't always read one another as well in large groups, so play ends before a fight might ensue.

I'm hoping that, as this study continues, more data will clarify just what is happening. Elisabetta Palagi and her colleagues have data that suggest that dogs maintain a play mood based on rapid mimicry and emotional contagion, a building block of empathy, but perhaps these things break down in large groups of dogs.

An interesting aspect of Dr. Palagi's study is that "the distribution of rapid mimicry was strongly affected by the familiarity linking the subjects: the stronger the social bonding, the higher the level of rapid mimicry." This supports the conclusions of Alexandra's science-fair project (which I described in the "citizen science" entry): Familiar dogs play more quickly and roughly than unfamiliar dogs, who take more time to get to know the dog with whom they are about to play by doing more sniffing and nose bumping. Simply put, it would be wonderful if someone studied play and group size in more detail. *See also* **citizen science**; **fun**; **golden rules of play**.

play bows. Bowing occurs when a dog crouches down on their forelegs while keeping their hindlegs straight or slightly bent. Barking and tail wagging may accompany bows. Play bows are usually used to initiate social play, as well as to maintain a play mood during play. The bow tells playmates something like, *I didn't mean to bite you so hard, let's keep playing*, or *I'm going to bite you, but it's only in play*. Using well-placed bows that punctuate ongoing play can help maintain the "golden rules of play," which is a commitment to play fair. Fair play requires dogs to stick to mutually agreed-upon codes of conduct.

In a study of play bows, researcher Sarah-Elizabeth Byosiere found that play bows most often occurred after a brief pause in play. Synchronous behaviors by the bower and the partner, or vulnerable/escape behaviors by the bower (such as running away) and complementary offensive behaviors by the partner (such as chasing) occurred most often after the play bow. These results indicate that during adult play, play bows function to reinitiate play after a pause rather than to mediate offensive or ambiguous actions. *See also* **fairness**; **golden rules of play**.

play face. A facial expression in dogs characterized by a relaxed open mouth and often panting.

play fighting. *See* **mock fighting**.

play panting. Rapid breathing during play. Panting might be a play signal or have something to do with what dogs "say" to one another when they play. *See also* **laughing**.

play scents. A type of pheromone that is unique to play. Bank voles who live along the River Thames in England emit a play scent from the skin at the back of their head that can stimulate play in other voles. There is no evidence that dogs do this, but we don't know either way.

play wiggle. When a dog lies on their stomach and slowly creeps or slides toward a potential play partner. Often when they're slinking, their tail is slowly wagging or going up and down.

pointing. When a dog stands still with one forepaw raised while looking intently at something. Hunting dogs have been bred to point, but other dogs can be trained to do so.

pooping along Earth's magnetic field. Dogs may use their magnetic sense as a compass in order to decide where to poop. I have to admit that I was a bit skeptical when I first heard about this study, but the data support the conclusions. A two-year analysis of more than seventy dogs from thirty-seven breeds showed that our furry friends "preferred to excrete with the body being aligned along the north-south axis under calm MF [magnetic field] conditions." When the MF was thrown out of whack, the dogs were "less picky about their crapping preferences."

population of dogs worldwide. It's very difficult to know how many dogs there are in the world. The generally accepted estimate is a billion dogs. Getting a handle on where they live, and the diversity of their living arrangements, is even more challenging. Several sources put the number of free-ranging dogs living mainly or entirely on their own at around 80 percent, while about 20 percent of the world's dogs live as companion animals or homed dogs, aka pets. If those percentages are correct, then there are about 800 million free-ranging dogs (including stray, street, village, privately owned but free-running, and feral dogs) and about 200 million homed dogs. However, Darcy Morey believes that only about 15 percent of the world's dogs are homed, while Andrew Rowan believes the percentage of homed dogs is closer to 50 percent, though his estimate includes dogs who are "homeless" and living in the shelter system. Either way, many people are surprised to learn that such a small percentage of dogs are actually homed dogs.

When asked, "What is the dog's natural habitat?" many people — scholars and dog guardians alike — typically answer, "The human home, of course." But clearly, fewer dogs live in homes than do not.

positive training. Teaching or educating dogs using force-free positive reinforcement — "soft" methods — rather than punishment, such as reprimanding or shocking them. Swedish psychologist Anders Hallgren says: "What you would not dream of doing to your child, you should not do to your dog." *See also* **training**.

posthuman dogs. In our book *A Dog's World*, Jessica Pierce and I explore what might happen to dogs, and how they might adapt, in a world without humans. We propose that three different classes of dogs will emerge:

- **Transition dogs:** Dogs who are alive when humans disappear and who have had some level of human contact. After approximately fifteen years, there will be no more transition dogs.
- **First-generation dogs:** Dogs born to mothers who had contact with humans. After roughly thirty years, there will be no more first-generation dogs.
- **Later-generation dogs:** Truly posthuman dogs.

post-traumatic stress disorder (PTSD). A condition in humans and nonhumans, including dogs, who have been abused or who have experienced or witnessed extremely upsetting, stressful, and traumatic events. Some symptoms include not eating, pacing, sleeping problems, fear, watchfulness, being easily startled, aggression or rage, and lack of interest in play.

precautionary principle. This decision-making principle suggests that when knowledge is incomplete or scientific evidence is uncertain about whether using a technology or taking an action might cause harm, people should proceed cautiously or not take action until more is known. For example, I believe that, while we may not know everything that goes on in an animal's or a dog's mind and heart, we know enough about the emotional lives of animals to protect them more than we do.

I believe, if we abide by the precautionary principle, we can bridge the knowledge translation gap around animal sentience and improve conservation efforts and the lives of nonhuman animals in many situations, including in our homes. Any doubt about what animals understand should make us more cautious about causing harm, not less.

As the article "The Precautionary Principle in Environmental Science" states, the precautionary principle has "four central components: taking preventive action in the face of uncertainty; shifting the burden of proof to the proponents of an activity; exploring a wide range of alternatives to possibly harmful actions; and increasing public participation in decision making."

Simply put, the "golden rule" of the precautionary principle is to first do no harm. This applies to medicine and to scientific decisions in general, and it should apply to any situation in which human action could cause pain and suffering to other beings. First do no harm is one of the foundational principles of compassionate conservation, which also includes individuals matter, value all wildlife, and peaceful coexistence.

While the precautionary principle is directly relevant to conservation and animal welfare in agriculture and industry, and many other arenas, we can also embody it with our companion animals and the animals we meet in our daily lives. Use it to take the best care you can of the dogs and other animals who share your life. *See also* **compassionate conservation**; **knowledge translation gap**.

precocial. An animal born in an advanced stage of development and able to get around by themselves. Ungulates such as deer and elk produce precocial young who can locomote along with the adults, although they're not as coordinated or as fast. This is important for avoiding being left behind and eaten by predators. *See also* **altricial**.

predatory behavior. Like wolves, dogs are predators, and predatory behavior includes looking for animals to eat, chasing and taking them down, and killing and eating them. Free-ranging and feral dogs can kill other animals. However, because of domestication, dogs have modified certain predatory behaviors, like developing an inhibited bite, which means they don't have as strong of a bite as wolves or coyotes. *See also* **antipredatory behavior**.

predatory drift. A term coined by dog trainer Ian Dunbar that refers to situations when one dog thinks another dog is prey because of their wolf ancestry. In this situation, dogs are not being aggressive, but rather doing what "comes naturally" because it's what their ancestors did in these situations.

pride. People sometimes ask me if dogs have egos and feel pride. I simply don't know, but sometimes dogs certainly appear to be pleased with themselves when they accomplish something. *See also* **accomplishment, sense of**.

privacy. Many dogs have a need for privacy or alone time, and they should be granted this. There is not anything necessarily wrong with a dog who needs quiet time and solitude. *See also* **alone time**; **introvert**.

pronouns for dogs. The words we use to refer to dogs and other nonhuman animals can directly influence how we treat them and how connected we feel to them. I believe that dogs and other nonhumans should be referred to as *who* or *whom*, rather than *it*, *that*, or *which*. Unlike countless animals who are kept in laboratories and on factory farms, who are numbered rather than identified by name, dogs typically are named, and so too should lab dogs and other animals used by humans in other venues.

Dogs also have *children*, but most scientists prefer to use less-personal words, such as *offspring* or *young*. When I first used the word *children* to refer to a female coyote's progeny, a few people said something like, "We don't use that word for animals." I politely reminded them that we, too, are animals and that there is no reason whatsoever not to refer to the young coyotes as children. One said, "It just doesn't feel right." When I asked why not, the person couldn't think of any reason other than it wasn't conventional. If we're going to change the ways in which we interact with dogs and other animals, we need to change our vocabulary. The same goes for writing about husbands, wives, nieces and nephews, and aunts and uncles, for that's who some individuals are. When we use "personal" words, it forces us to realize just who these individuals are and how their lives intersect among themselves and with us.

property. Legally, dogs and other animals are categorized as property, as things belonging to someone. Thinking of dogs as "owned" things is harmful and a double cross on these amazing beings who, although many live highly restrictive captive lives, still aren't mere objects but rather sentient subjects of a life. *See also* **legal status**.

prosocial behavior. Positive social behavior that helps build and maintain social bonds and friendships. These behaviors include greeting, spooning, and playing.

protean behavior. Aka random, unpredictable, and irregular behavior. This is what we witness when dogs are overcome with zoomies — zigzagging, spinning, looping, and bouncing frenetically. Animals also engage in protean behavior when fleeing from rivals and predators. *See also* **zoomies**.

psychohydraulic model of motivation. An "energy" model of motivation developed by Konrad Lorenz. Basically, energy builds up when an action hasn't been performed, and so it takes less of a stimulus to get an individual to perform it. Eventually, an individual may perform a behavior in the absence of any stimulus because a lot of energy has accumulated, which causes the individual to get rid of the energy by doing whatever needs to be done. For example, a dog who hasn't been exercised may get restless and begin running here and there frenetically to get rid of the energy that has built up.

psychopathology. A behavioral disorder or mental illness. Dogs and other animals can become psychopaths, but it's very rare and it is extremely difficult to apply this label with much reliability. A 2021 study of cats wrongly conflated normal species-appropriate cat behavior with psychopathology and sent out the wrong message about cats who are "going crazy." The researchers' lack of consideration of the *context* in which different behavior patterns are expressed by cats was surprising and problematic. Context involves critical information like who's involved, where they are, and what caused them to do what they're doing.

psychosomatic disorders. A condition when someone will show physical symptoms when not actually ill. Some veterinarians have told me they are very careful about making this diagnosis with dogs and other animals because they can't talk directly with the animal, and I understand what they're saying.

puppy. Any young dog between birth and as old as two years of age. At and soon after birth, dogs are called neonates.

puppy breath. A distinct sweet odor caused by a young dog's diet of mom's milk and possibly puppy food.

puppy dog eyes. A young dog's innocent or naive facial expression, one that's very difficult to say no to. Indeed, the expression "puppy dog eyes" describes any begging or pleading look like a puppy would give you!

Puppy dog eyes are an example of paedomorphism, or the retention of infant or juvenile characteristics. Humans tend to consider these traits "cute," and they often attract attention and care. So it's interesting and relevant that one study showed that dogs who display puppy dog eyes are rehomed more quickly from shelters than those who don't.

Why did dogs develop this trait? We really don't know, but they evolved a particular muscle, called AU101, that is responsible for this eyebrow lift. So it may be that dogs who displayed seductive puppy dog eyes gained a selective advantage over those who didn't, since humans are attracted to this facial expression.

The data on rehoming support the idea that puppy dog eyes help form and maintain close relationships between dogs and humans, and even might have prompted the muscle AU101 to evolve. Dog expert Juliane Kaminski and her colleagues concluded in their study: "Overall, the data suggest that selection — perhaps mainly unconscious during social interactions — can create selection pressures on the facial muscle anatomy in dogs strong enough for additional muscles to evolve."

That said, puppy dog eyes are not intentionally dishonest or manipulative. Even if certain dogs might occasionally adopt this expression in a deliberate or deceptive way, that would never result in the evolution of a muscle, and that isn't canine "business as usual." Dogs don't "use us," which is among the many different myths that need to be put to rest once and for all.

Human selection clearly influences the evolution of a wide variety of canine traits. Some of these traits benefit dogs, whereas others clearly do not. *See also* **eyebrow lift**.

puppy mills. A term for highly abusive dog-breeding facilities that churn out puppies for profit, while ignoring the needs of the pups and their mothers. It's estimated there are at least ten thousand puppy mills in the United States, and more than two million puppies are bred in these hellholes each year.

According to the Puppy Mill Project:

- There are two primary sales outlets for puppies bred in puppy mills: pet stores and the internet.
- Nearly all puppies sold at pet stores come from puppy mills. Pet stores are the primary sales outlet for puppy mills and are essential for keeping puppy mills in business.
- Both licensed and unlicensed mills sell to pet stores (many mills sell to pet stores without the required license and are not held accountable).
- Puppies are bred in mills and then shipped all over the country. For example, puppies bred in the Midwest may be shipped on trucks to Southern California or Florida. The shipping conditions are inhumane. Puppies can be forced to go up to twelve hours without food or water, and they are confined in a small space where diseases can be easily transmitted. Many puppies do not survive.

purebred dogs. Dogs bred from parents of the same breed or variety.

Q

quality of life. What makes a good and fulfilling life for a dog? At minimum, it involves allowing dogs to be dogs and to engage in dog-typical behavior, such as sniffing to their nose's content, including the butts of other dogs; allowing them downtime; giving them the opportunity to exercise their bodies and their senses; and getting quality veterinary care. While scales of quality might be somewhat helpful, it is essential to view each and every dog as an *individual* and consider what is the best life for them. When I asked singer and artist Joan Baez what question she wished she could ask her dog, she replied simply, "Are you happy with me?" Emmylou Harris said she wished she could ask her rescued dog, Roxie, "What do you want? What am I not giving you?" Jessica Pierce has written a lot of excellent pieces on quality of life for dogs.

R

radio tracking. Aka telemetry. This involves following an individual's movements via radio signals sent from a collar or chip an animal wears. Depending on the type of collar or chip being used, it can provide a lot of useful information about where they are, travel patterns, who is with whom, and if they're active. Wearing a radio collar can change behavior. I don't know of any formal long-term studies of radio-tracking free-ranging or feral dogs, but some people track sporting dogs, and some use these technique to keep track of where their household companion spends their time. I've seen some records of mountain dogs, and on occasion they roam far from their homes to meet up with some canine friends of whom their humans are unaware.

rage syndrome. Also called "sudden onset aggression." This occurs when a dog displays unprovoked aggression. For example, a few people I know have told me that their otherwise docile and friendly dog will spontaneously jump up and attack them for no apparent reason. These are people who know a lot about dog behavior, and when they say they have no idea what caused this to happen, I believe them.

raised-leg urination (RLU). Males raise a hindleg to pee, whereas females will raise and tuck a hindleg. *See also* **dry marking**; **peeing**.

random sampling. Scanning a group and seeing what individuals are doing with no time scale. *See also* **research techniques**.

rapid eye movement (REM) sleep. Dogs and other animals go through this stage of sleep during which the irises move rapidly and dreaming occurs. It is the deepest stage of sleep and happens around ninety minutes after falling asleep. This is when it looks like a dog might be chasing another dog or a deer.

reciprocity. Giving and taking with mutual benefits for the individuals involved. A phenomenon called reciprocal altruism occurs when there is a long-term relationship between two unrelated individuals and each benefits from this cooperative relationship. Not surprisingly, biologists debate whether reciprocity and reciprocal altruism occur in nonhumans and to what extent. No one has studied this in free-ranging or feral dogs, but I've seen some examples among the dogs who used to hang out around my mountain home, especially involving food. Jethro and especially his best friends Maddy and Zeke seemed to share treats among themselves more than they did with other dogs who also came to my place to play and sleep during the day. *See also* **altruism**.

recognition of siblings. Dogs seem to be able to recognize littermates and younger and older siblings when they're reunited after a long separation. They do this perhaps based on odors or vocalizations. Recognition might also depend on how long the individuals were together before being separated and how long they were apart. People have told me stories of littermates who learned to greet one another in a unique way and then, when they were reunited over a year later, do the same thing instantaneously. There has been no formal research on sibling recognition, so we don't have any specifics about how frequently it occurs and what factors are involved.

Jessica Wasieleski wrote to me about her dog Zylah meeting some of her littermates and her father after a year of not seeing one another:

> For Zylah's first birthday, we gathered with her littermates for a playdate. Her sister from the first generation also came to play. We all met at a dog park where she and her sisters and brother could run off-leash. They were jumping on one another, wrestling, and playing leapfrog. There was a lot of excitement and her brothers even attempted to hump her! They all frolicked for hours and seemed very happy. Afterward we brought Zylah to reunite with her parents for the first time since we picked her up at eight weeks. Her dad, a big athletic black Lab German shepherd, was whining and eager to greet Zylah. He even rolled over on his back with his belly exposed and legs wiggling in the air. Her mom, a fluffy Pyrenees, was wagging her tail and gently engaging with Zylah. There was a lot of squeaking from Zylah, as she expressed what seemed like excitement and joy.

Did the littermates recognize each other and did Zylah's parents know she was their daughter? Anecdotal observations like this make it seem so, and this behavior warrants formal studies.

Conversely, a study was done to see if humans could recognize their own dogs using only scent, and it turns out that some people can. Stanley Coren writes, "In general, younger individuals were better at identifying dogs than older individuals.... The best dog identification ability was found in young male participants.... So it appears that humans can identify their own dogs when the only information they have is the dog's scent." *See also* **mirror recognition**; **olfactory recognition**.

redirected behavior. Behavior that is redirected to an alternative individual or object. For example, a dog who doesn't want to attack another dog who threatens or tries to fight with them might redirect their aggression toward another individual or object and bite and shake it vigorously.

referential signaling. Pointing to, naming, or talking about another individual or object. I don't know of any formal studies, but it would be interesting to know if dogs, for example, tell others where there is food or anything else using these sorts of signals. *See also* **gesturing**.

regret. Do dogs feel sad or disappointed over lost opportunities, missed chances, or mistakes? We know that rats feel regret. There's no reason to think dogs don't, but I'm not quite sure how to know this. I had an interesting conversation with a woman at a dog park who felt sure that her dog Matilde once regretted not playing with another dog, Roseanne, who had invited her to play. The next day Matilde seemed more interested than ever to get Roseanne's attention. She succeeded and Matilde and Roseanne played and became lifelong friends.

regurgitating. Dogs and many other animals bring swallowed food back up to the mouth to share with others, especially with their children. Homed dogs generally don't do this, but I've seen this in free-ranging dogs.

reinforcement. Rewarding a behavior so it will happen again or discouraging a behavior so it won't. Reinforcement can be positive or negative during training, and I'm a fan of force-free positive training rather than using punishment to get a dog to do what their human wants them to do.

reproductive behavior. An inclusive term referring to different aspects of making babies, including flirting, courting, mating, birthing, lactating, and caregiving.

reproductive suppression. Preventing a healthy adult individual from mating. It can include delayed sexual maturation or it can be enforced behaviorally by higher-ranking individuals. It has been observed in wolves, but I don't know of any formal studies on dogs. I wouldn't be surprised if this occurred in groups of free-ranging or feral dogs.

research techniques. The ways dogs are studied. In this book, I've included explanations of many types of research or data sampling techniques (and provided cross-references to these at the end of this entry). Each is useful and might be preferred in any particular situation. Indeed, I encourage you to try these yourself with your own dog or a group of dogs, at home or at a dog park. By practicing citizen science, you will invariably learn a great deal about dogs in general and your own dog in particular.

That said, I always caution people before drawing conclusions from their research. With all research, formal and informal, it's important to consider how data are collected, where research is conducted, and who the subjects are. It can be easy to jump to conclusions over small sample sizes and neglect to notice how specific conditions influenced results. I'm very familiar with countless dog studies of all kinds, I have studied the behavior of domestic dogs and their wild relatives for years, and I have pondered this question a lot. And I have come to the conclusion that there's a lot of good science about dogs, but we need to be very careful about making sweeping generalizations.

I want to stress that, by saying this, I'm not implying that the science conducted on dogs is bad or necessarily questionable — though of course, some studies are more rigorous than others. Rather, the results from similar studies often vary from one another, and there are often very good reasons for this. One study might find that dogs tend to do one thing, and another study might find that they tend to do another, and that doesn't necessarily mean that one study was wrong or badly conducted.

Why might results differ when it seems they should agree? I often feel that researchers should consider a disclaimer of this sort: "These results apply to the conditions under which these dogs were studied, so differences among different studies are not surprising." Comparisons among different studies can be complicated because different dogs are being studied in different conditions in different laboratories or at different dog parks or in different field conditions.

Here are a couple of stories that help to explain not only why results may differ from one study to another, but also why the same dog might behave differently from one time to another within the same study. These variables are also important to consider when training or socializing dogs to live in our homes.

For instance, I was once watching a study being done, and one of the participants mentioned to me that he'd had a busy day and had just fed his dog around three hours later than usual. He wondered if that would influence how his dog responded in the experiment, which used food as a reward. I cautioned him that it might, he told the researchers, and they all decided not to test the dog that day.

Another time I was "secretly" watching researchers collecting data on dogs at a dog park, and they became a bit too intrusive for my liking. On that day, for whatever reason, the dogs clearly didn't want to play and preferred to sniff here and there or simply hang out with other dogs. The researchers started coaxing the reluctant dogs to get up and play, and then they stopped play whenever they felt it got too rough. Later, I was told by the dogs' humans that, compared to when the dogs chose to play, their interactions were different — they were shorter and consisted of more solo zoomies, and the dogs didn't follow the "golden rules of play," which they usually did.

Variation in research results isn't noise, but rather important information — at least, so long as we pay attention to what might have caused the variation. Further, I also feel that most researchers follow protocols as closely as they can. In a nutshell, variation should be expected and shouldn't be ignored, but we should also be very careful about serving up grand conclusions about what dogs can or cannot do, what dogs know or don't know, or what dogs can and cannot learn. There is no "universal dog." *See also* **ad libitum sampling; focal animal sampling; instantaneous sampling; matrix of social interactions; one-zero sampling; random sampling; scan sampling; splitting and lumping data**.

resemblance between dogs and their humans. Some people think that humans choose their canine companions because they look alike, or that, like married couples, they start to look alike over time. This is a source of funny internet memes, and every now and then even news articles triumphantly proclaim "Dogs Look Like Their Owners — It's a Scientific Fact." Actually, as it turns out, a resemblance between dogs and their humans is not all that common, though it exists to some degree. In one study, judges were shown forty-five pictures of dogs and potential owners, and there was no relationship between the ability to pair a human and their dog and the length of time they cohabited. However, it was easier for the judges to match purebred dogs and their humans based on physical similarities. Another study showed that similarities in the region of the eyes was the most important variable. And one study showed that when human-pet pairs were compared in pet beauty contests, the dog and their human showed higher facial resemblance than expected by chance. Dogs and their humans also often show similar personalities, and shared personalities may be what's actually important when choosing a companion to bring home.

resident effect. When being on one's home turf confers an advantage in aggressive or competitive interactions between dogs, sort of like a home-court advantage in sports. Anecdotes abound about dogs being bolder or more assertive on their own turf, but I don't know of any detailed studies. Many of my dogs seemed bolder when they were near my home, perhaps because of where they were or because I was there. My friend Marie told me she was sure her dog Theodore was "ballsier" at home. He pranced around with a dog treat hanging out of his mouth when his friends visited, perhaps teasing them, but he didn't do this off his own turf.

resource guarding. Protecting a resource such as food, a toy, or a place to rest and sleep. This is also called "possessive aggression."

rewards. Doing something to get a dog to do something (or continue doing something). A reward could be praise or encouragement, a treat, or playtime with a toy or a friend. Rewards of various types are an essential part of most training, whether it's handled formally or informally.

rhythm. Some dogs seem to have a sense of rhythm when they hear music. Dog expert Zazie Todd notes that dogs often respond to their human's behavior when they are listening to music but they don't "catch a beat" like we do. She notes that many YouTube examples of dogs with rhythm are really dogs responding to human cues. Nonetheless, they are fun to watch.

risk-taking behavior. Some dogs show a willingness to do dangerous things that provide an adrenaline rush but which might also cause injury or death, while other individuals are clearly risk-adverse and do not want to be unsafe or take chances. Usually, it's a human who puts a dog in a risky situation that the human finds enjoyable. There's no evidence that dogs are inherently thrill-seeking, adrenaline junkies.

ritualization. The evolutionary process by which an action or behavior pattern loses its original function and becomes a signal. It's possible, but not proven, that play bows may have originated when dogs who were lying down then stood up and stretched, and other dogs saw this and came over to play. *See also* **displays**; **play bows**.

road trips. Some dogs like road trips and some don't. If your dog enjoys traveling with you, be sure that their needs are met, and if they don't, it might be best not to take them along.

role reversing. A situation when a dominant dog behaves submissively with another smaller or lower-ranking dog. The dominant dog doesn't assert their full strength to even the playing field so the two dogs can play or hang out. *See also* **self-handicapping**.

rolling in stinky stuff. At the dog park, someone occasionally shouts a familiar warning: "Watch out! My dog Brutus just rolled on another dog's turd. He's pretty proud and is trying to let everyone know what he did." If I'm there when this happens, someone usually turns to me and almost pleads, "Why do dogs do this?" Unfortunately, we really don't know why dogs roll in poop and all sorts of other disgusting, stinky stuff. Some dogs dive in like it's not just fun but their dream come true. I used to call two of my dogs "holy rollers" because they looked like they went into a trance when they found something disgusting in which to roll, which on occasion they shared with me. I'm glad I had a lion- and bear-proof outdoor run in which they could safely rest and lose the pungent odor before they came into my house or my office.

Some people suggest dogs roll in stinky stuff because they want to mask their own odor by taking on a more pungent odor or one that's more prevalent wherever they are, whereas others say they're trying to spread their own odor around. Judging from what I've seen, dogs usually roll in things that are far smellier than they are, and they often want everyone to know. Lending credence to the theory that they're trying to mask their own odor, research suggests that red foxes appear to roll on scent left by pumas (mountain lions) to mask their own scent so as not to call attention to themselves and to confuse predators.

My friend's son, Greg Coffin, wrote to me about a rolling rating system he developed for his dog, Sophia:

> On our walks on and around the beach, there are many delightful things my Rhodesian ridgeback enjoys rolling in. She does it frequently

> enough that I have developed a simple rating system, classifying the nicest to the nastiest. Dead birds are the best you can hope for. A little musty, but nothing too gag-worthy. Fish, just really fishy. Land mammals are next. A special kind of vulgarity. Yes, it escalates quickly. But her favorites are dead sea mammals. They're full of all that rotting blubber, slathered in delicious fatty oils.

I'd love to be able to ask Sophia why she does this. *See also* **odor preferences**.

rolling over. When a dog rolls onto their back, the gesture can mean different things and send different messages depending on context. It could be a submissive move, an invitation to play, a form of self-play or simply back-scratching that feels good.

roommates, meeting new. I'm occasionally asked about how to make sure someone's dog feels safe and comfortable with a new roommate or partner. There are no one-size-fits-all solutions, but it's important for the dog to like new people in a household. One strategy is to have the new person and the dog meet in a neutral place, and then have plenty of treats and toys, which can go a long way toward fostering a positive relationship. After a few introductions, go home with both of them and see how that works out. Dogs, like people, have different personalities, and their past experiences can play a large role in how these introductions go. Be patient, as for some dogs this might take some time.

The same strategies work when having a partner spend time on their own with the dog for the first time. If the relationship is smooth, then try it for short periods, even a few minutes, and slowly build up to longer periods of time. And when you leave, say a goodbye to your dog and partner, and when you come home, perhaps greet the dog first.

rooting reflex. When newborns automatically turn their face toward a stimulus, in most cases a nipple providing milk.

rough-and-tumble play. *See* **mock fighting**.

S

safety, sense of. Dogs like to feel at peace and safe, just like we do. Some dogs also need a safe zone, a place to go where they feel secure, even places we can't access. Mishka, a large husky, loved to slink under my bed and often would lift a leg of the bed off the ground. She simply needed alone time and came out feeling her good old self. Even the most social dogs need time on their own, and when they do, there's no reason to take it personally or feel snubbed. *See also* **alone time**.

salivating. Dogs secret saliva in anticipation of food and when they feel nervous or uncertain. Most dogs salivate to some extent, which is also called drooling and slobbering, but if it seems excessive for your dog, see a vet to make sure there isn't a problem.

sampling. Collecting data about dog behavior as part of research. *See also* **research techniques**.

satisficing. A term for accepting an option as satisfactory or good enough. In contrast, optimizing or maximizing is trying to get the best deal possible. Most of the dogs I've known and lived with have been satisficers, and they seemed much happier than those who were pickier. My dog Jethro loved playing with his buddy Zeke and would prefer him over other dogs, but when Zeke wasn't in the mood to play or wasn't around, any dog who wanted to play was just fine. Jethro also loved to sleep under my desk, but when Zeke or another dog was there, he'd go elsewhere and didn't seem to have any problem getting the rest and sleep he needed.

sayings. There are numerous dog-related sayings and metaphors, which isn't surprising given how intimately and long we've shared our lives with dogs. Interestingly, according to Robert Palmatier in his book *Speaking of Animals*, we have the most sayings related to horses, followed by dogs. I've included some sayings in this book, and others include "dog-eared" for the turned-down corner of a page in a book; "dogged" for being persistent, obstinate, or stubborn; "doggie bag" for leftover food to bring home from a restaurant; and "doggone" as a substitute for swearing.

scan sampling. When the behavior of individuals in a group is recorded at regular intervals, perhaps every minute. The simplest technique is to record whether at least one animal is engaged in the behavior of interest at the set time intervals. This method does not yield detailed data. *See also* **research techniques**.

scapegoating. When dogs pick on or harass another dog, who is often called an omega animal.

scat. Wild animal poop or droppings.

scatology. An interest in or preoccupation with excrement. Dogs are competent scatologists.

scent marking. Intentionally peeing, or occasionally pooping, in a specific place to convey information to other dogs, aka "pee-mail." Marking is different from merely peeing or pooping anywhere when a dog simply has got to go; then it doesn't matter where they do it. The message of scent marking could be related to gender, mood, status, or territory, something along the lines of, *This is my space, stay out.* I think most dogs wish they could pee on everything in the world.

In an essay in James Serpell's edited book *The Domestic Dog*, John Bradshaw and Nicola Rooney note, "Among free-roaming dogs, males may urine-mark as a component of territorial behavior, while females mark most frequently around their den sites."

Meanwhile, in an important 2012 study on free-ranging domestic dogs, the researchers found "evidence that markings are used by dogs to form a 'property line' and to threaten rivals during agonistic conflicts. Both males and females utilized scent marking to assert dominance and probably to relocate food or maintain possession over it. Raised-leg urination and ground scratching probably play a role in olfactory and visual communication in both males and females. Urinations released by females, especially through flexed-leg posture, may also convey information about their reproductive state.... Our results suggest that many of the proposed functions of marking behaviors are not mutually exclusive, and all should be explored through detailed field and laboratory studies."

These observations are important because most research has been conducted on laboratory or homed dogs, and more data are needed for free-ranging individuals. *See also* **allomones**; **dry marking**; **peeing**; **pheromones**; **pissing matches**.

scientific research, dogs used in. Dogs are used in many different research programs, including highly invasive projects in which they're tortured and killed. I am against these sorts of studies on dogs and other nonhumans. It's estimated that around seventy thousand dogs are used in a wide variety of studies every year, but it's difficult to get reliable numbers because labs often don't report them accurately. In July 2022, more than forty-five hundred beagles were freed from a laboratory in Virginia by the order of a district court judge. I've known some researchers who tout how they love dogs and have companion dogs at home and then go into a lab and do horrific things to so-called "research dogs," many of whom are numbered rather than named. *See also* **abuse**; **legal status**.

scolding. Aka saying "bad dog." Often when dogs are doing dog-appropriate behavior that we don't like, we scold them for "being bad," but the fault lies with us. Dogs aren't misbehaving; they are simply behaving like dogs. In general, many people tend to scold rather than praise their dog, which can be problematic when the dog has no idea why they're being reprimanded. *See also* **"good dog" / "bad dog"**; **helicopter parenting**.

scruff biting. During play, a dog might bite another dog's scruff, shaking the head from side to side while delivering the bite, and yanking a dog here and there. This can also be observed during aggressive interactions, and the best way to know what's happening is to pay attention to context — to carefully watch the dogs and see where the interaction goes. Dogs who know one another might play rougher than those who don't, and even high-intensity scruff biting might be fine with them. *See also* **biting**.

selective breeding. This is another term for artificial selection, when humans control breeding with specific goals in mind, and it plays a large role in domestication. *See also* **artificial selection**; **domestication**; **natural selection**.

self-care. When dogs lick and groom themselves or rest when they're not feeling well.

self-handicapping. Performing different behaviors less intensely than is possible. Dogs often self-handicap during play and other friendly encounters. They inhibit their bite or minimize aggressive tendencies. Doing this can even the playing field so large dogs can play with smaller dogs and high-ranking individuals can play with lower-ranking individuals.

For example, best friends Zylah, a 45-pound mix, and Floyd, a 160-pound Great Dane mastiff, are able to play intensely because Zylah feels safe and Floyd controls his strength. *See also* **role reversing**.

self-play. When a dog plays on their own, such as with objects, chasing their tails, or engaging in zoomies. *See also* **play**; **zoomies**.

self-recognition. Dogs have a sense of self, though it isn't the same as humans experience. In studies, dogs clearly distinguish between their urine and that of other dogs, and thus display a sense of "body-ness" or "mine-ness," if not necessarily a sense of "I-ness." That is, they indicate they know something like "This is me." However, they don't do well on the visually oriented mirror test for self-recognition. Years ago, my mentor, Michael Fox, and I tried to do a mirror study on wolves and dogs, and they didn't respond and had no interest in what we were doing. This isn't necessarily because they don't have a sense of self, but rather they are more "nosey" animals than nonhuman primates.

That said, it's well-established that there are degrees of consciousness and of self-recognition among animals. Further, Charles Darwin argued that these differences in cognitive abilities and emotions are differences in degree rather than differences in kind. That means we should expect for self-recognition to differ among species, including humans, and these differences don't reflect some hierarchy of consciousness. *See also* **mirror recognition**; **olfactory recognition**.

senior dogs. It's difficult to say exactly when a dog becomes a senior citizen, but when they slow down and seem to want to rest more and behave like senior humans, this label can well apply. Of course, we must take care of them if something is wrong, but let's also remember that we can learn a lot from elder canines.

senses. *See* **hearing**; **sight**; **smell**; **taste**; **touch**.

sensitive period. *See* **critical period of development**.

sentience. Simply put, the ability to feel and to experience subjective states. Many, if not most, nonhuman animals, including dogs, are now recognized as sentient beings. That is, they have "inner lives" and are capable of experiencing pain and pleasure and making self-directed choices. In 2009, the Treaty of Lisbon recognized animals as sentient beings, and this encouraged an ongoing "sentience shift" that has been expanding ever since. More recently, in December 2021, Spain joined approximately thirty-two other countries — including France, England, the Netherlands, Sweden, New Zealand, and Tanzania — in recognizing sentience in many animals. In 2018, Slovakia revised the definition of animals in its civil code "to reflect that they are living beings, not things." Under the new definition, "animals will enjoy special status and value as living creatures that are able to perceive the world with their own senses." And the list of animals who are recognized as being sentient continues to grow. In the United Kingdom, octopuses, crabs, and lobsters have been included in the sentience club.

An abundant database of scientific research supports the clear fact that many diverse nonhumans are deeply emotional, sentient beings who care about what happens to themselves and others. This provides a pillar of strength for people who want to use "being sentient" to protect and respect the lives of other animals. In 2022, the Institute for Animal Sentience and Protection was founded at Denver University in order to expand the scientific understanding of the cognitive and emotional capabilities of animals. This institute is the first of its kind and a major step forward for studies of animal sentience, and I'm sure other universities will follow in these important footsteps. *See also* **consciousness**.

separation anxiety. Intense fear and distress of being alone. Dogs certainly experience separation anxiety, which causes emotional suffering and can lead to destructive behavior. Due to high stress, or the desire to get out of the place they are being kept, dogs may pace, pee, poop, bark, howl, or chew. According to the American Kennel Club, dogs shouldn't be left on their own at home during the day for more than six to eight hours without a dog walker or dog daycare. While all dogs need some time alone, too much can cause stress, so recognize the signs of separation anxiety. Individual differences among dogs are important to consider. Some dogs are more tolerant of alone time than others, so if it seems to be a problem, consult a user-friendly force-free positive trainer or a veterinarian. Punishing a dog who displays separation anxiety is counterproductive. *See also* **alone time**; **home alone, leaving dogs**.

service dogs. According to the Americans with Disabilities Act (ADA), "a service animal is defined as a dog that has been individually trained to do work or perform tasks for an individual with a disability. The task(s) performed by the dog must be directly related to the person's disability." Service dogs are not emotional support dogs or therapy, comfort, or companion animals. They do not have to be professionally trained, and there are no regulations for training service dogs, which can be very expensive. While there is a high demand for them, there have been problems with dogs not doing what they're supposed to do.

Many people worry that service dogs are more stressed than other dogs, but research shows that they do not necessarily experience more stress — including PTSD service dogs for veterans. However, some therapy dogs can be more stressed, which is why it can't be emphasized too many times that matching dogs with clients who will work with each dog's "strengths, abilities, and temperament" is critical.

In the United Kingdom, some dogs have received the PDSA (People's Dispensary for Sick Animals) Order of Merit, the "animal OBE (Order of the British Empire)," for public service. *See also* **animal-assisted therapy (AAT)**; **emotional support animal (ESA)**.

sex ratio. *See* **litter size**.

sexual selection. A form of natural selection for traits that confer advantages in mating. Examples include large size, bright coloration, and adornments such as antlers that help males compete with one another and that females often find attractive. For homed dogs, people make these sorts of decisions, but it would be interesting to know if free-ranging or feral dogs show examples of sexual selection.

shame. As with pride, there is no reason to doubt that dogs feel shame, but there haven't been any good studies to date.

shared emotions. *See* **emotional contagion**; **empathy**.

shelter dogs. Shelter dogs often suffer higher levels of stress compared to homed dogs.

shock collars. Also called e-collars, these collars deliver an electric shock and are used as a form of aversive conditioning. Many trainers and others are not fans of these devices, and there are heated debates about whether they should be totally banned. A number of countries have already done so, including Wales, Scotland, Switzerland, Austria, Slovenia, and Germany. In 2020, Quebec banned choke, prong, and shock collars.

Personally, I think shock collars are often used as the easy way out for dealing with behavioral problems that, with persistence, can be solved through positive force-free training. However, some people find that shock collars can be a helpful last resort, particularly in situations where a dog could harm others. In January 2022, one man shared his experience involving this. He was conflicted about e-collars, but eventually used one in a minimal way that solved the problem. Here is part of what he wrote:

> We absolutely did not support even the thought of shock collars. It is not learning from the dog about the dog itself, but just correcting it for the sake of having it behave exactly like you want. In 2007 we adopted our smooth fox terrier, Lemon, from a high-kill shelter and fell in love with him. After a long life he passed away earlier last year at the age of almost eighteen, and we miss him dearly.
>
> Of course, he was a handful in the beginning. He could escape crates (which we also don't like to use) and was constantly barking at everything.... As new dog owners we just had to learn to manage these things. But we also had a cat, Bubu. Our dog could not stand cats, and he would go in for the kill. Not playing, not threatening.... He was dead set on killing her. We tried for weeks to introduce them carefully, but it did not help.
>
> It got so bad that once, when our cat was stuck and I was freeing her, our dog got into the room and was so focused on getting her that he bit me. That was the straw.... We knew we had only one option left, a shock collar. If the dog had to go back, it would definitely be killed in the shelter.
>
> At the store, the clerk was really good and strict. He explained what it was (a training collar, not shock collar) and explained how to use it (sound first, then the mildest shock that makes an impact).
>
> So, at home, we sat with the cat and dog in the living room, and let the dog loose. He charged at the cat, and when he came close, we did one beep, then followed by the shock.
>
> We only needed one. From that moment, he thought our cat had magical powers and had so much respect for it. In the years that followed, they became such good friends until both of them passed of old age.
>
> I understand why people want to ban these collars, but it would take away the last piece of help someone might need to correct

dangerous behaviors. Maybe selling them with the same short lesson our clerk gave when he sold it to us would be better.

I still think that positive force-free training might have solved this issue — as did some trainers I spoke with — but I appreciate the man's thoughtfulness and minimal use of the device. What concerns me is that, more often, people don't use shock collars once and remove them; they leave them on, which means their dog is living in continuous fear of being shocked.

Here's an e-collar story that exemplifies the problem with these devices. A friend of mine who had a relatively minor problem with her dog found a local trainer on the web. When the trainer arrived to see the dog, she announced that she used e-collars and wanted to take the dog to her home for a few hours to observe her. Thankfully, my friend said no. The trainer didn't pay any attention to the context of the problem and showed no interest in the dog-human relationship. To me, this is a good example of someone who shouldn't be training any dog. *See also* **collars**; **positive training**; **training**.

sibling rivalry. Competition among littermates and older siblings definitely exists in dogs. Depending on their age and the situation at hand, they could be competing for food, space, or attention from another dog, including a parent or other caregiver. *See also* **adolescence**.

sight. To become fluent in dog, it's essential to know how their eyes work and to consider the canine visual cosmos. We tend to think of humans as visual mammals and dogs as olfactory and auditory mammals, but science is challenging these stereotypes. Visual acuity in humans is often described using what's called the Snellen fraction, which is the well-known ratio of 20/20 or 20/40 that represents the quality of one's eyesight. Dogs have a Snellen fraction of 20/75. This means that what we can see at 75 feet, a dog can see only at 20 feet.

Using this method of measuring acuity, dogs have worse vision than humans. But it would be wrong to claim that dogs don't see as well as humans, since the Snellen fraction provides only one small window into the larger sense of sight. It would be more accurate to say that dogs and humans see the world differently. The visual acuity of dogs evolved to meet dogs' unique needs, and different doesn't necessarily mean better or worse.

Dogs are visual generalists, meaning that their eyes work well in a range of different light levels. They can see better than humans at dusk and in the dark — it's estimated that their night vision is around 20/250. Dogs can see in light about five times dimmer than humans can. They also are better adapted than humans for identifying movement in their peripheral vision. However, dogs are not as good as humans at seeing things in detail. One reason for this may be that dogs can't easily distinguish between the colors red and green. A red ball thrown in a field of green grass will be challenging to see even for a Labrador retriever. They also may see more blue than we do.

Other aspects of vision include depth perception, visual field of view, and sensitivity to motion. For humans, when a light is flickering around sixty times per second, it looks to be a steady light — this is called the critical flicker fusion — whereas for dogs a light has to flicker around seventy-five times per second to appear to be steady. *See also* **color blindness**; **composite signals**.

size. I'm sure dogs somehow evaluate and use the size of dogs who are around to make decisions about how to interact with them, especially if they're strangers. How they do it remains a mystery, but there is evidence that some dogs match acoustic and visual cues to assess size.

sleep. Dogs typically sleep between eight and fourteen hours a day. Of course, how much a dog sleeps can depend on a lot of different things, like how much they exercise, if they're sick or stressed, if they had a bad day, if they're having a bad dream, if they're sleep deprived or suffering from a cognitive dysfunction, their human's schedule, and their relationship with their human. Stanley Coren reports, "More strongly bonded dogs have more deep restorative sleep when they are with their owners than dogs who lack the same degree of attachment. They also can suffer from narcolepsy and other sleep disorders such as sleep apnea in brachycephalic dogs." *See also* **dreaming**.

sleepwalking. The jury is still out on whether dogs sleepwalk like humans. Some people consider the running movements dogs sometimes make when sleeping to be a form of sleepwalking, but no one knows.

That said, I've shared my home with two dogs who *seemed* to be sleepwalking together on at least one occasion. They were moving around my bedroom and were clearly not aware of what they were doing as far as I could determine, and when one seemed to wake up on his journey, he seemed somewhat surprised and beelined back to his bed. I wouldn't be surprised to learn that dogs and perhaps other mammals occasionally sleepwalk as we do.

smell. It is said that a dog who has lost their sense of smell is no longer a dog. It's estimated that dogs can smell objects or people as far as around sixty feet away. Dogs also may be able to detect subtle differences in odor from one footstep to the next as they follow a scent trail.

Dogs love to use their noses. When unrestrained, dogs spend around 33 percent of the time sniffing, which allows them to pick up all sorts of information: who's been there, whether a female is reproductively active, how big other dogs are, and perhaps what other dogs are feeling. They can also smell our stress pheromones in our breath and sweat. I was pleased to learn of a breeder who asked her clients to send her a T-shirt with her client's odor, which she gave to whatever dog they were taking home.

We all know that dogs' noses wind up in and around places we'd rather they didn't, such as the butts and groins of canine and humans. Butts and noses often go together because butts are a critical communication center for dogs. If dogs used social media, their version of Facebook would be nose-centered and called Buttbook. For dogs, it's perfectly normal and dog appropriate to sniff wherever their noses lead them.

Humans are visual creatures, so the canine sense of smell is difficult for us to understand and appreciate. We can't see odors. However, the dog's nose is the organ most people are curious about because it's so much more sensitive than our own, and dogs use it most of the time.

On many occasions, we simply don't understand why they're doing what they're doing as their nose leads the way.

In fact, one study has shown that allowing dogs to exercise their noses is good for them and makes them think more positively. Apparently, sniffing makes dogs happier. A woman at a dog park once said to me, rather seriously, that she thought that not allowing dogs to use their noses the way they want could cause serious psychological problems. While that might be extreme, except in cases of extreme deprivation, it certainly seems true that their lives are improved when they're allowed to fulfill their need to sniff and pee as they choose. And if it's good for them, surely we should let them without rushing dogs along because we are in a hurry. We should let them savor and properly assess the various odors they come across, which we know provides detailed information to which we're not privy about the world and canine society.

People also wonder if dogs can smell water. Anecdotal evidence from dog owners suggests that maybe they can, and this citizen science can help generate more formal research into the sensory world of dogs. For example, in January 2017, I was sitting outside a coffee shop in Boulder when I made friends with a handsome bloodhound, Tommy, who happened to be walking by. After receiving permission from Tommy's human, I rubbed Tommy's shoulders as we talked about his lovely disposition, his beautiful long ears, and his amazing nose. Then Tommy started pulling toward a water bowl he couldn't have possibly seen. Tommy's human casually remarked, "He can smell water." I was astounded, as I had never thought about this possibility. Bloodhounds have amazing noses with more scent-detecting receptors than any other dog. *See also* **composite signals**; **noses**; **olfactory recognition**.

smiling. Dogs can make their faces appear to smile. This happens when they open their mouths and pull back their lips, letting their tongues lap over their teeth. This "dog smile" usually occurs in situations when they are relaxed and appear happy, which is why dog owners think it is a smile — and it may well be.

snarling. Aggressively growling with bared teeth. Snarling usually indicates something along the lines of *Leave this area* or *Leave me alone. See also* **lip curling**.

Snellen fraction. A measure of visual acuity. Humans have a typical or ideal Snellen fraction of 20/20, while dogs have a Snellen fraction of 20/75. This means that what we can see at 75 feet, a dog can see only at 20 feet. *See also* **sight**.

social catalysts, dogs as. Dogs can facilitate or "lube" people meeting other people and social interactions. Research shows that the behavior of people in groups when dogs are present is "more cooperative, comfortable, friendly, active, enthusiastic, and attentive." Pets can serve as conversation starters and influence the way people view potential dates; studies show someone with a dog is considered more attractive and approachable, with women being more discriminating than men. When dogs play, people seem to relax and smile more, social barriers break down, and people talk more with others, including strangers.

social cognition. How animals gather, process, store, remember, and use information in their social interactions with other individuals. Essentially, social cognition focuses on how dogs behave in social contexts, which is discussed throughout this book. However, as one more example, it turns out that dogs snub people who are mean to their guardians and even reject their treats, while cats tend not to do this.

social intelligence. A broad term used to describe a dog's ability to engage in different types of social interactions, ranging from play to aggressive encounters, and from resolving conflicts to cooperating with other dogs. Dogs display social intelligence when they understand what's happening and what's expected of them, along with the emotions and needs of other individuals, and account for different personalities and their social status in a wide variety of social contexts. Many of "rules" of social interaction are acquired early in life and can be learned during play.

social investigation. What dogs do when sniffing another individual.

sociality. The tendency for animals to form groups, usually with members of the same species, and to live together in organized ways.

socialization. The process by which dogs become "card-carrying" members of their species and learn dog-appropriate behavior. *See also* **critical period of development**.

social play. Play that involves another individual. *See also* **play**.

social work. Social work stresses the importance of both sides of the human-animal bond. At Denver University's Institute for Human-Animal Connection, which is part of their Graduate School of Social Work, students and faculty try to understand the best ways for dogs to work with and "serve" humans so that these arrangements work for the well-being of both dogs and humans.

sociobiology. A field of study that focuses on the biological bases of social behavior, which was popularized by the esteemed American biologist Edward O. Wilson.

socio-emotional intelligence. *See* **emotional intelligence**.

socio-infantile behavior. When adults perform infantile behavior. Derived socio-infantile activities are used to reduce social distance and maintain proximity. *See also* **derived activities**; **infantile behavior**; **neonatal behavior**.

socio-sexual behavior. Actions that contain elements of sexual behavior when used in other contexts. Mounting and humping would be examples when used in play or aggressive interactions. *See also* **derived activities**.

solidity principle. The solidity principle states that solid objects cannot pass through one another or exist in the same place at the same time. Do dogs understand this? Experimental data are mixed, but I've received a few emails from people telling me that their dogs understood this concept and would not look for a solid object that rolled into another solid object, for example, a rubber ball that rolled into a tennis ball. This is an area of research that calls for more study in dogs and other nonhumans.

souls. Whether dogs have souls is a religious or spiritual question that's beyond the ability of science to answer. Many people believe that if humans have souls, dogs must as well, but not everyone does. However, for some, having a soul means connecting with others in deep relationships of empathy, communication, and care, and dogs certainly do that.

spatial learning. The process by which an individual acquires a mental representation of their environment. Dogs exhibit spatial learning, but this ability declines as they age.

spaying. Removing female sexual organs. *See also* **castrating**; **neutering**.

speciation. The evolutionary process by which populations evolve to become distinct species. The biologist Orator F. Cook coined the term in 1906. It's possible that in a posthuman world, dogs might speciate into new species. *See also* **evolution**; **posthuman dogs**.

species. A group of organisms consisting of similar individuals capable of exchanging genes or interbreeding. Species is the principal natural taxonomic unit, ranking below a genus and denoted by a Latin binomial, such as *Canis lupus familiaris*. *See also* **taxonomy**.

spiritual experiences. Debates abound about whether dogs and other animals have spiritual experiences. Roughly speaking, spirituality is the belief in something bigger than ourselves. It's that sense of connectedness to all life that inspires awe and wonder, as well as altruism or selflessness.

A well-known example is Jane Goodall's observations of waterfall dances in chimpanzees. Sometimes a chimpanzee, usually an adult male, will dance at a waterfall with total abandon. Could this be a joyous response at being alive, or an expression of awe in response to natural beauty? Where, after all, might human spiritual impulses originate?

Dr. Goodall describes a chimpanzee approaching one of these falls with slightly bristled hair, a sign of heightened arousal. She wrote:

> As he gets closer, and the roar of the falling water gets louder, his pace quickens, his hair becomes fully erect, and upon reaching the stream he may perform a magnificent display close to the foot of the falls. Standing upright, he sways rhythmically from foot to foot, stamping in the shallow, rushing water, picking up and hurling great rocks. Sometimes he climbs up the slender vines that hang down from the trees high above and swings out into the spray of the falling water. This "waterfall dance" may last ten or fifteen minutes.

Chimpanzees also dance at the onset of heavy rains and during violent gusts of wind. Goodall asks, "Is it not possible that these performances are stimulated by feelings akin to wonder and awe? After a waterfall display the performer may sit on a rock, his eyes following the falling water. What is it, this water?"

Goodall wonders, "If the chimpanzee could share his feelings and questions with others, might these wild elemental displays become ritualized into some form of animistic religion? Would they worship the falls, the deluge from the sky, the thunder and lightning — the gods of the elements? So all-powerful; so incomprehensible."

I've had several people seriously tell me that they are sure their dogs have had similar awe-filled experiences, such as when they stare into a sunset or simply lie still and take in the beauty of where they are. I don't see any reason to close the door on this possibility.

splitting and lumping data. When organizing research data, *splitting* refers to distinguishing data in highly detailed or nuanced ways;

lumping refers to compiling (or pooling) data from different sources into one category. Typically, when data are collected, they are first split into refined categories before those categories that are similar or nearly the same are lumped together into larger categories in more generalized ways. For example, when we studied social play and aggressive behavior in dogs, coyotes, and wolves, we initially looked at how frequently around fifty different behaviors were used and strung together into sequences, but we found that to get an accurate picture of what was going on, we could focus on only around fifteen of them. *See also* **research techniques**.

squatting. The posture that female dogs typically assume when urinating.

standing over. When a dog places their forelegs on the shoulders or back of another dog and stands still, sometimes very stiff and sometimes more relaxed. Many people argue that standing over is a mark of dominance, but it can happen during play when it does not represent dominance.

state dogs. Thirteen states have designated an official state dog breed. Colorado and Tennessee have listed rescue dogs and cats as their state pets, and California named shelter pets as their state pet in 2015 because of all the abandoned shelter pets each year.

statistical significance. A research term that means the results of a study, rendered as a probability or percentage, are not solely due to chance. For instance, as a hypothetical example, if researchers were studying whether room size impacted dog play, they might compare a control group (dogs playing in an average size room) with dogs in a large room, then track (or sample) any differences in play. If a certain behavior in a large room occurred 90 percent of the time, but in an average room 30 percent of the time, researchers would call that difference "statistically significant." We would expect some variation in dog play in any room, but a difference of 60 percent indicates room size had a real influence.

Often, researchers calculate chance with the equation “$P < 0.05$.” This simply means that 5 percent of the time the difference in outcomes could be due to chance alone. Conversely, 95 percent of the time the difference is due to real differences between the two variables. In this case, that would mean the difference in dog play observed in a large room would be expected 90 percent of the time. While that difference is important, it’s essential to remember that this still doesn’t mean 100 percent of the time. It’s never the case that *all* individuals will behave in a certain way.

stray dogs. Dogs living on their own or mostly on their own; also called street dogs or “streeties.” There are as many as 700 million strays globally. They might use “street smarts” to get food and shelter, but receiving veterinary care is uncommon. Stray dogs are viewed and treated differently by different cultures. For instance, in Turkey and Russia, strays can’t be euthanized. And in India, the government has declared that feeding “streeties,” as they’re called, is an essential service. There also are global projects centering on the humane management of stray dogs. *See also* **free-ranging dogs**.

subitizing. Estimating numbers by scanning rather than by counting one by one. *See also* **counting**; **numerosity**.

submission. When a dog yields or gives in to another individual by rolling over, pawing, or moving away from a resource. Dogs sometimes exhibit a submissive “grin,” in which their lips pull back into what resembles a smile. *See also* **dominance**.

subordinate. Lower in social rank or status. Subordination is when a dog accepts a lower position in a group.

subspecies. A category below species that includes individuals of the same species who live in different areas but are physically and genetically different. However, interbreeding is possible among them. *See also* **species**.

sudden onset aggression. *See* **rage syndrome**.

sundowner's syndrome. An increased period of agitation and confusion in the early evening in individuals with dementia. Dogs can suffer from dementia and exhibit sundowner's syndrome. Signs can include restlessness and agitation, irritability, confusion, disorientation, ignoring directions, pacing back and forth or wandering, suspiciousness, aggression, and becoming demanding. *See also* **dementia**.

surfing dogs. Some dogs seem to like surfing and others do not. Some of the videos I've seen of dogs on surfboards tell me many dogs don't like it, but they're doing it because their humans want them to. Then there's Ricochet, a surfing dog who clearly loves the water and who helps people in need. Ricochet helps steady surfboards so people with physical and emotional disabilities can ride. He clearly enjoys it, so surfing is good for him and the humans he helps. *See also* **risk-taking behavior**.

sweat glands. A dog's sweat glands (or merocrine glands) are located in their paw pads, and they might be useful for cooling off.

swimming. Many dogs, but not all, enjoy swimming and occasionally diving into water. The dogs with whom I've lived have shown marked differences about swimming, so I have honored their wishes. I learned quite rapidly something that should have been obvious at the start, namely, that if a dog swims, say, fifty feet out into the water to fetch a ball, they have to be able to swim the same distance back to shore. This seems so obvious that I was embarrassed to tell people about my "discovery": I'd thrown a ball too far for Jethro and learned not to do it again with other dogs. But when I told other people about what I learned, many thanked me because they, too, hadn't thought about this obvious fact. On a more serious side, two summers ago I was cycling around the Boulder reservoir, and I heard a woman screaming hysterically. She had thrown a tennis ball into the water, a slight current had carried it farther than she planned, and her dog could not get back to shore against the current. Her dog was saved by a brave man who jumped into the water and was able to drag the dog back to safety.

T

tag, dogs playing. A few times I've seen dogs play what could reasonably be called tag. One dog would run toward another and might touch them, and then run away and get chased. Years ago, when I was studying free-ranging dogs outside of Nederland, Colorado, a woman told me that her three dogs regularly played what looked to be tag. On a few occasions they'd trade off a marrow bone — one dog would run toward another dog, drop the bone, and run away, and the other would chase and do the same. I only wish I could have seen it to see if I agreed.

tags. Dog tags are an essential piece of equipment, since they are imprinted with information that allows a lost dog to be identified and their owners contacted. However, many tags can be noisy and a pain in a dog's ears.

It's important to pay close attention to all the sounds we expose dogs to, which can hijack their sense of hearing and interfere with their ability to gather important dog-relevant information. Perhaps the easiest hearing-related aid you can provide for your dog is to silence their dog tag. If dogs could talk, that might be their number-one noise complaint.

When dogs are walking, running, or playing, the constant jingling of the tag on their collar can easily get in the way of listening to the world around them. Tag silencers — little neoprene covers that hold the tags together — are a cheap intervention that will be greatly appreciated by your dog. I'm sure we wouldn't like wearing devices that interfere with how we sense the world. *See also* **hearing**.

tail flagging. Flagging occurs when a dog holds their tail stiff and high while slowly and rigidly moving it back and forth. This can indicate potential aggression.

tail gland. Aka the supracaudal or violet gland. The tail gland secretes chemicals, including oils and lipids, that can be used for communicating with other dogs or as scent marking. In some dogs, it is absent or vestigial, which means it serves no function.

tails. In his book *Canine Terminology*, Harold Spira writes about more than twenty-five types of tails. Dogs use their tails to communicate with other dogs and humans, and we've learned to recognize their signals and understand them ourselves. A happy dog usually wags their tail, while a frightened dog often tucks it between their legs. In general, puppies do not wag their tails until they are about thirty to fifty days old, but I've seen what I'd call tail wagging earlier than that as a prelude to play wrestling or what seemed to be a "hello."

Interpreting what a tail position means depends on context — who the dogs are, their social relationship, and how tail position fits with other composite signals. A loose wag is probably friendly, whereas a stiff wag likely signals assertiveness or aggression. However, there are no hard-and-fast rules, and a wagging tail does not always indicate friendliness or a happy dog.

We also know that tail wagging with a bias to the right tends to indicate that a dog is happy and relaxed, whereas left-bias wagging may indicate anxiety. In one study, dogs seeing their owners were more likely to show high-amplitude wagging with a bias to the right side (showing left-brain activation), while dogs seeing dominant, unfamiliar dogs tended to wag to the left (showing right-brain activation). These findings are consistent with the hypothesis that dogs have a left-hemisphere specialization for approach behavior and a right-hemisphere specialization for withdrawal behavior.

What if a dog loses their tail? Stanley Coren tells a story about a dog whose tail had to be amputated after an unfortunate dog-motorcycle collision. Other dogs seemed unable to understand what this dog was trying to communicate.

Marisa Ware told me the story of her dog Echo, who lost her tail in an accident. After the loss, Echo changed the way she communicated with dogs and people by using her body and ears to compensate for the loss of her tail. Tailless Echo now relies more heavily on her ears to express her feelings. When she is excited to see someone, she puts her ears very far back and will almost wiggle them. She also has developed a kind of "hop-wiggle," taking a little hop and wiggling her butt very quickly if she is excited to see someone. Echo never did the "hop-wiggle" before losing her tail. *See also* **docking**.

"talking" dogs. On new devices, dogs can press a range of buttons that say certain words, and some people believe they can use these to teach their dogs to "talk." By learning what each button means, like "food," "outside," and "play," dogs can seemingly "ask" for what they want, but I'm not inclined to call this "talking." It's still not clear whether these dogs are understanding human words or simply associating certain buttons with particular outcomes, like being fed. However, I'll wait to see where formal research leads before closing the door on this possibility.

taste. A dog's sense of taste is far less sensitive than our own. They only have around seventeen hundred taste buds, whereas humans have about nine thousand. Humans can taste salty, sweet, sour, bitter, and umami (savory). Dogs (as far as we know) taste only salty, sweet, sour, bitter, and water. It's interesting to note how much variation there is in how well and what sorts of things dogs and other animals eat, perhaps because they're tasty for them but surely not me. For example, pigs have a more sensitive sense of taste than we do, possessing about fourteen thousand taste buds. Chickens have only about thirty taste buds, while cats have less than five hundred. During their evolution, cats lost the gene that detects sweet flavors.

taxonomy. The branch of science concerned with classifying animals. There are nine taxonomic ranks: domain, kingdom, phylum, class, order, family, genus, species, and subspecies. The diagram on the next page lists the taxonomy of dogs.

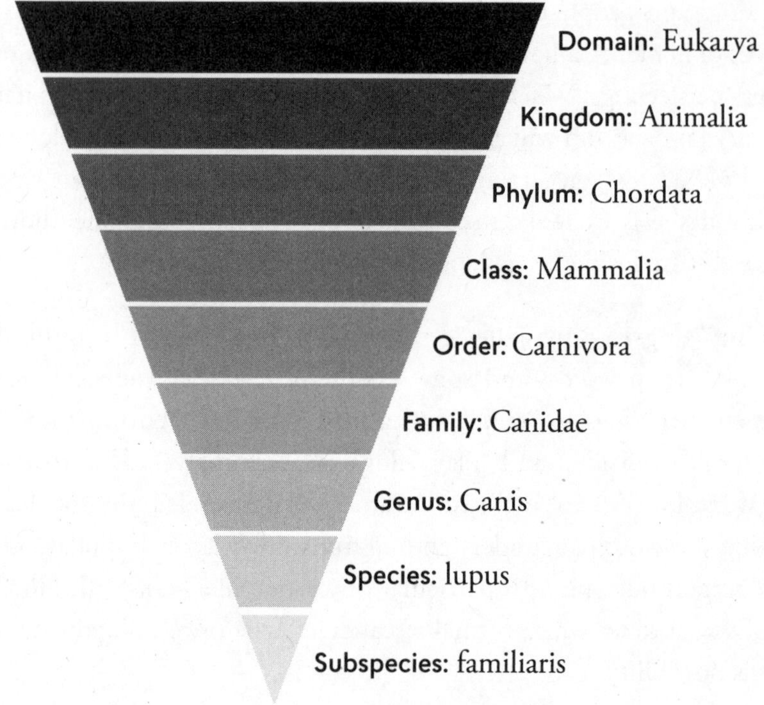

Taxonomy of the dog

tear stains. Reddish-brown discoloration from tears that drip from a dog's eyes. The color is due to the presence of porphyrins, molecules that contain iron. Treatments range from simply trimming the fur around the eyes to washing them away to using probiotics.

teeth. Puppies have twenty-eight temporary deciduous milk teeth. Adult dogs typically have forty-two permanent teeth; twenty on top and twenty-two on the bottom. However, some dogs don't grow all forty-two adult teeth. It is essential to follow good dental hygiene, including the gums and oral health in general.

teeth baring. We tend to assume that when a dog bares their teeth, they are being aggressive or threatening, but this is not always so. It might simply mean *Please leave me be.*

television, dogs watching. Some dogs pay close attention to the picture and sound emanating from a TV. No one has studied what dogs might understand about what they're watching, or if they prefer *Seinfeld*, *Law & Order*, or *The Addams Family*. To entertain a dog, many people keep TVs on when they're gone, but whether this really works is up for grabs. It might for some dogs, but it should go without saying that television is not a substitute for human company.

Ten Freedoms for dogs. In *Unleashing Your Dog*, Jessica Pierce and I expanded the Five Freedoms to the Ten Freedoms for dogs. The goal is to give dogs as much freedom as possible so a dog can be a dog.

1. Freedom from hunger and thirst
2. Freedom from pain
3. Freedom from discomfort
4. Freedom from fear and distress
5. Freedom from avoidable or treatable illness and disability
6. Freedom to be themselves
7. Freedom to express normal behavior
8. Freedom to exercise choice and control
9. Freedom to frolic and have fun
10. Freedom to have privacy and "safe zones"

See also **Five Freedoms**.

territorial behavior. One reason dogs can be "guard dogs" is because they have a sense of territoriality. They will defend a specific defined area that they consider their own, but sometimes they have to be trained to do so. Some people have wrongly claimed that dogs aren't territorial, although a dog defending their living room or a den is being territorial in the true sense of the word. Free-ranging and feral dogs defend territories where they find food or hunt or when they're denning. Territorial defense can be active — such as when a dog chases another dog or individual out of their "home" — or it can be passive, such as when a dog pees around the perimeter of their territory to mark their boundaries with their scent. Their wild canid relatives use visual displays, sounds, and scents to mark and defend territory, so it's not surprising for dogs to do the same. *See also* **core area**; **home range**.

theory of mind. Understanding that others have their own minds, their own perspective, and their own thoughts and feelings. This includes considering someone else's perspective and predicting what they might think or feel. Some people dismiss the possibility that dogs have a theory of mind, or they say dogs only have a "rudimentary theory of mind," but I and others disagree. Stanley Coren notes that the ability of dogs to engage in deceptive behavior indicates that they must possess theory of mind, since deception is all about what you want someone else to think or believe. When dogs play, they also demonstrate that they can take the perspective of other dogs. There also are differences in the ways in which theory of mind is studied, and some methods may not reflect what it means for dogs to have theory of mind. *See also* **deceiving**; **perspective taking**; **play**.

therapy dogs. *See* **animal-assisted therapy (AAT)**; **emotional support animal (ESA)**; **service dogs**.

thermoregulation. Maintaining one's body temperature in whatever is considered the "normal" range. For dogs, the average normal body temperature is 101 to 102.5°F.

thigmotaxis. Moving or orienting toward touch. Young animals including dogs orient toward a nipple when it touches their cheek. *See also* **rooting reflex**.

threat behavior. Dogs communicate their desire to be left alone, or that they don't want you to do something, by using several highly ritualized signals, including baring teeth, snarling, growling, and/or displaying a high tail. It's best to respect these warning signs, but they can mean something else in different contexts. My advice is when you see these behaviors, leave the dog alone — better safe than sorry. They don't necessarily indicate the intention to do harm, but more the willingness to do harm if the unwanted actions continue.

"three-dog night." A saying that refers to a night so bitterly cold you'd need three dogs in bed to keep warm. Also the name of a rock band founded in 1960s.

time, sense of. It's a myth that dogs only live in the present, with no concept of the past or the future. Their past influences them and they think about the future. Many dogs also seem to have a sense of passing time, as in, they know when it's time for their walk or when it's time to eat. They pay close attention to human cues, our movements and voices.

Anyone who's rescued an abused dog knows that dogs remember what happened to them and how long it can take for them to recover and be rehabilitated. Their memories are not always short-lived.

I've shared my home with many dogs, and each came from a different background, and it was thoroughly clear to me that their past experiences influenced how they responded to the same situation, including living with me. Indeed, because I hang out at dog parks a lot, I hear numerous people talk about how they have to work very hard to overcome their dog's negative past experiences.

Dog researcher Alexandra Horowitz hypothesizes that dogs might also "smell" time. They're not really telling time like we do, but they may associate a certain odor when, for example, someone arrives home, and then wait for that person or persons as if they know they will be there. Horowitz describes the case of a dog named Donut who shows how this might be so. At the same time each day, Donut would hop up from her rug, go to the back porch, and sit by a window waiting for a school bus that dropped off two brothers, who then walked home. When I mentioned this to a group of friends, two of them said they were sure that their dog also did something similar, but they had no idea how they did it.

Tinbergen's four areas of ethological research. Ethologist and Nobel laureate Niko Tinbergen stressed that studies of behavior should center on four areas of inquiry, namely, evolution, adaptation, causation, and ontogeny (development). In an essay called "Amending Tinbergen: A Fifth Aim for Ethology," Gordon Burghardt added a fifth area to

Tinbergen's list he called "private experience." Dale Jamieson and I wrote a paper called "On Aims and Methods of Cognitive Ethology," in which we showed just how fruitful and influential Tinbergen's work has been in the study of animal minds. For example, when considering why dogs play, we can ask why it evolved, why it is adaptive (what's it good for), why dogs play, what causes play, how it develops, and what dogs are feeling when they play.

tongues. Tongues are a vital organ for dogs. They contain numerous taste buds and are important for eating and tasting food, drinking water, swallowing, regulating body temperature, influencing the sound of barks, and grooming. *See also* **taste**.

tool behavior. I get asked often about whether dogs can make and use tools. They do, which of course requires the cognitive skills necessary to strategize what tool will help them accomplish a certain task. Here are some stories I've received:

Jimmy Dunn said his dog named Dammit Janet "uses a Frisbee to move around her food bowl where she wants it."

Valerie Balkwill sent me a video of her dog Bertie using a brush to push around a tennis ball, who did this on his own.

Valerie Cheney said her dog Moose often uses a llama-shaped toy as a bat to hit a ball along the floor. I thought this was a fluke, but I've seen him on numerous occasions.

Jennifer Rapowitz said her dog Maizee uses furniture to hold her Y-shaped bone in place.

Pamela, from Melbourne, Australia, wrote to me about her dog Daisy: "I have a second-generation toy cavoodle, nine months old. Since she was very small, she has used soft toys as 'bats' to send hard toys whizzing across the floors by shaking the soft toy. She also manipulates and holds (with one paw) the 'ball' in position before she bats it across the room. To me this is tool use in play." After watching her video, I agree.

Renee Sutherland sent me a video of her dog Satsuki fishing for minnows with a stick.

Then there is Grendel, a dog who made a back scratcher out of a marrow bone. Many years ago, Grendel's human friend, Lenny Frieling, told me the story:

> It would have been about 1973 that Grendel made her first tool. Because of her short legs and long torso, she could not reach the center of her back to scratch. One day we gave her a bone that was likely sawn from a large leg bone, perhaps lamb, because it was quite hard. It was cylindrical, with parallel flat sides. About a week (at most) after we gave her the bone, we noticed that she had chewed it so that one side was still flat, and the other side had two raised ridges (shaped like a sine wave going around the outer rim of the bone). She would place the bone, flat side down, on the floor, and roll over onto the two raised ridges using the protrusions to scratch the center of her back. I was convinced that she had made a tool, but in my mind, I thought that behavior had to be repeated to be scientifically significant. She had that first bone, as I recall it, for quite a while, maybe a year. It disappeared. We gave her another bone and within days, or a week, she had carved the second bone into a very similar shape and used it for the same purpose. She had repeated the making of the tool.

Finally, should anyone ever doubt the ingenuity and persistence of dogs to get food, watch the YouTube video entitled "What My Beagle Does When We Aren't Home." What caught my attention was the careful planning and creative strategizing of the beagle, who eventually moves a chair into position to reach the kitchen counter, and then carefully removes the chicken nuggets from the hot toaster oven so they can be enjoyed at leisure on the floor.

"top dog." A phrase that means the highest-ranking dog, or person, in a group.

touch. Dogs touch the world quite literally as they walk, run, play, and sniff. Dogs touch noses when they say hello, they may touch nose-to-butt to gather information about one another, and they touch us when they rub against our legs or curl up next to us in bed. And obviously, we touch our canine friends when we pet, groom, and hug them.

Concerning petting and hugging, these are usually OK so long as they are done on the dog's terms. The best advice is to err on the side of caution: When or if you're unsure, don't pet or hug a dog. As always, pay close attention to the personality of the dog. Understand their preferences and signals of consent.

The bottom line is simple. Always pay close attention to the personality of each and every individual dog, to what they like and don't like, and pay careful attention to what they're telling you. By understanding and honoring their preferences and signals of consent, we can respect their individuality and not trespass into their personal space. *See also* **hugging**; **leashes**; **whiskers**.

trainability factor. In a study on trainability in dogs, Yuying Hsu and James Serpell define this as "a dog's willingness to attend to its owner and obey simple commands, combined with a high 'fetch' motivation, and low levels of distractibility and/or resistance to correction." These researchers found some breed differences in trainability but no overall sex differences. Neutering didn't have any effect on trainability in females, but it had positive effects on male Shetland sheepdogs.

training. I like to think of training as teaching or educating a dog to learn what you'd like them to do or not do in different situations.

Most frequently, people seek out dog trainers to correct a dog's behavior so that the dog fits into the person's world. Sometimes dogs have problems with other dogs, so trainers can also help to remedy that. In the United States and most other countries, training is unregulated and anyone can call themselves a dog trainer. I am a fan of force-free positive training, and in my conversations with these sorts of trainers I've become convinced that these methods can work for the wide range of dog problems that most people deal with. There is no reason to use aversive techniques.

When people ask me specific questions related to training, I always stress that I am not a dog trainer. Further, it's impossible for me to give any advice at all without knowing the dog and witnessing the situation or problem behavior. Frankly, I don't see how anyone can offer training advice without seeing what's happening up close and personal. As I stress throughout this book, every dog is different, and it's essential to consider any dog behavior in *context* — who's involved, where something is happening, and what caused them to do what they're doing. For example, there are marked individual differences in how dogs learn to solve problems and remember how they did it that are important to incorporate into training. *See also* **affective dog behavior (ADB)**; **behavior modification**; **clicker training**; **LEGS dog training**; **positive training**; **voice and sight training**.

trigger stacking. A toxic accumulation of stress due to exposure to multiple triggers over a short period of time, which doesn't allow an animal's reactivity / stress levels to return to normal. Unnoticed trigger stacking is anecdotally one of the primary causes of "outbursts" from companion dogs. My friend and dog trainer extraordinaire Mary Angilly has seen this while working as a dog trainer and behavior consultant. Some examples include a dog who doesn't like to be left alone, doesn't know whether their human will be nice to them or angry, and doesn't like what they're fed.

tug-of-war. Sometimes called tug-a-war or just tug, this game is usually played by two dogs (but a few times I've seen three dogs), or a dog and a human, who each pull on one end of a piece of rope to try to get it away from the other. Tug-of-war is not necessarily linked to dominance or aggression. Dogs are not trying to dominate the other player. Dog trainer Pam Reid also notes that when dogs play tug-of-war it does not foster aggression.

I've watched dogs play tug-of-war countless times and heard people offer various explanations for what's happening. For some reason, people can get pretty fiery or feel very adamant about their views over this. The most common interpretation is that dogs are competing, which is certainly what the game looks like. But are dogs actually competing when they play tug-of-war? To explore this, at one point I enlisted some dog park helpers to observe fifty random tugs-of-war, and this preliminary data showed clearly that tug-of-war is mostly standard dog play with a competitive element thrown in. We considered a number of variables, including the relative size of the dogs, their social relationship and familiarity with one another, gender, context — what they were doing right before they began playing tug-of-war — age, and even breed.

When dogs of different sizes played tug-of-war, we observed what ethologists call self-handicapping — that is, the larger, stronger dog held back to some extent so the game could continue. They did not pull on the rope as hard as they could. When a large dog pulled so hard that the smaller dog couldn't play, the game usually ended. On one occasion, a large mutt pulled so hard he almost lifted his small friend off the ground. When he saw this happen, he dropped the rope, ran right at her, skidded to a stop, and did a play bow. The larger dog wanted to play — and they continued to do so — but clearly tug-of-war wasn't going to work.

Familiarity also was important. When two dogs who were close friends played tug-of-war, there were more exchanges and a willingness to let the other dog have the rope. These interactions didn't indicate real competition at all. It was more difficult to assess context, or how what was happening previously — whether the dogs were playing, just walking about, or were wired from other encounters with other dogs — influenced the outcome of tugs-of-war. However, once again, the impression we got was that if a rope was picked up during an ongoing play interaction, or right after one dog had been playing, the play continued as the dogs yanked on the rope and exchanged it on the run. On seven occasions we agreed that there was a competitive element, and four times there were some growls and a clear indication that one dog wanted the rope all for themselves. We only saw one instance where there was a strong likelihood that, if one of the dogs didn't give up the rope, there would have been a fight. We didn't observe any gender differences or breed differences, and many of the dogs were mixes.

Clearly, this isn't conclusive research, but it shows that tug-of-war is more complex than simply "competition," and citizen science can help us learn more. *See also* **play**; **self-handicapping**.

turn taking. During social play, dogs exhibit cooperative turn taking, such as when one dog chases and then the other dog does the same.

U

ultraviolet light. According to Stanley Coren, "dogs who evolved from nocturnal hunters may have maintained their ability to see ultraviolet light because they need that sensitivity when there is little light around."

umwelt. A term that refers to an individual's surroundings and their experiences of their environment. Dogs and other animals have their own umwelts. Umwelt is often translated as "self-centered world" and was coined by German biologist Jakob Johann von Uexküll. *See also* **innenwelt**.

unconditional love. Despite the widespread myth that dogs love people unconditionally, this is not true. Like people, dogs do not love everyone regardless of how they're treated. There is nothing wrong with a dog who is choosy about who they want to hang out with.

unconditioned response. In behavioral terms, this would be an "unlearned" response to a stimulus, such as the smell of food or a loud sound. For example, the smell of food is a natural stimulus (a dog does not need to be conditioned or taught to respond to it), and the salivation that occurs is the unconditioned response. *See also* **classical conditioning**; **conditioned response**.

"underdog." A term for a person or team who is unlikely to win a contest.

V

vacuum behavior. A term coined by Konrad Lorenz that refers to unexpected behavior that occurs without the stimulus that typically produces it. These behaviors include snapping in the air, barking, and whining, which would normally be seen or heard when a dog is riled up or feeling vulnerable.

vasopressin. An antidiuretic hormone (ADH) that has been associated with heightened aggression in humans and dogs.

vegan diets. People often wonder if vegetarian or vegan diets are OK for dogs. Yes, dogs can do well on vegan diets. A large research project published in April 2022 showed that vegan diets were healthier and safer than meat-based meal plans and did not compromise dog welfare. Dogs fed vegan diets visited veterinarians less often and took fewer medications. In a related study, the researchers learned that vegan dog food was generally not less palatable to dogs. *See also* **diet**; **obesity**.

veterinary behaviorist. Veterinarians trained in animal behavior who can detect and treat different behavioral problems. According to the American College of Veterinary Behaviorists (ACVB), who provide certifications, "Veterinary behaviorists are trained to address the relationships between an animal's health, environment, experiences, and its behavior. They have extensive knowledge of psychotropic medications, their uses, potential side effects and interactions with other medications, and are licensed to prescribe them when indicated."

veterinary ethics. The moral principles that guide what veterinarians do to dogs. Veterinarians must be concerned with every single individual animal's well-being.

veterinary medicine. The branch of medicine that focuses on nonhuman animals. The traditional science-based approach is called allopathic medicine. While it is rewarding to help a wide variety of companion and other animals, it is not easy to be a veterinarian — they experience high rates of suicide, and during the Covid-19 pandemic, there was increased burnout and abuse by humans who accompanied their animals. There is a shortage in veterinarians, vet techs, and other staff.

Veterinary education needs major improvements. In her book *Learning Animals: Curriculum, Pedagogy, and Becoming a Veterinarian*, Purdue University's Nadine Dolby followed veterinary medicine students through their education, from their initial enthusiasm and passion, through their encounters with animals — both alive and dead — to the crushing pain many of them experienced in their clinical year. Along the way, students were faced with dozens of moral, ethical, and personal struggles with their relationships with animals and people, but they never had the time or space to think about these issues. Nadine told me, "The stories in the book can be tough to read. Some of the book was very difficult to write. Why are vet students required to snare pigs? Asked to bond with and then euthanize a chicken? During their clinical year, why are students crying in their cars for an hour after their shift is finished before they can even drive home? Why does one student tell me that she developed anxiety during vet school but has come to accept this as a normal part of the profession? Why are their experiences systematically ignored?" Nadine loves the veterinary profession and only wants to make it better. Kudos to her. *See also* **holistic veterinary medicine**; **homeopathic veterinary medicine**.

village dogs. *See* **free-ranging dogs**.

voice and sight training. A method of dog training that emphasizes an immediate response to voice and hand gestures so that the dog can be off-leash in public areas. These techniques can be incorporated in different methods of training, and force-free positive training works just fine. That said, no training technique ever works 100 percent of the time. After completing voice and sight training, my friend Heather wrote to me, "I just completed the voice and sight dog tag training. They really expect your dog not to be off-leash. What dog always listens?" Heather is correct; no dog of the thousands I've known is perfect (and how many humans are?). Training helps humans control dogs most of the time, but when a dog is on a strong scent or zooming about here and there, it is hard to be heard, and even if dogs hear, they might not be able to stop themselves from doing what they're doing. It is reasonable to have dogs learn to be under voice and sight control, but it's best to still keep a dog on a long lead. Then they can have as much freedom as possible while avoiding problem encounters with humans, dogs, or other animals. We need to let dogs be dogs and accept that we need to compromise as well. *See also* **training**.

vomeronasal organ (VNO). Aka Jacobsen's organ. The VNO is often called the "second nose." It is a structure located above the roof of the mouth and detects nonvolatile olfactory stimuli. It plays a role in the flehmen response. The VNO was first described as a structure by the Dutch botanist and anatomist Frederik Ruysch in 1703 while dissecting a young male cadaver. *See also* **flehmen response**; **noses**.

W

walking a dog. Some people think that dogs should be walked a few times a day for a minimum of around thirty minutes per walk. However, dogs differ in what they need, and many if not most dogs would prefer to spend most of their time outdoors, so the more the better. If dogs don't exercise enough, they can become obese, bored, and stressed, so their health is in our hands.

Also, it's important to remember that taking a dog for a walk is *their* time; it's for the dog. So try to make it fun, enriching, and exciting and let them exercise their bodies and senses. It's also good for their mental health. Let the dog lead the way and choose where to go and how slow or fast; make each walk dogcentric. Every walk is a chance to strengthen your dog-human relationship, so make the most of it.

In addition, it turns out that neighborhoods in which dogs are walked have lower rates of homicide, robbery, and aggravated assault because potential criminals are deterred by seeing people and dogs in the streets.

Perhaps the biggest issue with walks centers on the leash. When walking a dog becomes a continual tug-of-war between a person and their dog, this has the potential to weaken the dog-human relationship and physically harm the dog and perhaps the human walker. While some dogs have a tendency to strain on the leash, the bigger issue is people yanking and pulling the leash to stop, corral, or redirect their dog. For more on this, see the "leashes" entry.

The gender of humans and dogs can also influence how walks unfold. One study found that male dogs pulled more frequently and created higher leash tension than female dogs, and that all dogs were more stressed when interacting with men than with women. Women were more likely than men to use verbal commands, including baby talk, whereas men were more likely to have physical contact with dogs.

In a separate study focused on shelters and how shelter volunteers walked dogs, researchers found that more-conscientious workers pulled on leashes less, had more physical contact with dogs, used verbal communication less, and didn't use high-pitched voices.

Clearly, walking a dog is not as simple as it seems, but it's good to approach it with a sense of humor. I'm particularly fond of the many "How to Walk a Human" lists online, like this one:

1. Allow your human to tether themselves to you. This keeps them from wandering off or running away.
2. Your human will probably need breaks. Be considerate and stop and sniff often.
3. Bark frequently. Humans have short attention spans.
4. When you go to the bathroom, walk away. If you have trained your human correctly, they will pick it up. Good aerobics.
5. Periodically drag your human as fast as you can. This is called interval training.
6. Do not allow your human to shorten the walk. They are being lazy. Sit in protest if you must.
7. Once you return home, allow your human to remove their tether, then lick their face many times. This is positive reinforcement for a job well done.

See also **leashes**.

weaning. The time when youngsters aren't allowed to suckle milk any longer, and puppies transition from milk to solid food. For homed dogs or those who have humans looking after them, humans often start weaning pups around three to four weeks of age. The age at which weaning occurs among the wild relatives of dogs varies, depending on available food and the number of brothers and sisters. In one field study of wolves, weaning conflict between mom and her children began at seven or eight weeks of age. *See also* **developmental stages**.

welfare, animal. Animal welfare concerns — how well animals are treated and their living situations — include homed and free-ranging dogs. But in particular, it applies to dogs used in observational studies and more invasive types of research, and dogs used in entertainment and as food (which is common in certain countries). In the context of these various uses, animal welfare advocates ask, Are dogs getting what they need physically and emotionally? Are they comfortable and do they have access to good food and exercise? Are we doing the best we can to reduce their pain and suffering? That said, animal welfarists don't necessarily argue against certain uses that are inherently abusive or require killing the animals (as in agriculture and research). Animal welfare standards can often be extremely self-serving, and as I like to say, they're used "in the name of humans" rather than "in the name of the animals." Compare with the "well-being, animal" entry. *See also* **Five Freedoms**; **Ten Freedoms for dogs**.

well-being, animal. In contrast to animal welfare (see above), which is concerned with how animals, including dogs, are treated while alive, animal well-being focuses on the quality of life experienced by each and every *individual*, and the standards of care it promotes are much more restrictive than animal welfare concerns. The difference between animal well-being and animal welfare is important to recognize. Animal well-being seeks to protect the inherent value of each *individual* and to end uses that ultimately abuse and kill animals. This is not to say that researchers are necessarily coldhearted (though I've heard some disheartening and chilling stories), but rather they are willing to allow dogs to be harmed and killed if they are following approved welfare standards and doing the best they can to be as "humane" as they can. Unfortunately, so-called humane guidelines and laws allow for the brutal abuse of dogs and other animals, and many researchers engage in humane-washing that somehow allows them to do what they do because it's an acceptable, legal practice. I often wonder how some people sleep at night or look at themselves in the mirror. Jessica Pierce and I write much more about this in *The Animals' Agenda*.

whale eye. When the whites of a dog's eyes are visible, indicating they are afraid or feeling threatened.

whimpering. A soft weak sound indicating pain or discontent.

whiskers. Aka vibrissae. Whiskers are specifically tuned sensory equipment that guide a dog through daily activities. These specialized hairs aid vision and help dogs navigate their environment by providing additional sensory input, much like antennae on insects. Although whiskers are called "tactile hairs," they do not actually feel anything. *See also* **touch**.

wildlife, impact of dogs on. Dogs can and do change the behavior of wildlife, and they will harm and kill wild animals. Just their presence can change the travel patterns of other animals such as deer, who want to avoid them, and this could also influence the behavior of animals who also want to eat the deer. In some areas, free-ranging and feral dogs are a major threat to wildlife, though in other areas, they're not. *See also* **free-ranging dogs**.

Willie the Wiener. Sir Willie is the FKD, the fastest known dog, and a legend of cycling. A miniature dachshund, he often accompanies one of his humans, professional cyclist Alexey Vermeulen, riding in his backpack on his training rides.

Willie on a ride with Alexey Vermeulen (Credit: Josh Lawton)

winner-loser effects. This effect poses the question: Do dogs who win a lot of contests become winners more often than expected, and do dogs who lose a lot of contests become losers more often than expected? No one has studied this in dogs, but in coyotes, Lee Dugatkin and I have found clear winner and loser effects that were rank-related. Highest-ranking (alpha) coyotes showed winner effects, lowest-ranking (omega) individuals showed loser effects, whereas there were no winner or loser effects for middle-ranking animals.

wolves. Members of the family Canidae and progenitors of dogs. Wolves are larger than most dogs, have to hunt for their meals — something many dogs, including free-ranging dogs, who live around human settlements, don't have to do — and are shot by humans who find them dangerous, who don't like them, or because they like to kill animals.

working for food. *See also* **contrafreeloading**; **enrichment**.

worrying. It's a myth that dogs and other nonhumans don't worry. They do.

Plenty of research shows clearly that nonhuman animals worry, by any definition, about what happens in their lives. Dogs, cats, and other animals lose sleep when they are uneasy, anxious, distressed, troubled, or on edge. Dogs suffer from separation anxiety and can fear loud noises like thunder. I've shared my home with a number of dogs who paced around nervously or hid under the bed or wrapped themselves in the sheets and lost sleep when there were severe thunderstorms. Often, after a night of raucous weather, the dogs would walk around obviously groggy from a lack of sleep. Many other people have told me the same about their dogs.

Particularly among wild animals, but also among dogs, patterns of antipredator vigilance display signs of worry, and animals unsure about where they stand in a social hierarchy will exhibit worry. Perhaps the only thing that makes humans unique when it comes to worry is that we have the luxury of obsessively focusing on and indulging whatever causes us stress. In the wild at least, animals have to get on with what they have to do to survive, since excessive worry, if it causes lack of sleep, can be costly. *See also* **alone time**; **separation anxiety**.

X

xenophobia. This is usually defined as a dislike for or prejudice against foreigners, and I've seen dogs behave in a xenophobic way, such as when they avoid interacting with strange dogs. Some dogs show a strong preference for dogs they know, especially those with whom they live or with whom they interact at a dog park or on a trail, whereas others are not at all friendly or even passive and will chase off strange dogs for intruding into their personal space. Stanley Coren notes that dogs can pick up prejudices from their humans. After reviewing a study focused on perceptions of racial bias in pet dogs, he wrote, "So, to answer the question, 'Is it possible that a dog can be racist?' the answer seems to be 'Yes,' particularly if its caregiver has explicit or implicit negative attitudes toward other races and has limited experience interacting with them. In this case, as in many others, dogs, like children, are modeling their behavior after what they see in the actions of their caregivers."

Y

yawning. Dogs most likely yawn for the same reasons people do: when they are sleepy, bored, or experiencing excessive stress. However, we have little detailed data on why dogs yawn. An article called "Dog Yawning Decoded: Why Do Dogs Yawn" summarizes how little we know, along with the many different reasons dogs might yawn. If a dog is yawning excessively, consider consulting a veterinarian.

yellow snow. Urine-soaked snow. *See also* **olfactory recognition**.

yelping. An attention-getting loud cry of pain, fear, or surprise. Dogs typically only yelp when they're in pain, such as when their tail gets stepped on by accident, but if they're startled and afraid, they might also yelp. As always, consider the context.

Z

Zen dogs. This term embodies the myth that dogs live in the present and have no worries in the world. Dogs might wish this was true. *See also* **time, sense of**; **worrying**.

zoomies. Aka frenetic random activity periods (FRAPs), zoomies are when dogs run wildly here and there with no obvious aim or direction. When dogs see another dog zooming, it might be a signal to come join and play. Play can be a kaleidoscope — a frenetic potpourri — of the senses. *See also* **play**.

zoomorphism. Attributing characteristics of nonhuman animals to humans. *See also* **anthropomorphism**.

zoonoses. Infectious diseases spread by animals.

zoothanasia. I coined this term for when healthy animals are killed in zoos when they can't contribute to a genetic lineage or when there isn't room for them. Zoothanasia is not euthanasia or mercy killing. In some zoos, it is rather common. While dogs are not kept in zoos, it's the same utterly heinous practice of killing otherwise healthy individuals when breeders or people who run puppy mills kill dogs who don't meet breed standards or who have become too old, ill, or worn out to continue being used as breeding machines. *See also* **euthanasia**.

ACKNOWLEDGMENTS

The number of people to whom I owe a great deal is extremely long, and I apologize if I've missed someone. My superb PhD mentor, Michael W. Fox, got me rolling on my long career, and I can't thank him enough for all he did way back when and continues to do for me and people around the world. His 1971 book *Behaviour of Wolves, Dogs, and Related Canids* remains a classic in the field, and much of what I and many others do is derivative of his pioneering work.

I've been thinking about a book like this for decades, and just as I was putting my ideas together, I was out on a cycling training ride with my teammates Andy Pruitt, Heather McWilliams Mierzejewski, Bill Simmons, and Steve Paul. When I fell off the back of the group and as I chased back, I outlined a proposal that had been gestating somewhere in my brain and was thrilled that New World Library liked it. Andy, Heather, Steve, Bill, Tom Gordon, Margell Abel, and many others have listened to me talk about "all things dog" for countless years, and I thank them all and many others — Christy, Angela, Hunter, Don, Carron, Rob — for asking questions and for telling me wonderful stories. So, too, have Jessica Pierce, with whom I've written four books and to whom I owe a very special thanks, and Mark Derr, who knows as much about dogs as anyone I know; and Mary Angilly, force-free positive dog trainer extraordinaire, who always has wonderful ideas and asks tough questions. Sindhoor Pangal kept me in the loop on what was happening on the ground in India. Colorado's First Gentleman Marlon H. Reis always wants to talk dogs, and I so appreciate his insights into their behavior, including reports on his highly skilled food-snatching dog, Gia, Colorado's first dog. Paul McGreevy also helped me fill in gaps of my knowledge of various aspects of normal dog behavior, including chewing. It always was and remains a pleasure to talk with Jennifer Holland about dogs and all things animals. And many thanks to my friend and colleague Dr. Jane Goodall, dog lover extraordinaire, for writing the foreword.

At New World Library, I thank executive editor Jason Gardner, with whom I've worked closely for eighteen years, Monique Muhlenkamp, Kristen Cashman, and Danielle Galat. They are a wonderful crew. My copyeditor, Jeff Campbell, has been helping me clean things up for eighteen years, and I am deeply indebted to his valuable insights about dogs and other nonhumans. Thanks also to the amazing proofreader Tanya Fox.

I thank Irwin Redlener for introducing me to Joan Baez, who graciously created illustrations for this book and has talked with me about the various nonhumans who live with her on her property. Joan has wonderful stories about dogs and many other animals, some of whom stray into her home and are treated with great care, dignity, and respect. Joan introduced me to Emmylou Harris, and Emmylou also shared with me her passion for dogs and other nonhumans. Ingrid Newkirk asked Paul McCartney if he could answer a few questions for me, and I'm thrilled that he sent a story about his rescued dog, Rose.

I also thank everyone who sent me stories and answered my questions about what they would ask their dog and what their dog would ask them. Betty Moss and Valerie Belt kept me current on "all things dog," as they have for many years. Hal Herzog and Stanley Coren also kept me in the loop about their and others' research, for which I am very grateful. I also thank Amanda Layton at the local Kinkos for making quick copies when I really needed them.

ABOUT THE AUTHOR

Marc Bekoff is professor emeritus of ecology and evolutionary biology at the University of Colorado, Boulder. He has published thirty-one books (or forty-one if you count multivolume encyclopedias); has won many awards for his research on animal behavior, animal emotions, cognitive ethology, compassionate conservation, and animal protection; has worked closely with Jane Goodall; and is a former Guggenheim Fellow. He also works closely with inmates at the Boulder County Jail. In June 2022 Marc was recognized as a Hero by the Academy of Dog Trainers. His latest books are *The Animals' Agenda: Freedom, Compassion, and Coexistence in the Human Age* (with Jessica Pierce), *Canine Confidential: Why Dogs Do What They Do*, and *Unleashing Your Dog: A Field Guide to Giving Your Canine Companion the Best Life Possible* (with Jessica Pierce). He also publishes regularly for *Psychology Today*. Marc's most recent book with Jessica Pierce, *A Dog's World: Imagining the Lives of Dogs in a World without Humans*, was published by Princeton University Press in 2021. A revised, second edition of Marc's *The Emotional Lives of Animals* will be published in spring 2024. In 1986 Marc won the Master's Tour du Haut, aka the age-graded Tour de France. His homepage is marcbekoff.com.

NEW WORLD LIBRARY is dedicated to publishing books and other media that inspire and challenge us to improve the quality of our lives and the world.

We are a socially and environmentally aware company. We recognize that we have an ethical responsibility to our readers, our authors, our staff members, and our planet.

We serve our readers by creating the finest publications possible on personal growth, creativity, spirituality, wellness, and other areas of emerging importance. We serve our authors by working with them to produce and promote quality books that reach a wide audience. We serve New World Library employees with generous benefits, significant profit sharing, and constant encouragement to pursue their most expansive dreams.

Whenever possible, we print our books with soy-based ink on 100 percent postconsumer-waste recycled paper. We power our offices with solar energy and contribute to nonprofit organizations working to make the world a better place for us all.

Our products are available wherever books are sold. Visit our website to download our catalog, subscribe to our e-newsletter, read our blog, and link to authors' websites, videos, and podcasts.